MW01030173

MIGHTY LIKE A RIVER

Previous Books by the Author

The Social Worker in a Child Protective Agency

Black Families in White America

Children of the Storm: Black Children in American Child Welfare
(with Jeanne Giovannoni)

Black Families and the Struggle for Survival

The Evolution of Black Families

Climbing Jacob's Ladder: The Enduring Legacy of
African American Families

MIGHTY LIKE A RIVER

The Black Church and Social Reform

—⚬—

Andrew Billingsley, Ph.D.

OXFORD UNIVERSITY PRESS
New York   Oxford

Oxford University Press

Oxford New York
Auckland Bangkok Buenos Aires Cape Town Chennai
Dar es Salaam Delhi Hong Kong Istanbul Karachi Kolkata
Kuala Lumpur Madrid Melbourne Mexico City Mumbai Nairobi
São Paulo Shanghai Taipei Tokyo Toronto

Copyright © 1999 by Andrew Billingsley and the University of Maryland

First published in 1999 by Oxford University Press, Inc.,
198 Madison Avenue, New York, New York 10016

www.oup.com

First issued as an Oxford University Press paperback, 2003

Oxford is a registered trademark of Oxford University Press

All rights reserved. No part of this publication
may be reproduced, stored in a retrieval system, or transmitted,
in any form or by any means, electronic, mechanical,
photocopying, recording, or otherwise, without the prior
permission of Oxford University Press.

Library of Congress Cataloging-in-Publication Data
Billingsley, Andrew.
Mighty like a river: the black church and social reform / by
Andrew Billingsley.
p. cm.
Includes bibliographical references and index.
ISBN-13 978-0-19-516179-3 (pbk)
ISBN 0-19-510617-2 : 0-19-516179-3 (pbk)
1. Afro-American churches.   2. Church and social problems—United
States. I. Title.
BR563.N4B534   1999
277.3'082'08996073—dc21   98-13875

5 7 9 8 6 4

Printed in the United States of America
on acid–free paper

*The author gratefully thanks the following people
for assistance in preparation of this book:*

Judith Denise Crocker, LMSW
Social Worker, South Carolina Department of Juvenile Justice

Cleopatra Howard Caldwell, Ph.D.
Assistant Professor of Psychology, University of Michigan, Ann Arbor

Robert B. Hill, Ph.D.
Director, Institute for Urban Research, Morgan State University, Baltimore

Terry Stephens, M.S.
Assistant Professor of English, Morgan State University, Baltimore

And also

Angela Dungee Green, M.A.; Fleda Mask Jackson, Ph.D.;
Otis Johnson, Ph.D.; Mona T. Phillips, Ph.D.;
Sandra Crouse Quinn, Ph.D.; Suzanne Randolph, Ph.D.;
Roger Rubin, Ph.D.; Alicia Simon, M.S.; James M. Shopshire, Ph.D.;
Stephen Thomas, Ph.D.; Willie Tolliver, Ph.D.; Naomi Ward, MSW.

Permission to reprint selections from the following sources
is gratefully acknowledged:

Lloyd Gite: "The New Agenda of the Black Church: Economic Development" from *Black Enterprise Magazine*, December, 1993, pp. 54–59. Reprinted by permission of *Black Enterprise Magazine*, New York, NY. All rights reserved.

Ira Berlin, et al. (eds): From *Free at Last: A Documentary History of Slavery, Freedom, and the Civil War*. Copyright 1992 by The New Press. Reprinted by permission of The New Press.

Andrew Billingsley, et al. "The Black Church" from Special Double Issue, *The National Journal of Sociology*, vol. 8, nos. 1 and 2, Summer/Winter, 1994, pp. 1–159. Reprinted by permission of John Sibley Butler, editor.

The Editors of the *New York Times*: "New Time Religion: Editorial" from the *New York Times*, May 23, 1988. Copyright 1988 by the New York Times Co. Reprinted by permission.

Otis S. Johnson: From *The Social Welfare Role of the Black Church*, copyright Otis S. Johnson, Brandeis University, 1980. Reprinted by permission of Otis S. Johnson.

Courtland Milloy: "A Collective Source of Black Power" from *The Washington Post*, Sunday, Dec. 5, 1996, p. B–1 and B–7. Copyright 1996 by *The Washington Post*. Reprinted by permission.

DEDICATION

*To the memory of the Reverend Doctor Henry C. Gregory III,
to his family, and to Pastor Wallace Charles Smith
and all the members of Shiloh Baptist Church, Washington, D.C.*

"How do you see the Black church today? Is it enlarging its vision and mission in the Black community? Is it still a bulwark for Black people? Is it undergoing a leadership crisis? Is the church relevant?"

—Dr. Kenneth Smith, president, Chicago Theological Seminary;
former chair, Chicago Urban League; former president,
Chicago Board of Education; former senior minister,
Trinity United Church of Christ, Chicago

"Given their collective history, why have many contemporary Black churches chosen to be detached from those efforts aimed at societal transformation?"

—Alex Poinsett, veteran journalist

"The days of coming to church for personal salvation alone are over. Now we are looking not only for personal salvation but for social salvation. If we don't change the community, the community corrupts the individual."

—Cecil L. (Chip) Murray, senior minister,
First A.M.E. Church of Los Angeles

Contents

Foreword   *Lawrence N. Jones*, xiii
Preface   *Andrew Billingsley*, xv
Acknowledgments, xvii
Introduction   *C. Eric Lincoln*, xix

PART I
EVOLUTION OF THE BLACK CHURCH
AS AGENT OF SOCIAL REFORM

1 The Storm Is Passing Over: The Black Church in Perspective, 3

2 If Tombstones Could Talk: The Evolution of the Black Church in Savannah, 13

3 General Sherman and the Black Church, 22

4 The Crisis of Emancipation and Reconstruction in Savannah, 35

5 Rev. Ralph Mark Gilbert and the Civil Rights Movement in Savannah, 53

6 First African Baptist Church, Richmond: Seedbed of Social Reform, 62

PART II
THE CONTEMPORARY BLACK CHURCH REACHES OUT TO THE COMMUNITY

7 New-Time Religion, 87

8 The Black Church and the Male Youth Crisis, 102

9 The Black Church Confronts the HIV/AIDS Crisis, 110

10 A Tale of Two Cities: Black Churches in Denver and Atlanta, 119

11 Often Seen, Seldom Called: The Legacy of Jerena Lee, 132

12 Twelve Gates to the City, 144

13 Unashamedly Black and Unapologetically Christian, 170

14 One More River to Cross: The Black Church Faces the Future, 185

Appendix A: Project Advisory Committee Members, 195
Appendix B: Studying Contemporary Black Churches, 198
Appendix C: Tables, 207
Notes, 227
References, 245
Index, 251

Foreword

BY LAWRENCE N. JONES

Though several benevolent societies were the first organized institutions created by Africans in America, the black churches that followed soon after proved to be the most viable and inclusive. From their earliest beginnings in the 1790s, black churches became and have continued to be the focal point of virtually every movement for change that affects their communities. Andrew Billingsley's *Mighty Like A River: The Black Church and Social Reform* documents the truth of this assertion. Based upon extensive research over several years, this volume will prove to be a valuable contribution to the growing body of research about the religious life of the African American community. *Mighty Like A River* is testimony to an intellectually well-informed and skillfully executed design.

The research was restricted, primarily, to Protestant Christian bodies with which most African Americans have been affiliated historically. There are passing references to the work of some Catholic churches and to the Black Muslims, but their contributions must await further research, hopefully with the comprehensive scope of Billingsley's volume.

This book is especially valuable because it demonstrates that the significance of a religious institution cannot be calibrated solely in terms of the number of conversions it records, in the growth of its membership, or in other measurements utilized by ecclesiastical bodies. These statistical indices inevitably reflect, to some degree, perceptions of the seriousness of the church's commitment to enhancing the quality of life in the community in which it is located. Favorable perceptions invariably result in church growth.

The point is also made that faithfulness to the Christian Gospel, which they proclaim, requires gathered communities of faith to be involved in the changing panorama of political, economic, social, demographic, educational, and cultural realities in which persons live out their lives. Though often cloaked in secular jargon, the ever-increasing involvement of churches in the world is rooted in the Gospel's requirement that believers must care for "the least of these." One thing is clear: Any institution that hopes to survive must take account of dynamism that characterizes the life of its community. It must have grasped the truth that "service and concern for those God loves is worship."

The research reported and analyzed here is focused primarily on established churches. The investigators highlight a number of activist congregations. An implicit negative assessment is levied upon "conservative" fellowships that appear to be oblivious to the suffering in their midst. I share this assessment, but I and the researchers are well aware that many individual Christians who are members of nonactivist churches participate in other venues concerned with quality-of-life issues. Obedient to the faith of the church, they labor tirelessly, sometimes in anonymity, to enrich the life of the community. This activity of the "body of Christ" is not readily accessible to any researcher, and reports will usually be anecdotal. The faithfulness of believers cannot be fully captured in a statistical net or in reports of what they may do collectively.

The community of scholars will benefit from the research recorded here, as well as from the conclusions drawn from it. At the same time clergy and laity will discover in the volume role models with whom they can identify and whom they can seek to emulate.

It is fortuitous that Dr. Billingsley and his associates are primarily academic sociologists. As sociologists they bring objectivity and precision to the volume. At the same time, it is salutary that they are involved in the institution they are studying. As a consequence, a balance is achieved between the research data and the living reality of the churches as worshiping, proclaiming, and serving communities of faith. This is responsible scholarship because both scientific methodologies and institutional vitalities are appropriately weighted and related.

—LAWRENCE N. JONES
Dean and Professor Emeritus
Howard University School of Divinity

Preface

S ometime around 1986, the late Reverend Henry C. Gregory III, of Shiloh Baptist Church in Washington, D.C., invited a group of men in the church called "Men of Shiloh" to a meeting on the rooftop of the Family Life Center operated by the church. I was among them. Gregory pointed to the inner-city neighborhood surrounding the church at Ninth Street and P Street Northwest: "There are hundreds of young boys out there," he said, "who are in danger of losing their way. Each day they confront all the problems of modern urban life." Then, turning to us, he said, "But you men are strong, and I want you to lend some of your strength to those young boys and their families." Thus was born the "Shiloh Male Youth Health Enhancement Project," a mentoring program linking the church, the youth, their families, schools, and other agencies. A decade later, hundreds of boys and their families have benefited from the vision of Reverend Gregory and the strong support of this church. When Lynn Walker Huntley of the Ford Foundation came for a site visit in 1987, the idea was generated for a study to see what churches around the nation were doing for children and families and communities beyond meeting the spiritual needs of their members. Thus began the series of research studies on which this book is based.

I extend special appreciation to C. Eric Lincoln of Duke University, Lawrence Mamiya of Vassar College, A.M.E. Bishop John Hurst Adams, and other members of the National Advisory Committee, who gave valuable assistance. They are noted in Appendix A.

My colleagues at the University of Maryland have been most supportive. I am especially indebted to Dean John Burt, Sally Koblinsky, Suzanne Randolph, Roger Rubin, Noel Myricks, Jacqueline Wallen, and Mitch Mochtari. For invaluable assistance in the conception, design, and execution of the large-scale surveys, I am grateful to Dr. Robert B. Hill, Dr. Cleopatra Howard Caldwell, Dr. Victor Rouse, Terry Stephens, Angela Dungee Greene, Valery Denise Williams Drake, Jeanne Giovannoni, Pamela Carter, and Diane Wells-Tabron. Also my students Helen Hopson, Juliette Jones, Brooks Menessa, James Taylor, Brian Jackson, Walter Alston.

Part I, "Evolution of the Black Church as Agent of Social Reform," contains a series of chapters (Chapters 2 to 6) which feature case studies of antebellum churches still in existence today and how they have periodically moved beyond their religious work to confront social, economic, and political problems facing the African American community. Black heroes and heroines are profiled, together with a few whites, who helped to take the church into the community in remarkable ways, often with fateful consequences both positive and negative.

Chapters in this part are based on intensive ethnographic case studies of particular surviving antebellum churches principally in Savannah, Georgia, and Richmond, Virginia, conducted during the period from 1992 to 1996. Information is also drawn from visits to churches in Montgomery and Birmingham, Alabama, as well as Augusta, Columbia, Atlanta, and Marietta, Georgia. Judith Denise Crocker, LMSW, served as principal research assistant and director of field operations.

Part II, "The Contemporary Black Church Reaches Out to the Community," moves beyond case studies to embrace large-scale social surveys among nearly a thousand black churches in different parts of the country.

The six chapters in this part (Chapters 7 to 12) seek to answer such questions as, How widespread is the community outreach activity of black churches today? What are the types and patterns of activities being undertaken? Why are some churches activist, and others not? How do the activist churches go about confronting some of the pressing problems today, including family instability, youth development, problems of the elderly, and HIV/AIDS and other health issues?

A concluding chapter (Chapter 14), "One More River to Cross, " sets forth my conception of the future role of the black church as agent of social reform.

Acknowledgments

This book would not have been possible without the assistance of many other people and organizations. Although it is not possible to mention everyone individually, I thank you all. The research on which the book is based has been made possible by the generous, steadfast financial assistance and timely input of Lynn Walker Huntley, Emmett Carson, Robert Michael Franklin, and others of the Ford Foundation, and Jacqui Burton of the Lilly Endowment. A special word of thanks also goes to the University of Maryland and to Spelman College for financial, personnel, and social support for this project. The Rockefeller Foundation and its Villagio Center for Scholars in Lake Cuomo, Italy, the Virginia Center for the Creative Arts at Sweetbriar College in Virginia, as well as the Institute for Families in Society and the African American Studies Program at the University of South Carolina all provided valuable time and resources for reflection and writing. So, too, did Mary Ladd, Linda and John Sullivan with David Banks, Andrea Anderson, Alice Turner, Oliver Davis, Alicia Darenberg, and Linda Bracken. For conducting the Denver survey, Grant Jones, Jessica Pearson, Rachael Harding, the Rev. Teressa Frye, and the Rev. Robert Wolfolk.

For assistance with the Atlanta survey I am indebted to Professor Naomi Ward, Alicia Simon, Norman Rates, Harry Lefevre, Daryl White, Mona Phillips, Evelyn Chisholm, LaConya Butler, Coye Williams, and returning students Judith Crocker, Lila Anderson Lucas, Gail Armstrong Johnson, Pauline Geter, Glenda Hodges, Tamara Mann, Jo Ellen Paige, Wanda Perry Hardemann, and Helen Richmond.

For assistance in the collection of extensive ethnographic case studies from dozens of antebellum churches highlighted in the several chapters of Part I of this book, I am indebted to Judith Denise Crocker. And for assistance with the actual writing of several chapters, I am grateful to Dr. Cleopatra Howard Caldwell, Dr. Robert B. Hill, Dr. Roger Rubin, Dr. Suzanne Randolph, Dr. Stephen Thomas, Dr. Sandra Crouse Quinn, Dr. William Tolliver, Dr. James Shopshire, and Dr. Otis Johnson.

For clerical assistance, Sandra Kay Ashley has been superb.

Special appreciation to Angela Billingsley, Terry Stephens, and Judith Crocker for reading and critiquing the entire first manuscript. At Oxford University Press, I am indebted to Gioia Stevens, who first saw the value and potential of this book, and to Joan Bossert, who expertly guided this book to completion. Not enough can be said of Malaika Adero of Blue Media Editorial Services. Her expert editorial and literary talents helped me to convert this manuscript from a collection of research reports for a limited range of scholars to a more readable book for the general reader. At the same time the authenticity of the whole treatise has been maintained.

Of course, none of this would have been possible without the excellent cooperation we received from the ministers, their associates, and others who agreed to be interviewed and observed, and who provided access to their facilities, programs, and documents.

For the survey of ministers in three rural South Carolina counties, I am indebted to Robin Kimbrough, Jim Donally, Barbara Morrison Rodriguez, Catherine Ward, Hartmut Fege, Charles Smith, Lillie McGill, Cecelia Wragg, and Sylvia Barr. I also thank the nearly 100 ministers who participated.

Finally, members of my nuclear, extended, and augmented families have provided invaluable support.

All the persons above and others too numerous to mention have combined to make writing this book a remarkable learning experience, a marvelous adventure, and a decade-long labor of love.

Needless to say, the shortcomings of this book are mine alone.

—ANDREW BILLINGSLEY

Introduction

BY C. ERIC LINCOLN

This new book by Andrew Billingsley and his associates contains an expanding body of research on the black church in America. It provides the reader with a synoptic view of the travail and triumph of the black church as a social institution from antebellum times to the present. Such an approach contributes substantially to a more comprehensive understanding of what I have elsewhere termed "the Black Sacred Cosmos." This introductory chapter aims to set forth for the reader the multiple contexts—intellectual, cultural, religious, and historical—which condition the black church as a critical agent of social reform, and the jurisdiction of first appeal.

Like other expressions of the uniquely human experience we call religion, the Black Sacred Cosmos—the peculiar spiritual mantle which identifies and distinguishes African American culture—is not monolithic. It lives and it operates in two realms of reality—the "spiritual" and the "public," or the "privatistic" and the "communal." Professor Martin Marty, one of the most reliable interpreters of the practice and the meaning of religion in America posits a duality of "private" vs. "public" religion.[1] This spiritual polarity recognizes the most vital personal interests of the individual without abandoning or avoiding the interests of the collectivity to which the individual is attached by bonds that include faith but may also transcend it. While this concept does not exhaust the catalog of possible interpretations for the private/public duality of the faith, it does offer valuable insights for understanding black religion as a response to a bastion of grace recognized and shared by millions of Americans whose underlying cultural roots are as varied as the first convocation at Pentecost.[2]

The critical significance of the dialectic which energizes the Black Sacred Cosmos will not be apparent wherever there is a precommitment to the convenient convention that the black church is merely a kind of folk rendition of white mainstream religion.[3] Given the peculiar social and religious history of America, this very common convention may be "understandable" because it is consistent with other conventions which structure social and religious understanding in our society. The fact is, however, that every authentic religion is a precipitate of the peculiar cultural experiences that shape the sense of identity and self-awareness as these relate to some ultimate presence beyond the self and other selves cast from the same clay but fired in a different furnace. The Black Sacred Cosmos is addressed to the critical urgencies pervasive to the black experience that seem to lie beyond effective human resolution. Even more problematic is the fact that the cultural "set" that produced or confirmed a "mainline American religion" is not only of a different order, but a different origin. It remains an unremitting backdrop against which the travail and triumph of the black church must accomplish its mission.

From the beginning, African Americans were involuntary adhesions to a "host" society in which their creative participation was severely limited by law, by tradition, and by caprice. Accordingly, the critical urgencies of the host society were inimical to the most compelling concerns of the black bondsmen, and vice versa. In consequence, black religion takes its origins not from established religion in America, but from *the black experience in America*, which was and is a very singular illustration of the complexities of the human predicament, and of the spiritual resources available to the black church's mission to overcome.

From its inception the black church set out to do for its peculiar constituency of black slaves and freed men what no one else was willing to do for them, or to have them do for themselves. There was no consistent effort to bring Christianity to the slaves in America until the (Anglican) Society for the Propagation of the Gospel in Foreign Parts[4] established a spiritual presence of sorts on the plantations of the South in 1701—almost a hundred years after the first Africans arrived at Jamestown in 1619. The price of permission to exhort the blacks which the planters exacted from this missionary society was the written assurance of the reigning bishop of London that in no case would "conversion work manumission." This concordat of understanding constituted an effective prenullification of any dreams the slaves may have had of burning their bonds in the fires of the faith by confessing Christ—as was the tradition in England, but never in America. Nevertheless, it was not until the sense of the bishop's spiritual ruling was codified as the law of the land that the slaveholders were willing to risk their property to the hands of the Christian missionaries. But the Anglicans were persistent, and by the middle of the 18th century, selected "big house" retainers often held "auxiliary" membership in some of the white churches.

The black Christians in white churches were cramped by their style and stifled by the requirements of racial conformity. Though they were finally "in church," it was demonstrably not "their" church, a communication that spoke pointedly and consistently through the sermons, the prayers, the spiritual suppression, and the absence of fellowship. In the white churches the Africans were offered a God who had cursed them and ordained their travail and debasement in perpetuity. When faith falters, idols tumble down and false gods flee for cover, but truth is its own best witness and will ultimately be manifest in the scheme of things. It became clear to black and white Christians alike that there were serious incongruities in the white church's faith and practice which could not be reconciled short of exhaustive spiritual and moral overhaul and reconstruction. Although some individuals and even some churches recognized the depravity of Christian racism, so drastic a reform was nowhere on the agenda of the white church. Hence, it was inevitable that black Christians would heed the call to "come ye out from among them." South Carolina and Georgia were the early incubators of black churches. The first viable black denomination was established under the leadership of ex-slave Richard Allen in Philadelphia in 1815.

The black church *came into existence* fully committed to the private or spiritual aspects of religion as *yin* to the *yang* of public religious concern. Like all other religions, black christianity has leaned syncretistically upon the forms and formulas of pre-existing religious norms, thereby sharing in a rich lode of continuous faith and practice. But the black church itself is a precipitate of its *own* culture, developed from, and in response to, its own experience. The black experience and the white experience in America may be parallel in history and they may share a common demography, but they are no more "interchangeable" than are, say, the Mormon Church and the Southern Baptist Church. Religion presupposes self-awareness, human vulnerability, and the availability of help from God. It is the uniqueness of the collective response to the experience of the holy in response to human need that determines the structure of faith and practice by which particular ways of faith are identified.

Religion begins where self-sufficiency ends. Or to be more precise, religion begins with the *awareness* that self-sufficiency is an illusion, and one that can seriously compromise the struggle on earth and the benefits of heaven. The function of religion is to make the human individual acceptable to God (who created him without blemish). The catalogue of *changes* addressed by religion is as inexhaustible as human weakness and perversity, but among the more generic expectations is that true religion turns darkness into light, foolishness into wisdom, deficiency into wholeness, strife into peace, hate into love, and bondage into freedom. Black religion begins with the unshakable faith that *all things are possible with God;* and in the confusing context out of which the black church developed, there was good reason to believe that *only* God could change the fate that had been designed for them by their "masters" on earth.

The black church knew from the beginning what its deficits were—and they were many; but it also knew that in the (ironic) words of Thomas Jefferson, "God's justice [would] not sleep forever." The black church knew that its paramount mission was freedom. All other beneficial changes it might garner along the way were only preparation to *true* freedom—the pearl of great price. Because the black church was born in a time and place of human bondage, it is generally "understood"—incorrectly so—that the church's emphasis on freedom was limited to liberation from the political encagement which made personal property of black men and women. It is easy and convenient to make this assumption because now that political freedom has been "achieved," and personal liberation is a "fact," freedom cannot possibly be a serious issue of consequence in or out of the black church—or any church. But in the black church, despite the millions of sermons preached, the prayers prayed, the solemn spiritual songs lifted up to heaven, freedom is as burning an issue today as it was when God first revealed Himself and His true relationship to His black children in America. The freedom the black church has been after transcends all of the petty impediments that human caprice can assemble. It is the freedom to belong to God, to worship God exclusively, and it is the freedom to participate in the divine agenda without selective hindrance from other human beings. Translated into practical terminology this means that since God made humankind the apex of his creative work on earth (and gave them dominion over all else), it follows that God's expectations for human development and human behavior are not maudlin. In the black church it was recognized quite early that the divine expectations could scarcely be fulfilled in the absence of full freedom. Responsibility is not responsible when it is conditional. The concern was not just for physical or political freedom; although such an achievement was a necessary first step. True freedom meant the absence of *any* inhibiting factors or conditions that could disrupt the divine agenda by arbitrarily conditioning the lives of selected human beings who are still held accountable to God and the community. Mankind was created with the powers of reason and creativity; hence, the absence of educational opportunity is a formidable assault on freedom. Hunger, improper health care, joblessness, drug addiction, debasement, and denigration all inhibit the full flowering of the human potential to belong wholly to God.

In the early black church the first emphasis was on getting to know God more intimately, and getting used to the idea that black people were not "cursed of God," nor condemned by God to be "hewers of wood and drawers of water" for the white people who called themselves "masters." The church brought the comfort and the security of God's love and redemption into the hopelessness of abject dereliction. The black response—the prayer and the preaching, the singing, the moaning, the shouting (or as Du Bois put it, "the frenzy")—kept human spirit alive and the presence of God an assured consolation.

A second urgent concern was to destroy the evil slave system by refusing to cooperate with it. Personal escape represented the ultimate act of non-cooperation. Punishment for "running away" or for assisting those who did was severe, but the black church was the primary resource that sent or led tens of thousands of slaves to new freedoms via the Underground Railroad. When the slave era was finally ended by the Civil War, much remained to be done to prepare the ex-bondsmen for full participation in the divine agenda and in the body politic. And so the black church sponsored schools, savings societies, insurance companies, banks, improvement clubs, and a variety of social services to speed the day when full freedom would come to a cadre of people who were among America's oldest residents but her newest and least recognized citizens.

The struggle for full freedom has kept the black church in dialectical tension from its inception, and it continues as we move into the 21st century. To cope with the formidable exigencies presently stalking this civilization the pendulum of religious responsibility will (and indeed *must*) continue to move in measured cadence between its traditional practices and communal responsibilities. Spiritual nurture and social reform are productive of freedom at its best, but the challenges of today and tomorrow will put the black church and its mission to the test of relevance and even survival. The rampant secularization and debasement of traditional values critical to the moral authority of the faith, and the increasing acceptance of black Christians in churches from which they were summarily excluded or by which they were spurned, will inevitably weaken the reservoir on which the black church depends for physical survival. A related problem which looms ever closer is the confusion of black identity brought on by racial and ethnic intermarriage, and by the increasing rejection of the "one drop of blood" convention which makes a person who has that fateful drop of African blood a "black" person. A new dialectic has been introduced. It is race versus racelessness in a church that had no options of racial policy or definition when it came out of the void. The black church has always been considered the most formidable bastion of black solidarity. To those who can visualize no other reality, *the Tiger Woods syndrome*, which rejects the race of one parent as being defining to the exclusion of the other, is awesome in its potential for the fragmentation of the church and the African-American community. Other problems include the continuing social and economic pathology of young black males, and the attractiveness of Islam over the black church for those who manage some form of salvage from the maelstrom. Finally, there is the zeal for economic development under church leadership, which is good for the church and good for the community. Yet care must be taken that the commitment to the spirit which has defined the black church in the past must not be permitted to slide imperceptibly into the commitment to mammon when the Fortune 500 comes to knock on a black church door that has stood open for two centuries.

The historic duality of mission is addressed (as it has always been) to both the spiritual and the social deficits of the human predicament, which made the black church the defining reference of the black community. It remains so today: The black church is the uncontested mother of black culture. As with all his other works on the black experience, Professor Billingsley's careful research and insightful analysis reward his readers with a new appreciation of how the black struggle is at the same time more, much more, than a preoccupation with group survival. It is a vitalizing resource for all Americans.

—C. ERIC LINCOLN,
William Rand Kenan Professor (Emeritus)
of Religion and Culture,
Duke University

I

EVOLUTION OF THE BLACK CHURCH AS AGENT OF SOCIAL REFORM

1

—ᴡᴡ—

The Storm Is Passing Over:
The Black Church in Perspective

When I was growing up in the St. James Baptist Church, Birmingham, Alabama, during the era of World War II into the 1950s, the focus of this church and all its activities was on helping to prepare its parishioners for life in the hereafter. There we would eat sweet milk and honey, chatter with angels, wear golden slippers, dance along streets of gold, and hear little David play on his harp—but until then, we would travel through this world of woe doing the best we could. Our real home was "over Jordan." And when the time came for us to be there, we wanted to be ready to "walk in Jerusalem, just like John."

Our beliefs and practices were what has been termed otherworldly. Our concern was sustaining ourselves as we resisted the evil influences of this world to survive and overcome it in order to go home to where we would have no more suffering.

The St. James Baptist Church was a warm and caring place that nurtured emotional and spiritual growth as well as latent talent in its members. It gave me the opportunity to sing in the choir, to play my trombone, to teach Sunday school, and to stand before the congregation giving reports on current events. At times it was even a romantic experience. Courtship was fostered among the young, a role often played by the church unintentionally. Among my fondest memories of St. James were the times my brother Bill and I walked the sisters Ruth and Catherine home after Tuesday night choir practice; the times I sat on the back seat of the church enduring the long service by holding hands with the pastor's stepdaughter, Wilhelmina.

There were some socially significant spinoffs to this St. James Baptist Church experience. In helping to prepare us for the other world, we were encouraged to live a good life, to work hard, to study, to be kind and considerate of others. We were taught to follow the Golden Rule and to think well of ourselves but not "more highly than we ought." We were taught to get along with other people, and to obey the rules of sacred and secular authorities. There was also a nod once in a while given to some secular activities. A Boy Scout troop was sanctioned for young male members. It was organized by one of the sisters of the church, Mrs. Watts, and I have long supposed that we were the only Boy Scout troop in the nation with a female as scoutmaster. But, for the most part, St. James Baptist Church was an example of what the Rev. Cecil Murray has called "coming to church for personal salvation alone."

St. James Baptist Church was not alone in this respect. All over town it would have been hard to find a black church in the early 1950s that was actively engaged in the community.

And then came the thunder. One short decade later, all hell seemed to have broken loose in Birmingham. The 1954 Supreme Court Decision in *Brown* v. *Board of Education of Topeka, Kansas* had aroused some local leaders to test its application. Notable in this regard was the Rev. Fred Shuttlesworth, who tried to enroll his children in the nearby white school. Later still, after the courts outlawed the Alabama NAACP, Shuttlesworth would organize the Alabama Voting Rights League, which would initiate direct social action in Birmingham. Meanwhile, the year-long 1955–56 bus boycott in Montgomery, some 80 miles away, had electrified the nation. Soon the black citizens of Birmingham would declare war on segregation. Dr. Martin Luther King Jr., Shuttlesworth, and others would lead a children's crusade. The police commissioner, Bull Connor, would lose his mind, unleashing hostile dogs and fire hoses on innocent black children. The civil rights revolution had come to Birmingham. And the black church was at the center of it. Birmingham would never be the same again.

In time, the great, quiet, sedate, upper-middle-class 16th Street Baptist Church would be catapulted onto center stage in the movement, in part because of its strategic location on the periphery of the African American community and downtown, across the street from Kelly Ingram Park, and in part because of the leadership of the pastor. It was in this church on September 15, 1963, less than a month after the heralded march on Washington, that four little girls—Denise McNair, Carole Robertson, Cynthia Wesley, and Addie Mae Collins— were killed by assassins while attending Sunday school in the basement. And moving out into the fray, with all the rest, was my beloved St. James Baptist Church. Not all black churches were actively involved in this movement. Indeed, not even a majority, but a significant critical mass was sufficiently active to make the civil rights revolution possible.

The movement would bring out the best in black Birmingham, and for several years it would bring out the worst in white Birmingham, including the white churches. And it would give the world King's famous "Letter from a Birmingham Jail," surely among the most eloquent literary treatises on social justice in American literature.

Finally, the movement would see the crumbling of the physical, social, psychological, and political walls of segregation. Birmingham would elect a black educator and Sunday school teacher, Richard Arrington, for repeated terms as mayor. The city would also witness the ushering in of good relations between the races. A memorial park and an institute have been erected to the civil rights movement and the history of the blacks in the South.[1] The Alabama Civil Rights Institute, a self-directed journey through the civil rights movement, was organized in the 16th Street Baptist Church. The large and modern building is appropriately fronted by a bronze statue of Fred Shuttlesworth. It contains 10 venues, among them the Introductory Theater, which plays a 10-minute film that introduces the history of Birmingham from its founding through the 1920s; the Barriers Gallery, which comprises 14 scenes conveying the quality of life under segregation from about 1920 to 1954; the Confrontation Gallery, which consists of three scenes depicting the climate of violence and intimidation that reinforced segregation; and a Movement Gallery, consisting of the 16 scenes showing progress through the history of the movement from 1955 to 1963.

And so throughout the institute. The adjacent Kelly Ingram Park, through which civil rights marchers treaded in 1963, has been redesigned as a monument to the Walk To Freedom and features a life-size bronze statue of King and snapshots of the movement. Indeed, the 16th Street Baptist Church, the Civil Rights Institution, and the Kelly Ingram Park monument taken together from the same street corner provide a dramatic and lasting memory of the movement. It is being copied in other cities.

Mayor Arrington, the driving force behind creating the institute, said Birmingham remains a city overly preoccupied with race. "We've learned to tolerate one another," Arrington said. "Every year, we come closer to understanding the common ground we share. We're beginning to work more and more toward common goals."

Like so many other things in Birmingham, though, building consensus and support for the institute was a struggle. Voters rejected two bond referendums before the mayor raised the construction money by selling off another city building.

Initially, many white corporate leaders shied away from the project, believing that dredging up the city's violent past would hurt its future.

Yet as construction neared completion, attitudes changed. In two months, a corporate fund drive raised $2.5 million seed money to pay for educational programs for the next five years and create a small endowment for scholars.

All this is testament to the success of the civil rights movement. And at the vortex of this overthrow of the old order stood the black church.[2] It was true not only in Birmingham and Montgomery and Selma and Albany and Savannah and Nashville, but all over the South.

The civil rights movement was not the first time black churches have been called upon to serve an activist role in the community. Nor did the civil rights movement represent the end of black church activism, as many have suggested. The chapters of Part II are devoted to setting forth this theme. Indeed, some of the most productive of scholars—W.E.B. Du Bois, E. Franklin Frazier, and C. Eric Lincoln—have established that the black church is a profoundly social institution and often serves as an agent of social reform.

W.E.B. Du Bois

The earliest sociologist to study the black church as a social institution was Du Bois.[3] He pioneered the use of the social survey, and many of his findings and theories are valid a hundred years after his writings. Beginning at the turn of the century he carried out empirical studies of black communities in the North and the South, in urban and rural areas, and in small towns and large cities. He found important distinctions between rural and urban settings, North and South, and the various social classes. He found differences between large and small churches, denominations, and preaching styles. But despite the differences, he found the church to be a central feature of black life and to serve as an integrating function. He also found a strong interaction between the family and the church, which resulted in mutually enhancing effects on both institutions.

This particular research of Du Bois's gives us some of his most mem-

orable findings and observations, including his famous three-part ty-
pology of the black church service. "Three things characterized this
religion of the slave," he concluded, "the Preacher, the Music and the
Frenzy."

Then he sets forth insightful descriptions of all three characteristics
in which the concepts, if not the exact words, survive until this day.
"The preacher is the most unique personality developed by the Negro
on American soil. A leader, a politician, an orator, a 'boss,' an intriguer,
an idealist."[4]

Du Bois continues: "The Music of Negro religion is that plaintive
rhythmic melody with its touching minor cadences, which, despite car-
icature and defilement, still remains the most original and beautiful
expression of human life and longing yet born on American soil."

Du Bois is also clear about the origin of this music. "Sprung from
the African forests, where its counterpart can still be heard, it was
adapted, changed and intensified by the tragic soul-life of the slave,
until, under the stress of law and whip, it became the one true expression of a people's sorrow, despair and hope."[5]

Then he comes to the third characteristic of black religion: "Finally,
the Frenzy or 'Shouting,' when the Spirit of the Lord passed by, and,
seizing the devotee, made him mad with supernatural joy, was the last
essential of Negro religion and the one more devoutly believed in than
all the rest."[6]

The frenzy observed by Du Bois has been interpreted by the Rev.
Wyatt Tee Walker of Canaan Baptist Church in New York and Dr. Jeremiah Wright of Trinity United Church of Christ in Chicago as "experience of the Holy Ghost."

Du Bois also observed that the black church, as a social institution,
is deeply connected with and affected by the larger society. It does not
exist in a vacuum, but rather is "the center of social life within the
Black community," and is the most characteristic expression of African
character.[7]

E. Franklin Frazier

E. Franklin Frazier spent 40 years studying the black church, and his
preeminence as an expert was assured at the time of his death in 1962.

In 1953, at the peak of his career, Frazier served as chief of the
Division of Applied Social Sciences in the Department of Social Sciences
of UNESCO in Paris. When he was invited to give the Frazier Lecture
in Social Anthropology at the University of Liverpool, he chose, without hesitation, to lecture on black religion and the black church in

America. This lecture was later expanded into his well-received book *The Negro Church in America*, published in 1963 in Liverpool and in 1964 in the United States.[8]

Like Du Bois before him, Frazier was not a churchgoing man. But he appreciated the social significance of the church as a central feature of black life and made the church a central feature of his scholarship. Indeed, in no other fields, with the exception of the black family and the black middle class, has Frazier's scholarship received such wide recognition among students of the black experience in America.

Frazier saw the black church as "a nation within a nation," and he credited it for being "the chief means by which a structured or organized life came into existence among the Negro masses" after emancipation. He also believed that this social cohesive or social integration function of the black church was a radical departure from the role played by the invisible institution" under slavery. Moreover, as he observed the whole history of the evolution of the black church, he also held that this cohesive effect broke down rather completely as the black population shifted from rural South to the urban industrial North during the 1940s.

A second important contribution made by Frazier is his concept of the black church as agent of social control. His conception allows us to isolate and study this particular function of the black church as a dynamic institution responding to the changes in its social environment.

Frazier was also eloquent in analyzing the economic functions of the black church, identifying four specific ways in which this economic function operated. By owning their own real estate, black churches made an economic investment in the community. They purchased and built churches, parishes, and other facilities. They also established Mutual Aid Societies after emancipation and throughout the 19th century, and these evolved into black-owned insurance companies. They created and organized black fraternal organizations, which served both social and economic functions.

A fourth area in which Frazier saw the black church exercising a social mission was in the area of education. Churches organized schools, helped to pay teachers, and provided scholarship funds to students.

Frazier also appreciated the role of the church as a political institution. "It was inevitable that preachers who had played such an important role in the organized social life of Negroes should become political leaders during the Reconstruction period when the Negro enjoyed civil rights."[9] He cites Bishop Henry M. Turner of the A.M.E. church as among those who rose to political prominence in Georgia.

Supported by his research on the church and on the black family, he saw the link between the two, including the support system each provided to the family and the community. Moreover, he saw that the Negro's status as an outsider in the American community deepened his loyalties to the one place where he felt safe and accepted: the church.[10]

The idea and reality of the black church as a refuge from a hostile and indifferent white society received strong currency in Frazier's sociology.[11] Frazier also saw the black church as a conservative and accommodationist social institution.[12]

Frazier brilliantly advanced the idea of the secularization of the black church. He observed that over time churches began to tolerate worldly pleasures among its members, including card playing, dancing, theatergoing, and the like. A more pervasive example of secularization was the interest of the churches in the affairs of the community.

Frazier also presented the black church as a deeply heterogeneous institution, and he pointed to the social stratification within and among black churches as a feature of their diversity.

In all Frazier's work, then, the picture of the black church that comes down to us is one of a multifaceted religious, social, economic, educational, cultural, political institution with a broad range of social structures and social functions. His is a conception that provides a highly usable framework for students of the black church as a social institution, even up to the present time.

As valuable as Frazier's work is, it is not perfect. His most conspicuous failure perhaps was his view of the church as exclusively a product of and reaction to white racism. He predicted the withering away of black churches as white churches began to open their doors to blacks. But this has not happened, and the likelihood of its not happening suggests that the origins and functions of the black church are much more complex than he believed and have a certain continuity with the African past which Frazier denied, even as Du Bois affirmed it.

C. Eric Lincoln

Unlike Du Bois or Frazier, who were not even church members, Lincoln is a theologian as well as a sociologist and thus an insider in the study of the black church. All in all, he brings to the subject a unique systematic sociological perspective.

Just as Frazier saw a sharp demarcation between the Negro church

in the postbellum agricultural era and the later period of urban industrialization, Lincoln saw a sharp demarcation between the entirety of
the Negro church, as Frazier knew it, and what Lincoln calls "the Black
church of today."[13]

Lincoln and Mamiya in their pathbreaking study of the black
church observe that "thus far, a general theory of the social analysis of
Black religious phenomena and a sociology of Black churches has not
yet appeared."[14] They set forth certain "theoretical assumptions" and
concepts designed to guide further research and to contribute toward
building a sociology of the black church. Part of their contribution is a
series of concepts in which he posits a "Black Sacred Cosmos" as reflecting "the Religious Worldview of African Americans (as) related
both to their African heritage, which envisioned the whole universe as
sacred, and their conversion to Christianity during slavery and its aftermath."[15] Moreover, they set forth a "dialectical model" of the black
church, which "holds polar opposites in tension constantly shifting between polarities in historical time."[16]

Then, delineating a half-dozen pairs of such polarities, they come
to the one that informs our study. In sum, he views the black church
as characterized in part by a "dialectic between the communal and the
privatistic" orientations. The communal orientation "refers to the historic tradition of black churches being involved in all aspects of the lives
of their members, including political, economic, educational, and social
concerns." On the other hand, "The privatistic pole of this dialectic
means withdrawal from the concerns of the larger community to focus
on meeting only the religious needs of its adherents."[17]

Peter Paris, professor of religion at Princeton Theological Seminary,
has delineated a similar conceptual framework describing the black
church according to "compensatory" and "political" models. His "compensatory model" corresponds roughly to Lincoln's "privatistic orientation." His "political model" corresponds roughly to Lincoln's "communal orientation."[18]

The social role of the black church is also recognized in the extensive studies of African American religion by Hans A. Baer and Merrill
Singer.[19] They find, on the basis of their widespread studies, that there
is a distinct protest tradition among black churches, similar to Lincoln
and Mamiya's "communal orientation," which periodically rises to the
surface as a counterpoint to the more consistent "accommodationist"
tradition, which conforms roughly to Lincoln and Mamiya's "privatistic
orientation."

Perhaps the most comprehensive view of the black church's involvement in social reform has been set forth by Aldon Morris.[20] In his

prize-winning book *The Origins of the Civil Rights Movement*, Morris holds that black churches were able to play such a defining role in this era because of their institutional characteristics—as formal organizations but not "bureaucracies"—and because of the characteristics of the ministers as leaders.

In addition to the influence of the minister and the church organization, we have noted a third source of influence on the community outreach role of the black church, and that is the community itself, which provides the social context for the action or behavior of the church.

During periods of severe and sustained crisis in the African American community, people tend to turn to the church for guidance and support and leadership. When they do, the church typically responds by moving beyond its purely spiritual or religious or privatistic mission to embrace its communal mission, provided that the church, as an organization, is strong, stable, and resourceful and provided that the minister, as leader, is strong, charismatic, innovative, and community oriented.

That is exactly what happened in Birmingham and elsewhere during the civil rights movement. In the 1940s and 1950s in Birmingham there was no general mission and sustained crisis in the African American community. The black church, epitomized by my own St. James Baptist Church, concentrated on the purely spiritual aspect of its mission. To be sure, there were severe problems in Birmingham at that time. Two of the most severe, seemingly as permanent as death and taxes, were segregation and poverty. But in the 1940s and 1950s, even though both were recognized and experienced as evil, there was no generalized heightened awareness of the possibility that they could be abolished and no generalized confrontation over them.

The 1954 Supreme Court decision outlawing school segregation changed all that. On December 1, 1955, when Rosa Parks refused to give up her seat in the segregated black section of a Montgomery city bus so that a white man could take it, she was thrown off the bus and into jail, precipitating a crisis in the African American community. The crisis rose to a crescendo during the yearlong bus boycott that followed. The African American community in Montgomery turned to the black churches, in part because of the strength and resourcefulness of the churches and in part because of the character of their leadership.

It was not the first time blacks in Montgomery had boycotted city buses. Dexter Avenue was not the only church involved. It was not the first time a minister at Dexter Avenue protested publicly against segregation. But when the Rev. Vernon Johns, King's predecessor, did so, the community was not in crisis over segregation. The community had not called on the churches for leadership against it. The Rev. Johns was fired for his confrontation with segregation, which brought discredit onto the church. In choosing King to replace Johns, Dexter Avenue Church thought it had opted for a safer and less confrontational pastor. King was expected to take care of church business and stay out of the streets, while Johns had been accused of doing the opposite. And until Rosa Parks precipitated the crisis, King did just that.

Leadership also came from laymen within the church. Dr. Jo Ann Robinson, a professor at Alabama State College and president of the Women's Political Action Committee, was a longtime advocate of such protest. By all accounts, the minister who was the most logical choice to lead the movement was the Rev. Ralph David Abernathy of First Baptist Church. Some say that he confidently expected as much when he arrived at the meeting. Indeed, most of the people at the meeting who elected King had never seen or heard him before that day.

The literature on the movement speculates on why King was elected. The most prevalent is that he was new in town and did not yet have any enemies. Yet another reason should be added: He was elected, in large part, because members of his church, including Robinson, realized that he was an eloquent and highly learned leader with a set of credentials made to order for times such as this. And so they actively worked for his election. The next day, when King gave his acceptance speech, the whole town knew that the right person had been selected.

So, in this crisis in the African American community precipitated by Rosa Parks and managed brilliantly by the likes of Jo Ann Robinson and A. D. Nixon, the people turned to the churches for leadership and support. Several strong and resourceful churches with highly able leaders responded by joining the battle.

The question is: Was this an isolated example of the black church as agent of social reform? The answer, we suggest, is that it had happened before, is happening now in some places and in some forms, and might well happen in the future on an even grander scale.

2

—ༀ—

If Tombstones Could Talk: The Evolution
of the Black Church in Savannah

A study of the historical evolution of the black church as agent of social reform could have no more authentic setting than Savannah, Georgia. Here stands the oldest continuous black congregation in all of North America. And throughout its 225-year history (since 1773), the First African Baptist Church repeatedly has been drawn into the community to deal with social issues of a nonreligious nature.

Laurel Grove South Cemetery

To understand this story and put it in its proper sociohistorical perspective, one must begin at the cemetery—specifically the Laurel Grove South Cemetery, located at the end of Victory Drive on the western edge of the city. Established in the antebellum period as a resting place for enslaved and free Africans, and moved to its present location after the Civil War, Laurel Grove South is the preeminent repository of African American history and culture, a history and culture that centers on the role of the black church in the city. Vocalist Nina Simone sings an ode to the city called "One More Sunday in Savannah." It is eminently appropriate because from the early development of the legendary "Praise Houses" to the present time, the black church has been at the center of community life and the keeper of African American history.

Any visitor to Laurel Grove South Cemetery, especially if under the guidance of local historian W. W. Law, will be immediately immersed in this history. At the gateway to these burial grounds is a marker bearing three names: the Rev. Andrew Bryan, the Rev. Andrew Marshall, and the Rev. Henry Cunningham. The sign points to their burial crypt. Not only do these three men represent the one church originated by George Leile, as his linear successors, but all three of them are buried together in one crypt. They have thus over the years come to symbolize the concept of "three in one" so central to the Christian faith.

To understand the contribution of these men to the evolution of the black church in Savannah, let us first consider the role of the Rev. George Leile, whose legacy they represent.

Rev. George Leile

George Leile was born into slavery in 1750 in Virginia. In his youth he was sold downriver to a rice plantation owner near Savannah who was a deacon in the white Baptist Church. Leile once wrote of his early development, "I was informed by both white and Black people, that my father was the only Black person who knew the Lord in a spiritual way in that country. I always had a natural fear of God from my youth, and was often checked in conscience with thoughts of death, which barred me from many sins and bad company. I knew no other way at that time to hope for salvation but only in the performance of my good works."[1]

Of his conversion in 1773 at the age of 23 he said: "I found no way wherein I could escape the damnation of hell, only through the merits of my dying Lord and Savior Jesus Christ; which caused me to make intercession with Christ, for the salvation of my poor immortal soul; and I full well recollect, I requested of my Lord and Master to give me a work, I did not care how mean it was, only to try and see how good I could do it."

That year he was baptized by the white minister at the same church where his employer was deacon. He then purchased his freedom and set out to preach on both sides of the Savannah River, in South Carolina and Georgia. He had learned to read and would often be found reading the Bible and teaching hymns to blacks on the plantations. He then assembled a small group of followers in Savannah to whom he preached regularly. Two years later, in 1775, Leile was ordained into the Christian ministry by the minister who had baptized him. Leile could now administer baptism and the other sacraments himself, and thus the first black church in Savannah was officially constituted.[2]

In the midst of the Revolutionary war, when Leile's church was only six years old and its leader only 29, the British captured Savannah. They occupied the city from 1779 to 1782, throwing the community into turmoil and crisis. The British invited the African captives to come over to the British side and work with them, promising that they would be treated as free persons. But the plantation owners, their holdings still intact, forbade their slaves to leave their servitude under threat of severe punishment.

To solve their dilemma, the Africans turned to their church and its young minister for guidance. The Rev. Leile led a movement encouraging black people to side with the British. He spent much of his time on Tybee Island, where the British forces were based, tirelessly working with the British. He also commuted to Savannah in his boat to minister to his flock and consult others. He and many other blacks played heroic roles in the capture and occupation of Savannah by the British. But after the British lost the war in 1782, many of those Africans who had joined in support of them were reenslaved. Others managed to escape, going to the West Indies, Nova Scotia, and Sierra Leone during the evacuation of the British.

The estimated total number of blacks leaving Savannah was 4,000. Another 6,000 were evacuated from Charleston and 4,000 from New York.[3] But the evacuation of the British did not mean the death of the black church. Indeed, four streams of black churches evolved from Leile's prodigious evangelizing in Savannah: in Jamaica, Nova Scotia, Augusta, Georgia, and Savannah.

Though Leile had bought his freedom, the heirs of his former owner sought to reclaim him as their slave. Because he resisted, they had him thrown into jail. He secured his release and his safe passage to Jamaica by hiring himself out as an indentured servant to a British officer. In Jamaica he worked off his debt and became an independent farmer, abolitionist, and missionary to Africa, and in 1784 he founded the First Baptist Church in Kingston, Jamaica. It was the first Baptist church established on the island, and it exists to this day.

David George, an associate of Leile's at the Savannah church, was the leader of the settlement of blacks who went with the British to Nova Scotia. Life there was very hard because the land was poor and infertile. In January 1792, he led a group of about 1,200 free blacks from Nova Scotia to form a colony in Sierra Leone. Later still, members of this community immigrated to Nigeria. Eventually, a group of these converts immigrated to the United States and opened a church in South Carolina.

A third continuation of George Leile's church in Savannah took place in Georgia. After the evacuation of the British, one of Leile's associates in the Savannah church, whom he had baptized Peter Galphin, went back to Augusta, Georgia, where he lived before the war, and founded the Springfield Baptist church.[4] Finally, the small congregation left by Leile in Savannah in 1783 was continued under the leadership of Andrew Bryan, who had also been baptized by Leile. (For the ministers of this church from Leile to the present see Table 1 in Appendix C.)

Rev. Andrew Bryan

After Leile departed for Jamaica, Andrew Bryan took up the task of holding the little band of worshipers in Savannah together.[5] They met frequently for prayer, singing, and discussions, and after about nine months, Bryan felt the call to preach. He continued for three years to lead this congregation, even without any formal authority. The Rev. E. G. Thomas has written of this time, "Taking up this work that had been kept alive in the midst of hostile whites, organizing and teaching a servile class who for more than three years had been taught to hate the very masters who continued to hold them in bondage, Andrew Bryan was undertaking a task that was threefold more difficult than he imagined."[6]

He continues: "Individuals were punished by their masters. Some were intimidated and cruelly dealt with by the militia. They were often waylaid and severely flogged on their way to and from their humble meetings. But none of these things moved them! Indeed the severer the persecution the more resolutely did these saints rely upon God and stick to their worship."[7]

In desperation, a group of whites seized Bryan and about 50 of his followers in the public square one day "and beat them so severely that their blood ran down and puddled on the ground about them. But Andrew Bryan, already inhumanly cut, and his body so lacerated that his clothes were saturated in his own blood, with uplifted hands cried to his persecutor: 'If you would stop me from preaching, cut off my head! for I am willing not only to be whipped, but would freely suffer death for the cause of the Lord Jesus.' Only then, did their tormentors walk away."[8]

How did these black people, held in bondage, sustain such courage of their convictions? How could they so utterly defy the slave masters, who, according to the law, owned them? From where did they find the strength to persevere? These must surely be among the events that prompted James Weldon Johnson to write about the days "when hope unborn had died."[9]

The ordeal of these black Christians was not yet over. After Bryan's expressed willingness to suffer death for his beliefs, he and his followers were no longer beaten in the streets. Instead their enemies decided to use the legal system. Bryan and his followers were accused of insurrection and plotting against whites in their meetings. And so the black believers were swiftly tried, found guilty, put in prison, and their meeting house was taken away from them.

This was the last straw for Jonathan Bryan, the plantation owner who claimed Andrew Bryan as his slave. He interceded on behalf of his property and had Andrew Bryan and his followers released from prison. Jonathan Bryan gave Andrew Bryan and the other worshipers permission to use a rice barn on his plantation, three miles outside of Savannah, as their meeting place. They met there for several years. This barn became memorialized as "Brampton's Barn," after the plantation on which it was located. The congregation grew. For a time they had a measure of peace, but that ended abruptly.

The enemies of the congregation began to circle around the barn during worship services. As the worshipers went to and from their meeting house, they were closely watched. One day, one of the eavesdroppers heard Bryan fervently praying inside the barn. As the eavesdropper got closer, he could make out that Bryan was praying for the man who had subjected him to a beating in the public square. The eavesdropper became so unnerved by this that he ran screaming from the barn, telling all within hearing what he had heard. Whites responded in various ways. Though some responded in fear, others had great sympathy for the worshipers who remained compassionate as they endured oppression. As word of Bryan's prayer spread among blacks, they reacted in a more consistently sympathetic way; those who were not already members joined this church in droves.

Some of the influential whites who were sympathetic to the worshipers' plight actively came to their aid. They took a petition to Chief Justice Osbourne of the state court, asking that these victims of persecution be provided legal protection. The judge ruled that they could worship freely as long as they did so between sunrise and sunset on the Sabbath. The court deemed that on weekdays they had more important things to do; and that in the evenings, being black, they could not be trusted to gather together for purposes whites considered unacceptable. The ruling was limited and limiting, but it still brought immense relief to the black Christians.

So, in the words of the Rev. E. G. Thomas, the author, "they obtained peace through peaceful methods, and won many friends among the more influential whites and multitudes of blacks were added to their number."

After the ruling, Jonathan Bryan acted again on behalf of these worshipers. He invited a black preacher from Augusta, Jesse Peters (whom George Leile had converted), to visit his plantation together with a white preacher, the Rev. Abraham Marshall of Kiokee, to assist in baptizing 45 converts. At the same time they were permitted to ordain Andrew Bryan, who was then officially installed as the pastor of the church.

Shortly after that, Jonathan Bryan died. In his will he left Andrew Bryan to his son, William Bryan, also a planter. William Bryan rose to a new level of magnanimity by permitting Andrew to purchase his freedom for what was considered the modest sum of 50 pounds British sterling. According to the Chatham County courthouse records, the transaction reads, "For the sum of 50 pounds sterling, and acknowledging also the faithful services of my Negro fellow Andrew . . . I give and grant the said Negro fellow Andrew his full and absolute manumission."[10]

Then William Bryan went a step further. At Andrew Bryan's request, he persuaded another local white man to sell the newly free black man some property. Thus on June 6, 1790, Thomas Gibbons sold to "Free Andrew," for 27 pounds sterling, a lot 95 feet by 100 feet, which Andrew Bryan used to build the first church building owned by blacks in Savannah. The newly ordained minister was now on his way to the top. Seven years later, on June 3, 1797, he sold this property to the church for 30 pounds sterling, making only a modest profit. He also operated a hauling business with white and black customers and became rather well-to-do.

Andrew Bryan died in 1812, at the age of 96. And while he had suffered much in his life, he died a free man, a wealthy man, and one highly respected by Blacks and whites alike. More important still, he had established a firm foundation for the church which would continue to the present time.

To mark his passing, the Savannah Baptist Association held a ceremony, where they adopted a resolution honoring his memory. An intimate friend of Bryan's, Dr. Henry Holcombe, had 16 years earlier written a description of him, which was read at the occasion:

Andrew Bryan not only honorably obtained liberty but a handsome estate. His fleecy and well-set locks have been bleached by eighty win-ters; and dressed like a bishop of London, he rides, moderately corpulent, in his chair, and with manly features of jetty hue, fills any person to whom he gracefully bows with pleasure and veneration, by displaying in smiles, even rows of natural teeth white as ivory, and a pair of fine black eyes sparkling with intelligence, benevolence, and joy.[11]

Reverend Henry C. Cunningham

The second name on the marker at the entrance to Laurel Grove South Cemetery is that of Henry C. Cunningham. As pastor of the First African Baptist Church in Savannah, Bryan led efforts to establish another church, the Second African Baptist Church. The Second African Baptist Church was established in 1802 after First African Baptist Church became overcrowded.

Both Cunningham and Henry Francis, another deacon in First African Baptist Church, expressed a desire to lead the new church. It is said that Bryan had a preference for Francis and had indeed purchased his freedom and brought him from Augusta to groom him for future leadership. As the establishment of the new black church approached, Bryan was preparing Francis to assume the pastorate. In the meantime, however, Henry Cunningham gathered strong support from the white Baptist Association. He was installed as pastor of the new church on January 1, 1802, even before he was ordained as a minister.

The next day, Francis was appointed pastor of a third black church, newly established at Ogeechee, some 14 miles outside Savannah. That church survived only a few years, but remnants of it became the current Littway Baptist Church. Meanwhile, Cunningham built the Second African Baptist into a strong church. An astute businessman, he operated a successful hauling company. His mostly white customers helped to make him a wealthy man. He bought slaves to assist him in his hauling business. As a free person his status of slave owner was legal, but indications are that he treated his slaves with the utmost in kindness. The church, which has always been located in Greene Square, was the site for Gen. Sherman's reading of the Emancipation Proclamation in January 1865 and for Dr. Martin Luther King's deliverance of his first "I have a dream" speech in July 1963, one month before the historic march on Washington.

Andrew Marshall

The third man buried and named on the marker at the entrance to the cemetery is Andrew Marshall. Marshall, a deacon, assistant to and nephew of Andrew Bryan, succeeded him as the third pastor of the First African Baptist Church. He was by all accounts a learned, effective, popular pastor and community leader who led a large and growing congregation for some 44 years.

Marshall had already been pastor for about two decades when a major crisis exploded in the community. Though this new crisis could not equal the crisis of the coming of the British in 1779 or their evacuation of Savannah three years later, it would have enormous ramifications all over town and down through history.

In 1832, a white evangelist, Dr. Alexander Campbell, came to Savannah preaching a doctrine of the fatherhood of God and the brotherhood of man, including the principle that all persons are equal in the sight of God—whether black or white, slave or free. As a consequence, the white churches refused to allow Campbell to preach from their pulpits. The First African Baptist Church and its bright, brave, and dynamic third pastor, the Rev. Andrew Marshall, invited Dr. Campbell to preach there. Upset over this affront to the slave authority, the white Baptist Association suspended Marshall and encouraged a rump group who disagreed with him to form a new church. The Sunbury Baptist Association passed three resolutions at the November 1833 meeting.[12]

> Resolution 29. Resolved, that this association having undoubted testimony of Andrew Marshall's holding the sentiments avowed by Alexander Campbell, (the visiting evangelist) now declare him and all his followers, to have thrown themselves out of the fellowship of the churches of this association, and it recommends all of its faith and order to separate from them. Resolution 26. Resolved that this association approves the conduct of S. Whitfield, J. Clay, and others who separated from the First African Church and recommends that they be accepted into full fellowship with all the churches (of this association). Resolution 25. Application was made by the Third African Church to become a member of this association. Granted by a unanimous vote.[13]

When the deacons of First African Baptist met with the white Baptist Association to ask for guidance on the selection of a pastor, since the Rev. Marshall had been suspended, they were told that they could select any preacher of their choice, black or white, slave or free, as long as he was ordained and as long as he was not Andrew Marshall.

When the deacons consulted Marshall himself, he reminded them that Baptist doctrine gave the authority of hiring pastors to the congregation and no other association. So the congregation assumed its rightful authority and elected him its new pastor. The officers then met with the association and gave their report. It was such a bold and skillful act of defiance on the part of these persons held in bondage that the association acquiesced, and Marshall served another 20 years as pastor. He ultimately died while on a tour up North to raise money for the new church building on Franklin Square. He was 100 years old.

What is striking about this schism is how the actions of the white Baptist Association encouraged those who disagreed with Marshall to form a new church. Later the Sunbury Association appointed a distinguished committee of black and white Baptists that recommended that the three African Baptist churches be accepted into the slaveholding authority in good standing.

A group of 155 members under the leadership of Deacon Adam Arguile Johnson, who had been a long and close associate of Marshall's, withdrew from First African Baptist and were given letters of dismissal to form the Third African Baptist Church. They were also given the original building purchased by the Rev. Andrew Bryan in 1790. Johnson led this new church until it elected its first pastor, the Rev. Thomas Anderson. Anderson would serve only from 1833 to 1835. The overwhelming majority of 2,640 members stayed with Marshall and moved into the new quarters on Franklin Square purchased from a white church.

After the schism the First African Baptist Church grew by leaps and bounds. It has never lost its preeminent leadership position in Savannah (as seen in Table 2 of Appendix C). All three churches showed strong membership. By 1857, nearly 25 years after the schism some five years before the outbreak of the Civil War, the First African Baptist Church had 1,137 members, the Second African Baptist Church had 1,012, members, and the Third African Baptist Church had 241 members (see Table 2).

If the Rev. George Leile was the hero of the first crisis, the capture and occupation of Savannah in 1779 by the British, and if his understudy and successor, the Rev. Andrew Bryan, was the hero of the second crisis, the evacuation of the British in 1782, then the Rev. Andrew Marshall was surely the hero of the third crisis, in 1832.[14] Meanwhile, Laurel Grove South Cemetery continues to tell their story and to serve as a symbol of the evolution of the social role of the black church in Savannah.

3

—ɱ—

General Sherman and the Black Church

G en. William T. Sherman's brilliant and bloody march through
Georgia and the Carolinas during the fall and winter of 1864–65
profoundly affected the black community and the black church. And,
the relationship was reciprocal. Just as profoundly did the black people
and their church affect the success of Sherman's mission.

This story begins when Gen. Sherman and his forces launched the
Kennesaw Mountain Campaign en route to Atlanta and captured Marietta, Georgia, in June 1864,[1] where he used the First Baptist Church
as a hospital. In his conquest the general freed the Black Zion Baptist
Church from its dependence on the white First Baptist Church, where
it had existed as an appendage for a number of years.

Black membership in the First Baptist Church of Marietta had
begun as early as January 9, 1836, when "Dicey," a slave woman
serving a prominent white family in the church, became the first black
person admitted to membership. By 1843 there were 59 black and
142 white members, including Brother Ephraim Rucker, a servant of
the famous Dobbs family, prominent members of the church. Since
1855 the black members had been petitioning for their own church
but were repeatedly denied. In 1863 Rucker was licensed to preach by
the First Baptist Church, but only to the black members. They were
allowed to have their own church conference but still no church of
their own.

After Sherman's conquest, however, the Zion Baptist Church would become separate and free, and Brother Ephraim would lead this independent church into the early years of freedom.[2]

Atlanta to Savannah

On September 2, 1864, Atlanta fell under the onslaught of Sherman's troops. The general wired the news to President Lincoln: "Atlanta is ours and fairly won."[3] Hailed throughout the North, the news virtually guaranteed the reelection of Lincoln in November that year, an election which most experts agree he would otherwise have lost.

After the presidential election, Sherman was ready to move on with his march through Georgia. On November 15, 1864, after setting fire to Atlanta, Sherman and his 60,000 infantry, 5,500 calvary, and tons of supplies, ammunition, and equipment set out on their journey to the sea. As he departed for his long march to the sea, the city's premier black church was among the few structures he left intact. Later generations would come to know the Big Bethel A.M.E. Church as the city's oldest and surely one of its most distinguished churches down to the present time. Big Bethel was founded as "Union Church" in 1847 by a group of captives, including Vine Ware, Sam Fisher, Andrew Montgomery, Melus Murphy, and Henry Strickland. The church was given a new lease on life by Sherman's conquest.[4]

On his way out of town Sherman would pass through Stone Mountain, Georgia, where the black captives set free by his march would gratefully name a portion of the town after him (Shermantown) and freely establish their own Bethseder Baptist Church.[5]

Still farther along, Sherman's forces entered Covington, Georgia, where they would liberate the Bethlehem Baptist Church, which had been in operation since 1847. The church founded by the Rev. T. Baker and served by him for 46 years would be led from 1896 to 1902 by the Rev. A. D. Williams, the maternal grandfather of Dr. Martin Luther King Jr. Later still, this historic church was led by King's uncle, the Rev. Joel King, "Daddy King's" brother, from 1935 to 1941.[6]

Sherman's march through Georgia could not have been successful without the extensive cooperation and support of black residents, even though they were not allowed to join Sherman's armies as fighting men.[7]

All along the way, Sherman repeatedly urged his men to encourage young able-bodied black men to join his ranks, even as he used blacks as scouts, guides, and informants.[8]

In addition to these work recruits, however, an additional 35,000 blacks left their plantations to follow Sherman's army, often camping near the soldier camps.[9]

Sherman in Savannah

When Sherman and his troops entered Savannah triumphantly on December 21, 1864, without firing a shot, the Confederate troops were allowed to escape across the Savannah River. Sherman's forces were accompanied not only by their battalions of black laborers, but by 10,000 other blacks who had tagged along successfully. One group of blacks had drowned trying to follow Sherman's troops across a river, an event for which Sherman would be widely denounced in the North.[10]

By the time Sherman reached Savannah in December 1864, the black ministers were ready for him. A small delegation of black ministers, organized by the 51-year-old William J. Campbell, pastor of the First African Baptist Church, together with pastors of Second African Baptist Church and Third African Baptist Church, called on Sherman to offer their assistance in the transition. They later reported that Sherman received them with the greatest courtesy.

This early contact with the black preachers in Savannah would prove helpful to Sherman and his mission. Their interaction would culminate in an historic meeting with 20 black religious leaders at Sherman's headquarters on January 12, 1865, a meeting that historian Ira Berlin has called "among the most important gatherings of the entire Civil War era."[11]

Another person who met Sherman on his arrival was the cotton merchant Charles Green, who offered Sherman the use of his mansion as a headquarters. At the time the mansion was one of the largest, most stately and richly appointed in all Savannah.[12]

Twenty Black Religious Leaders

They gathered one by one and two by two. They came from many directions, walking from across town, riding their mules, and in their horse-drawn carts. They had seen this house many times but only from the outside. They had never been invited in. And if they had, they would have been asked to enter through the back door. On this night, Thursday, January 12, 1865, less than three weeks after the fall of Savannah, twenty black religious leaders gathered in front of the house and entered through the massive mahogany front doors, ushered in by military guards. Tonight they were the special guests of the general.[13]

They passed through the grand foyer and down the long hallway adorned with American black walnut and elaborately carved crown moldings and cornices. The doorknobs, hinges, and keyholes were all silver plated. There were marble mantels throughout.[14]

These men had never seen anything like this. But tonight they were not on an art and architecture tour. They had been summoned for an urgent mission, to help Gen. Sherman, Secretary of War Edwin Stanton, and President Lincoln himself figure out how to implement the Emancipation Proclamation! For this occasion, they were dressed in their finest clothes. They were on their best, soberest behavior. They knew that they carried the weight and the fate of their people and of the fragile union itself on their shoulders and in their hearts, and minds, and souls. And history would record that they were fully up to this task. Though most had been recently set free from slavery, they were not ordinary bondsmen. All except two were ordained ministers, serving as pastors and assistant pastors of the city's five historic black churches. The other two were prominent laymen with important fiduciary responsibilities.[15]

What was the genesis of this remarkable meeting?

After Sherman's capture of Savannah, President Lincoln was eager to move ahead with implementation of the Emancipation Proclamation of January 1, 1863, but there were no plans for implementation. And so Lincoln dispatched his abolitionist secretary of war, Edwin Stanton, to Savannah, where he arrived by ship on January 11, 1865. He would depart on January 15.

Sherman has described the genesis of this particular meeting in his memoirs:

> Mr. Stanton seemed desirous of coming into contact with the negroes to confer with them, and he asked me to arrange an interview for him. I accordingly sent out and invited the most intelligent of the negroes, mostly Baptist and Methodist preachers, to come to my rooms to meet the Secretary of War. Twenty responded, and were received in my room upstairs in Mr. Green's house, where Mr. Stanton and Adjutant-General Townsend took down the conversation in the form of questions and answers. Each of the twenty gave his name and partial history, and then selected Garrison Frazier as their spokesman.[16]

Who were these 20 black leaders?[17] (Their profiles appear in Table 3 of Appendix C.) The principal leaders:

• William J. Campbell, age 51, was born in Savannah. Campbell was held in slavery until 1849, when he was liberated by will of his mistress, May Maxwell. At the time of the meeting, he had been pastor of the First African Baptist Church of Savannah for 10 years, with a membership of about 1,800 and church property valued at $18,000.

• The Rev. John Cox, 58, was pastor of the Second African Baptist Church. Born in Savannah, Cox had been held in slavery until 1849, when he bought his freedom for $1,000. He had been an ordained minister for the last 15 years, and his congregation numbered 1,222 persons, with church property worth $10,000.

• The Rev. Ulysses L. Houston, 41, was pastor of the Third African Baptist Church. Born in Grahamsville, South Carolina, he was held in slavery until the Union army entered Savannah in 1864. The congregation at that time numbered 400, with church property worth $5,000. Even though he was held in slavery, the Rev. Houston had been in the ministry about eight years. After the Civil War, he had a distinguished career in politics, and lost his pulpit because of it. But at the meeting with Stanton and Sherman he was a respected member of the leadership team.

• William Bentley, 72, was born in Savannah. Bentley was held in slavery until he was 25, when he was emancipated in the will of his "owner." He was pastor of Andrew's Chapel, Methodist Episcopal Church, the only one of that denomination in Savannah, and had been in the ministry for 20 years. Bentley's congregation numbered 360 members, and their church property was valued at $20,000.

• James Porter, 39, was born free in Charleston, South Carolina, his mother having purchased her freedom. He was a lay reader and president of the board of wardens and vestry of St. Stephen's Protestant Episcopal Colored Church in Savannah. He had been in communion nine years, with a congregation that now numbered 200 and church property worth $10,000.

• Adolphus Delmotte, 28, was also born free in Savannah. He was a licensed minister of the Missionary Baptist Church of Milledgeville. His congregation numbered 300 to 400, and he had been in the ministry about two years.

• Garrison Frazier, age 67, a minister for 35 years, was born in Granville County, North Carolina. He was held in slavery until eight years before, when he bought freedom for himself and his wife, paying $1,000 in gold and silver. He was an ordained minister in the Baptist Church but, his health failing, had charge of no congregation at the time.

The other 13 ministers were mainly associates at the above churches.

All of the men were literate and were experienced leaders. Together, they had a combined 271 years in the ministry. On average, they could boast of 14 years experience in their posts. Four of them had 20 years or more of leadership experience, while only seven had less than ten years. And though not the beneficiaries of formal education, they were learned and at the helm of already established, strong institutions. Primary among them were the First African, the Second African, and the Third African Baptist Churches.

The Episcopal Church was another strong institution established as early as 1855. In the winter of that year a church was established in a bakery owned by a William Cleghorn on Perry Lane. Originally called St. Stephen's, the church changed its name to St. Matthew's Episcopal Church after the Civil War.[18]

Stanton made introductions and put the first question to the group assembled. "State what your understanding is in regard to the acts of Congress and President Lincoln's (Emancipation) proclamation, touching the condition of the colored people in the Rebel states."

The Rev. Frazier, having been elected to speak for the leaders, responded promptly.

> So far as I understand President Lincoln's proclamation to the rebellious states, it is that if they would lay down their arms and submit to the laws of the United States before the first of January 1863, all should be well; but if they did not, then all the slaves in the Rebel states should be free henceforth and forever. That is what I understood.

Frazier's eloquence and precision astounded the government officials.

The secretary then put a second question to the leaders. "State what you understand by slavery and the freedom that was to be given by the president's proclamation."

It was the shortest question the secretary would ask all evening and perhaps the most profound. The Rev. Garrison and the others had given a great deal of thought to the issue of slavery and freedom. Frazier said simply:

> Slavery is receiving by irresistible power the work of another man, and not by his consent. The freedom, as I understand it, promised by the proclamation is taking us from under the yoke of bondage, and placing us where we could reap the fruit of our own labor, take care of ourselves and assist the government in maintaining our freedom.

The wisdom of these men came in part from the uncanny ability of oppressed people to know more about the doings of the oppressors than the oppressors know about them. It came from the capacity of these men to think deeply about the nature of the human condition. As learned men of the Scriptures, it came from their own interpretation of the biblical prescription for justice in human relationships. Finally, they were wise men because they were self-conscious Africans.

The secretary of war said to them, "State in what manner you think you can take care of yourselves, and how can you best assist the government in maintaining your freedom?"

The Rev. Frazier responded in language that suggested a well-delivered sermon.

> The way we can best take care of ourselves is to have land, and turn it and till it by our own labor—that is, by the labor of the women and children and old men, and we can soon maintain ourselves and have something to spare. And to assist the government, the young men should enlist in the service of the government and serve in such manner as they may be wanted. We want to be placed on *land* until we are able to buy it and make it our own.

Frazier knew back then what many contemporary advocates of social progress have not yet learned: The secret to independence is *land*. Ownership of property. That is what makes the black church such a strong, independent, and self-sustaining institution.

But how, the secretary wanted to know, could these uneducated masses, with a 250-year history of bondage, use land to develop their independent status in the new order? So he put the next question. "State in what manner you would rather live—whether scattered among the whites or in colonies by yourselves."

It is remarkable that so many of the issues these leaders were asked to grapple with are unresolved even today. Consider the Rev. Frazier's response.

"I would prefer to live by ourselves, for there is a prejudice against us in the South that will take years to get over; but I do not know that I can answer for my brethren."

All the other leaders were polled. The Rev. James Lynch said he thought they should not be separated, but live together. All the other men, questioned one by one, agreed with the Rev. Frazier.

At one point Stanton asked gratuitously whether blacks had the intelligence to look after themselves. The response was as brief as it was positive. The secretary continued:

> State what is the feeling of the black population of the South toward the government of the United States; what is the understanding in respect to the present war—its causes and object, and their disposition to aid either side. State fully your views.

The longest recorded response of the whole meeting came when The Rev. Frazier observed:

> I think you will find there are thousands that are willing to make any sacrifice to assist the government of the United States; while there are also many that are not willing to take up arms, I do not suppose there are a dozen men that are opposed to the government. I understand, as to the war, that the South is the aggressor. President Lincoln was elected president by a majority of the United States, which guaranteed him the right of holding the office and exercising that right over the whole United States. The South, without knowing what he would do, rebelled. The war was commenced by the Rebels before he came into office. The object of the war was not at first to give the slaves their freedom, but the sole object of the war was at first to bring the rebellious states back into the Union and their loyalty to the laws of the United States.
>
> Afterward, knowing the value set on the slaves by the Rebels, the president thought that his proclamation would stimulate them to lay down their arms, reduce them to obedience, and help to bring back the Rebel states; and their not doing so has now made the freedom of the slaves a part of the war. It is my opinion that there is not a [black] man in this city that could be started to help the Rebels one inch, for that would be suicide. There were two black men who left with the Rebels (when they abandoned Savannah) because they had taken an active part for the Rebels and thought something might befall them if they stayed behind; but there is not another man. If the prayers that have gone up for the Union army could be read out, you would not get through them these two weeks.

There was no rushing this meeting. This was serious business of the state. The men talked "until the small hours of the morning."[19] Quarles states that each of Frazier's responses was written down by Stanton and read to the others to make sure they agreed with it. Quarles continues:

"After such answers Stanton would put down his pen and finger his glasses in a surprised way, as if he could not comprehend how these men came to possess such a clear consciousness of the merits of the questions involved in the war."[20] Stanton would later report that the responses from these former slaves were so profound that he could not have received better responses if he had been speaking with the president's cabinet![21]

The secretary asked another half-dozen questions. He wanted to know whether rural blacks might hold views different from those of urban blacks, whether the blacks would fight against the Union if armed by the Rebels, what blacks thought about enlistment in the Union armies, and what they thought about the possibility of enlisting blacks in the army as replacements for whites to meet Union state quotas.

At this point an amazing incident occurred. The secretary of war asked Gen. Sherman to leave the room. Sherman was most insulted, as he would write in his memoirs.[22]

It should be noted that although Stanton was an abolitionist, Sherman was not. Sherman, as he often told his Southern friends and critics, was a career military man who was just doing his duty to crush the rebellion against his government. Sherman had two generals who served as his chief deputy field commanders. One was the abolitionist Gen. O. Howard, who would later head the Freedman's Bureau and become founder and first president of Howard University. A deeply religious man who prayed before sending his men into every battle, Howard was keenly aware of the evils of the slave system. The other of Sherman's generals, however, was more of a Rebel sympathizer and, some said, black hater; it was this general who had allegedly caused hundreds of blacks to drown and be massacred by Confederate soldiers while he and his army escaped across a river. Sherman's reputation as anti-black, based on tragic incidents such as this, and his refusal to accept blacks into his army and some of his unflattering descriptions of blacks had all floated back to Washington. The abolitionists were furious at Sherman. The president was uneasy, and Stanton wanted to clear the matter up. He would never have a better resource for clearing up the matter of Sherman's loyalty and devotion to emancipation than the audience before him this night. So he took the risk of insulting Sherman to put his audience at ease. He wanted to talk to them about the general.

It has been said that Sherman "paced the hall outside the closed door, grinding his teeth" over what he considered a gross effrontery.[23] He was no doubt puffing furiously on his famous cigar and blinking his eyes rapidly, as was his custom, especially when agitated. He wrote later in his memoirs:

> It certainly was a strange fact that the great War Secretary should have catechized negroes concerning the character of a general who had commanded a hundred thousand men in battle, had captured cities, conducted sixty-five thousand men successfully across four hundred miles of hostile territory, and had just brought tens of thousands of freedmen to a place of security; but because I had not loaded down my army with other hundreds of thousands of poor negroes, I was construed by others as hostile to the black race.[24]

It is in this context that the secretary put his final question to the men after Sherman was out of the room: "State what is the feeling of the colored people in regard to General Sherman; and how far do they regard his sentiments and actions as friendly to their rights and interests, or otherwise?"

The men were as well prepared for this question as all the others. Frazier again spoke first.

> We looked upon General Sherman prior to his arrival as a man in the providence of God, specially set apart to accomplish this work, and we unanimously feel inexpressible gratitude to him, looking upon him as a man that should be honored for the faithful performance of his duty. Some of us called upon him immediately upon his arrival, and it is probable he would not meet the secretary (of war) with more courtesy than he met us. His conduct and deportment toward us characterized him as a friend and a gentleman. We have confidence in General Sherman and think that what concerns us could not be under better hands. This is our opinion now from the short acquaintance and interest we have had.

The secretary went around the room, asking each leader to present his own view. All agreed with Frazier except the 26-year-old minister from up North, the Rev. Lynch. He stated that because of his limited acquaintance with Gen. Sherman, he was unwilling to express an opinion one way or another. At this point, Gen. Sherman was invited to rejoin the meeting, and informal conversation proceeded.

No wonder historian Dr. Ira Berlin called this meeting among the most remarkable gatherings of the Civil War period. Indeed, it was remarkable that this meeting was held at all; that the highest officials of the government asked black leaders for their views; and that the men were so well prepared. But these men represented not just themselves, or the people generally, but specific institutions that the people had built up even under the oppression of the slave era.

Even more remarkably, this meeting led to concrete and far-reaching results. One was that these black ministers became elevated in the eyes of their community, the local white community, and the government itself, as qualified spokespersons and leaders for the transition from slavery to freedom. Another result was these black leaders that night persuaded Sherman to address a mass rally of the black population and explain the Emancipation Proclamation and the commitment of the government to carry it out. He did so from the steps of the Second African Baptist Church.

But perhaps the most important result was a policy that eased the emancipation of blacks four months before the end of the war. Berlin writes:

Four days after the meeting, General Sherman issued Special Field Order 15, which set aside a large expanse of coastal land, stretching from Charleston, South Carolina, to Northern Florida, "for the settlement of the negroes now made free by the acts of war and the proclamation of the President of the United States." Each family would be allotted "forty acres of tillable ground . . . in the possession of which land the military authorities will afford them protection, until such time as they can protect themselves, or until Congress shall regulate their title."[25]

There is no doubt that this meeting with the black religious leaders on Thursday evening, January 12, 1865, was a major source of this policy. Within a few days, before he would set off for his march through South Carolina and North Carolina on his way to Richmond, Sherman authorized the beginning of this massive resettlement. Robert Smalls, the legendary Civil War hero, again took the wheels of his warship, the *Planter*, to carry families to these resettlements. The first to be settled on their lands were the 10,000 blacks who had followed Sherman into Savannah.

The order, written jointly by Sherman and Stanton and approved by President Lincoln, specified:

The islands from Charleston south, the abandoned rice fields along the river for thirty miles back from the sea, and the country bordering the St. John's River, Florida, are reserved and set apart for the settlement of the negroes now made free by the acts of war and the proclamation of the President of the United States.[26]

It forbade whites to settle on these lands:

At Beaufort, Hilton Head, Savannah, Fernandina, St. Augustine, and Jacksonville, the blacks may remain in their chosen or accustomed vocations; but on the islands, and in the settlements hereafter to be established, no white person whatever, unless military officers and soldiers detailed for duty, will be permitted to reside; and the sole and exclusive management of affairs will be left to the freed people themselves, subject only to the United States military authority and the acts of Congress.[27]

The order provided for enlistment of young blacks in the U.S. Army, contrary to the policy which Sherman had pursued. "The young and able-bodied negroes must be encouraged to enlist as soldiers in the service of the United States, to contribute their share toward maintaining their own freedom, and securing their rights as citizens of the United States."[28]

Moreover, it provided for voluntary black communities:

> Whenever three respectable negroes, heads of families, shall desire to settle on land . . . the Inspector of Settlements and Plantations will . . . give them a license to settle such island or district, and afford them such assistance as he can to enable them to establish a peaceable agricultural settlement.

Sherman appointed Gen. Rufus Saxon to supervise this massive relocation.

After issuing Field Order #15, and before departing Savannah on January 21, Gen. Sherman took Gen. Rufus Saxon with him to a meeting at the city's Second African Baptist Church, where several hundred black persons heard them explain the meaning and the significance of both the Emancipation Proclamation and the field order. It was a festive occasion. Hymns were sung, prayers offered, and a rousing reception was given the two generals.[29]

After Lincoln's assassination, Sherman's order was set aside by order of President Andrew Johnson, a Southern sympathizer. A similar plan was passed by the U.S. Congress during Reconstruction but was vetoed as well by President Johnson. For these and other actions supporting the Confederacy, Johnson was put on trial, impeached by the House, and came within one vote of being convicted by the Senate. The idea of "40 acres and a mule" and the unresolved issue of reparations lingers in the folklore and the culture of the African American people, resurfacing periodically in public discourse. In 1990, Congressman John Conyers introduced a bill in the U.S. Congress to honor the spirit of Sherman's famous order #15.[30] In July 1994, a national publication launched a series of articles and commentaries on "The Reparations Question."[31] And in 1996, at an emergency conference in South Carolina, the principal speaker, the Rev. Mac Charles Jones, representing hundreds of black churches that were burned, called for a program of racial healing. In order to deal with racism and bring blacks and whites together he advocated a national local and individual program of recognition of the problem, repentance, and a program of restitution that could lead to reconciliation. On the question of restitution he cited the need to find a way to deal with the reparation for blacks in a manner similar to the reparations the nation instituted for the Japanese Americans forced to live in concentration camps during World War II.[32]

But a striking feature of all these contemporary discussions of the reparations question or the modern equivalents of the legendary "40 acres and a mule" is that none of these discussions traces the origin of this idea to the 20 black religious leaders who met with Stanton and Sherman on the evening of January 12, 1865, on the top floor of Sherman's headquarters in the Green Mansion in Savannah.

Sherman Departs Savannah

After six weeks in Savannah, Sherman left the city for his campaign through the Carolinas. He did not burn or abandon Savannah, as he had done Atlanta. He left troops and officers to hold the city. Soon this small force was augmented by units of black Union soldiers from the South Carolina campaign. Sherman was widely expected to go through Augusta, Georgia, and then to capture Charleston, the place where the war was said to have begun with the Rebel capture of Fort Sumter. Sherman actually encouraged such speculation. But in his own mind he had laid other plans. He confided in a letter to his wife on January 15, 1865, that he planned to avoid Augusta and Charleston, and instead head for Columbia, South Carolina, and Fayetteville and New Bern, North Carolina.[33] Sherman embarked in a steamer for Beaufort, South Carolina, and spent one night there. He then headed northward to Columbia with two large columns of troops and equipment with the aim of meeting up with Gen. Ulysses Grant's forces and together capturing Richmond, thus ending the war. Sherman was not a man for making small plans. There were, however, two ironic developments during Sherman's march through the Carolinas. While he was moving on Columbia, Charleston fell at the hands of the black troops whom he would not have accepted in his army.[34] Then Sherman was prevented from his long-held goal of teaming up with Grant to take Richmond, because before he could arrive there, black troops had taken Richmond as well and virtually ended the war.[35]

As the black troops entered Charleston, the historic antebellum Emanuel A.M.E. Church, where Denmark Vesey plotted his insurrection in 1822, and whose minister, the Rev. Morris Brown, was banished from the state because of it, rose majestically from the underground. It became the rallying point for a thunderous display of welcome for the liberators. After the war, this and other churches led the movement to make Charleston the leading city in the South during Reconstruction.

4

—∿—

The Crisis of Emancipation
and Reconstruction in Savannah

B lack churches in Savannah responded in two distinct ways to the
collapse of the Confederacy and the crisis of emancipation. They
expanded their churches, in numbers and membership, and in the process established an institutional hegemony in the black community that
would last for more than a century and a half.

Robert Perdue described the rapid expansion of churches and how
they "educated the children, imparted morality, strengthened black
family life, married the young, and buried the dead."[1] In all these matters the church was functioning as social institutions as defined by Du
Bois, Frazier, and C. Eric Lincoln. In addition the church also moved
resolutely into community action, thus executing the "communal" di-
mension of its mission as set forth by Lincoln and Mamiya. Among the
areas of social reform in which churches were preeminent in the black
community were education, economic development, and politics.

Education

After emancipation, blacks in Savannah turned to education with a
vigor matched only by their allegiance to their churches and their families. Indeed, in little more than a month after Sherman captured Savannah, blacks had established 10 schools, with some 500 students
enrolled.[2] Drago recounts that "Northern missionaries were astonished,

and later chagrined, to find that members of the city's black clergy had established by January 1, 1865, the Savannah Education Association, which staffed its schools entirely with a black teaching corps."[3]

How is it that blacks could move so resolutely in providing for their own education after some 200 years of bondage? Because they placed high value on education, a value that originated in their African homeland, which slavery could not destroy, and because blacks in Savannah came out of slavery with a head start in education and self-help.

Antebellum Initiatives

There had been a strong history of black participation in education in Savannah even during slavery, despite laws and custom which tried to thwart it. Sometimes blacks were taught by sympathetic whites, sometimes by free blacks, and sometimes they taught themselves.

White sailors taught Ulysses S. Houston to read and write while he was working in the Marine Hospital.[4] Houston would use these skills to become a powerful pastor at the Third African Baptist Church and a prominent member of the state legislature in 1868. Houston became a strong supporter of education throughout his career.

Other blacks taught by whites attended classes clandestinely. Susie K. Taylor was taught to read by white students. It is said that on her way to class, she wrapped her book in paper so that whites would think she was carrying her lunch.[5]

Some slaves attended schools taught by free blacks. Julian Frotaine, a free black man from San Domingo, opened a school in 1819. The climate of race relations in Savannah at that time was such that Frotaine conducted his school openly from 1819 until 1829. After an apparent hiatus he conducted school secretly in his home from 1836 to 1864.[6]

Another free black to conduct school was James M. Simms, a deacon in the First African Baptist Church. He taught blacks to read and write in the 1840s, despite the law forbidding it. Simms was whipped publicly when city officials discovered him. Undeterred, he continued teaching until he was fined $100. He refused to pay the fine and fled to Boston, where he stayed throughout the war. While in Boston he was ordained as a minister. After the war, Simms returned to Savannah and the First African Baptist Church. He rose to a position in the state legislature and kept education as his highest priority.[7]

One of the most spectacular stories of free blacks teaching others is that of Jane Deveaux. Sent north to Boston for her education, Deveaux came back to Savannah and operated a secret school for black children from 1847 until the Civil War. "She held her clandestine and illegal school in a house on the northeast corner of St. Julian and Price streets in Savannah," historian Donald Grant writes.[8] Deveaux thus earned the place of honor she now occupies in Laurel Grove South Cemetery.

Susie King Taylor built upon DeVeaux's success. Born in 1848, She was brought up in Savannah by her grandmother, who sent her to learn to read and write at the home of a free black woman named Mrs. Woodhouse. Taylor was an avid student and moved north to Boston with her husband to further her education just before the outbreak of the war. She and her husband moved to Savannah after the war was over, and set up the first of many schools she would open in her lifetime of service.[9]

Another black woman who made an important contribution to the education of blacks in Savannah was Mother Matilda Beasley. Before the Civil War, she, too, risked imprisonment for teaching black youths how to read and write. She worked through the Catholic Church, and though early in life was a married woman, she went to England after her well-to-do husband died in the 1880s and eventually became a nun. She returned to Savannah and established an orphan's asylum in the area. She died in 1902.[10]

These then were the forerunners of black education in antebellum Savannah. They laid the foundation that would be built upon after the fall of the confederacy.

Postwar Initiatives

After the war black self-help initiatives in education expanded rapidly.

Efforts by blacks to educate their people were often nothing short of heroic, for violent attacks on black schools and teachers continued throughout the late nineteenth century. William and Ellen Craft, Georgia's most famous runaway slaves, returned from England in 1870 and managed a plantation just across the Georgia line in South Carolina but were burned out by night riders. They then moved to Woodville plantation in Bryan County near Savannah, where they established a school patterned after the Ockham School they had attended in England. Ellen ran the farm and the school while William traveled widely in the North, raising money for the two operations. The farm failed following Ellen's death in 1891, but the school lasted into the next century.[11]

Another type of self-help was also undertaken. In late 1865 the *Colored American*, a black newspaper, suggested that black educators hold a convention to plan a comprehensive strategy for education reform in the region. Thus, on January 10, 1866, more than 40 black delegates gathered in Augusta's Springfield Baptist Church. They elected the Savannah minister James Porter as temporary chairman. Porter, 40, had come from Charleston to Savannah before the war and was preaching at the local Protestant Episcopal church. He was one of the 20 black religious leaders who had met with Gen. Sherman and Secretary of War Stanton on January 12, 1865. A highly learned man and gifted orator, he would be elected to the Georgia legislature three years later.

As W. W. Law has insisted, the recognition of the preeminence of self-help in the field of black education takes nothing away—and should take nothing away—from the indispensable and, some say, providential help that came from the dedicated, mostly young, white middle-class Northerners who came down by the hundreds to assist in this undertaking. The South would not experience another outpouring of young, white Northern reformers until the civil rights crusades of 1964.

And while the ever religious blacks considered the teachers from the North as manna sent from heaven, they also had occasion to reflect on the adage that God helps those who help themselves.

Blacks from the North

The fact is sometimes overlooked, however, that not all Northerners who came south after the war were white. Of the hundreds of teachers sent by the Northern associations into Georgia, 18 (seven women and 11 men or about 5 percent of the Georgia teachers) were black.[12]

Conspicuous among these was the Rev. Hardy Mobley, who had been born into bondage in Augusta, Georgia. After he saved enough money to purchase his freedom and that of his family for $3,000, he moved to Brooklyn. At the end of the war he returned to the South, to "labor for the improvement of his old neighbors who had been less fortunate than himself."[13]

Another was the famous antebellum author Harriet Brent Jacobs, who wrote her autobiography about growing up in Georgia during slavery and her incredible escape north. She, too, returned to the South after the war and, together with her daughter, taught in Savannah for a year.

A strong partner to these private efforts, eventually coordinated by the American Missionary Association, was the federal government's Freedman's Bureau, established by Congress in March 1865, a month before the end of the war. President Lincoln swiftly appointed one of

Sherman's chief deputies, Gen. O. Howard, as director. Howard, an abolitionist before the war, moved with equal dispatch.

Following the wishes of the newly freed African Americans, the bureau gave strong priority to education. And though both these national efforts, the private (American Missionary Association) and the governmental (Freedman's Bureau), would turn out to be extraordinarily short-lived, they did a world of good. They pioneered a combination of black self-help initiatives, outside support from private and voluntary associations, and strategic support by their government.

In the fall of 1866 the Savannah Education Association changed its name to the Georgia Education Association (GEA). According to Grant, "By late 1867 there were 120 schools in 53 of the state's 131 counties affiliated with the 3,500-member GEA. The GEA did not confine itself to the '3 Rs' but added a fourth, 'Rights', and was a base for the political careers of many blacks, including Rev. James Porter, William Jefferson White, and Tunis G. Campbell, Sr. The GEA held its first convention in Macon in October 1867."[14]

Their efforts had substantial success. The 1868 Constitution required the next session of the legislature to provide for the *education of all children.*

In addition, State Representatives Philip Joiner of Dougherty County and the Rev. Henry McNeal Turner proposed that the old Milledgeville Capitol building and $100,000 be allocated for a Negro college. Though black leaders were pushing for a public college for blacks as early as 1868, they would not get one until 1891, with Savannah State. Instead, the Milledgeville site became a private white school that was still receiving state money in the 1990s.

In an extraordinary and illegal move, some Republican state legislators joined with white Democrats and voted to expel blacks from the legislature as soon as the 1868 democratically elected and first biracial legislature was convened as authorized by the new state Constitution. In the absence of these black legislators, the legislature failed to act on the issue of free public education.

When black legislators were restored to their seats in 1870 (25 in the House and three in the Senate) by federal intervention the legislature quickly passed the universal education act, and Gov. Bullock signed the law establishing Georgia's first statewide public school system.[15] There is no doubt that black legislators made the diference on this issue.

This most progressive step would be reversed in later years, after white Democrats regained control. Free public schools were abolished. So white children suffered, too, without free public schools. It would not be the last time whites would punish their own children in an angry effort to punish blacks. It happened again during the struggle for school desegregation after the United States Supreme Court outlawed segregation in 1954.

While black self-help was the key force in post–Civil War initiatives, there have been occasions where government, the private sector, and the black communities have collaborated for the good of all concerned. The establishment of the Beach Institute in 1867 was one such instance.

The Beach Institute

The Beach Institute was a result of a collaborative effort between public and private sources. A private citizen, Alfred E. Beach, an inventor and editor of the *Scientific American*, donated funds to the American Missionary Association to purchase a site for a school in Savannah for blacks. The Federal government spent $13,000 to construct the building that would house the Beach Institute. And in the same year the black community's Savannah Education Association added a $3,000 home for teachers to the institute. The teachers came from the North. Because of the shortage of black teachers, most were white missionaries.[16]

The Beach Institute ceased to operate as a school during the 1960s. But with the assistance of the Savannah Arts Academy and local business and civic leaders, the institute has become a private center for art and culture, informal education, lectures, and exhibitions. It is a centerpiece of African American culture in Savannah.

In recent years, under curator Carol Greene, the Beach Institute has become the permanent home of the 250-piece celebrated traveling exhibition of wood sculptures by Savannah folk artist Ulysses Davis.

The Beach Institute now anchors an historic African American community that bears its name and is part of the historic preservation district of the city, due largely to the leadership of W. W. Law, who for a time was chairman of the board. Dr. Annette K. Brock, who succeeded Law, has continued his leadership.

Higher Education

Black Savannah's higher-education movement greatly benefited from the organizing brilliance of the eloquent and deeply spiritual E. K. Love, pastor of the First African Baptist Church, rising to the forefront between 1885 and 1900. The church historian, Deacon Harry James, has written that among the pastors of this historic church, "the most prominent and aggressive before 1900 was Emanuel King Love."[17]

When the current pastor, the Rev. Thurmond Tillman, was asked to name his favorite predecessor, he readily chose the Rev. E. K. Love. It was no doubt the combination of his spirituality, his intellectualism, and his activism on behalf of youth that endeared him to Tillman. It was his pioneering work in higher education, however, that has endeared him to the community to the present time.

Love (1850–1900), born into slavery, began preaching when he was 18 and ultimately became pastor of the historic First African Baptist Church in Savannah in 1885. He filled several state and national posts and edited two newspapers, as well.

In 1871, he studied briefly at Lincoln Institute in Marion, Alabama. Then, with the support of his pastor and church, he attended Augusta Institute in Augusta, Georgia, founded by Springfield Baptist Church. The institute would later become Morehouse College. He entered on November 18, 1872, and graduated at the head of his class in June 1877 with a bachelor's degree. On October 1, 1885, he was elected pastor of the First African Baptist Church in Savannah, which was at that time "the largest and most prominent Negro church in the United States."[18]

Love's influence was the greatest single political force in Savannah. He was also a prominent figure in state and national Republican conventions. He was a prolific writer who at one time was associate editor of the *Augusta Weekly Sentinel*; he established and published the *National Watchman* in Albany before coming to Savannah. He was also acting president of the State Baptist Convention, and he edited *The Baptist Truth*, which developed a wide circulation.

After working hard and successfully to influence the state Legislature to establish the first college for blacks in Georgia, Love convinced the state authorities that Richard R. Wright Sr. should become this fledgling college's first president.

Richard R. Wright Sr.

Richard R. Wright was born in bondage on May 16, 1853, in Dalton, Georgia, near the Tennessee border, only three years younger than the Rev. Love, his distinguished benefactor. One of the many traumas in his early life occurred when he, his mother, and his sister were sold at a slave auction in 1859. He was six years old, and sold for the grand sum of $300.[19] Yet, because of his strong intellectual gifts, he would become what one of his biographers, Charles Elmore, calls "the most neglected Black intellectual and visionary of the 20th century."[20]

At the end of the Civil War, Wright's mother wanted desperately for him to get an education. She heard about the "boxcar schools" that were being set up in Georgia by the Freedman's Bureau for the education of the newly freed blacks. She and young Wright walked more than a mile from Dalton in North Georgia to Atlanta so that Wright could be enrolled in one of those schools. He was enrolled in the Storrs School in 1866, when he was 13 years old. He could barely read and write, but he was smart. And his mother knew that he would make something out of himself if given half a chance.

Wright made a name for himself at the school on the occasion of a visit from O. Otis Howard, the Civil War general, abolitionist, and founder of the Freedman's Bureau. Howard came to Atlanta to an assembly of children attending the Freedman's Bureau schools. A passionate advocate for black youth, he gave an emotional appeal to these young people to make the most of their educational opportunities. Then, at the end of his address, which was meant to encourage the students to develop their leadership skills, he asked his young audience: "What should I tell the children of the North about you when I go back to Washington?" Young R. R. Wright raised his hand and, on being recognized, said, "Tell them, sir, that we're rising."[21] Gen. Howard was so impressed by this response and by the young students generally that he told the experience to the poet John Greenleaf Whittier, a friend and fellow abolitionist. Whittier wrote a poem, "Howard at Atlanta," in which he recounted this incident, and young R. R. Wright became famous, just five years out of slavery and just before his 17th birthday. It was a harbinger of things to come.

After completing the elementary course at Storrs School in 1869, Wright enrolled in Atlanta University. The school would not have its first collegiate-level class until 1872. That year Wright entered the freshman class with 12 other carefully selected and promising young black men. Four years later, he and five others graduated. Wright immersed himself in the classical curriculum with specialties in Greek and Latin, and he was selected valedictorian of his graduating class, assignments. Meanwhile, Wright's future benefactor, the Rev. E. K. Love, was at Augusta Baptist College.

By now Wright had become captivated by the educational opportunities around him. He stayed on in Atlanta, enrolling in the graduate program at Atlanta University, where he earned a master's degree in 1879. Meanwhile, he had already begun teaching at the privately supported Howard Normal School in Cuthbert, Georgia, some 200 miles from Atlanta.

But in 1879 he was called away to Augusta by a group of leaders that included the legendary C. T. Walker, longtime pastor of the historic Tabernacle Baptist Church in that city and an important political leader, to establish the first public high school for blacks in the state of Georgia. Wright named his new school the Edmund Asa Ware High School, in honor of the white president of Atlanta University, who had greatly inspired him.

Wright would thrive in Augusta. It was there that he and E. K. Love would work together. Love was pastor of the First African Baptist Church in Thomasville, Georgia (1879–1881), but was associated with the Rev. C. T. Walker in Augusta in a number of ventures.

Wright served as principal of the Edmund Asa Ware High School in Augusta for 10 years. During the same period he became co-founder and editor of the *Augusta Sentinel Newspaper*, whose other founders included Walker and Love. All three were active Republicans.

When Wright brought his fledgling college to Savannah in the fall of 1892 he had three instructors, including himself, all of whom were Atlanta University graduates; and eight students, all of whom were graduates of Ware High School in Augusta. Wright would spend 30 years in Savannah as president of what became Savannah State College.

During this time Wright became a power in the Republican Party and was able to attract the interest of highly placed people. President McKinley spoke at his school in 1898, and William Howard Taft visited the campus two years later. Wright developed a curriculum influenced by the philosophies of both W.E.B. Du Bois and Booker T. Washington. He fought a constant battle to include liberal arts courses in the curriculum and enjoyed some success, despite continuous opposition to his goals by white leaders. However, he did not—could not—neglect the manual arts. He took a leadership position when he organized farmers cooperatives and conducted the first Negro county fair in Georgia. He testified before a congressional committee in 1912 that as president of the Georgia Negro State Fair he had raised $100,000 from blacks for the festival, which had been held annually in Macon since 1906.[22]

Booker T. Washington and Henry McNeal Turner were featured speakers at the first fair, and George Washington Carver often attended the fairs. Wright, like Washington, also worked to improve the farmers' incomes by showing them how they could improve their farm practices. In 1900 he initiated farmers conferences on the Savannah campus patterned on the Tuskegee model. Wright would go out and visit the farmers before each conference to encourage attendance. In 1905 he said, "More than 120 prosperous farmers, owning from 100 to 2,000 acres of cultivated land, have promised to attend."[23]

In addition to his work at the college, Wright was active in civil life, founding a Center for Orphaned Girls in 1912, working to hire the first black president of Atlanta University, and attending Republican national conventions. He was also a contributor to the pages of the *Savannah Tribune*, the first and most influential black newspaper in the state from 1875 until its demise in 1960. He also collaborated with Love and the Rev. James Simms, a former member of the state legislature, author, educator, and businessman, in the establishment of an independent Republican organization, founded in the basement of the First African Baptist Church.

When Wright left Savannah in 1921—in part, it is said, because a white man slapped his daughter in public—he moved to Philadelphia. There he established a career as a banker. He helped to establish the Citizens and Southern Bank, which flourished in Philadelphia until 1960. While in Philadelphia he founded the first national holiday to honor descendants of slavery, signed into law by President Truman in 1948.[24]

Wright and his wife had three sons and five daughters. One of his sons, Emanuel Crogman Wright—named for Emanuel King Love and William Henry Crogman, one of Wright's classmates at Atlanta University, who would become president of Clark College—became an officer of his father's Philadelphia bank. Another son, Whittier Wright, named for the poet that made Wright famous, became a physician with a longtime practice in Georgia before moving north.

A third son, Richard R. Wright Jr., became a famous educator and clergyman whose mark on history virtually eclipsed his father's. Wright Jr. was one of the earliest blacks to be trained in the then new discipline of sociology, graduating from the University of Chicago with a master's degree in sociology in 1903.[25] He earned a Ph.D. in sociology at the University of Pennsylvania in 1911. He became president of Wilberforce University and one of the nation's leading Methodist bishops. He was an outstanding activist in education, religion, and social work. Wright Jr. wrote his autobiography in 1965, titled *87 Years Behind the Black Curtain*.[26]

Richard R. Wright Sr. died and was buried in Philadelphia. And while his 20 or so years of leadership there in business and civic affairs surely entitles him to that resting place, there are those who knew him well who think that he really should be buried at Laurel Grove South Cemetery in Savannah, along with such luminaries as Edward King Love, Andrew Marshall, Henry Cunningham, James Simms, and all the fathers and mothers of historic black Savannah.

Business and Economic Development

In addition to their pioneering initiatives in education and higher education, black churches played a leadership role in business and economic development in the early years of emancipation.

One of the earliest, most successful, and longest-lasting black business enterprises was the *Savannah Tribune*, originally called the *Colored Tribune*, founded by John H. Deveaux of Savannah (1848–1909), an active Republican official.

Its first issue was dated December 4, 1875, and was available for purchase in five of the city's newsstands and stores. Deveaux's announced purpose was to defend and elevate black people, break down prejudice, and establish friendly relations with whites. Deveaux edited the paper until 1889, when Sol C. Johnson became editor.[27]

The churches were early and dependable supporters, users, and distributors of this newspaper. The paper ceased publication in 1960. It was later revived by the president of Carver State Bank.

The success of early business developments spawned by the churches, such as the mutual aid societies, led to black-owned insurance companies, which in turn led to black-owned banks. In Savannah, a black bank was established in the early years of Reconstruction.

Both Love and Wright, then president of Savannah State College, were instrumental in the founding of the first black-owned bank in Savannah. They had tried and failed to get the legislature to establish a bank for blacks. They observed that around the turn of the century Savannah was a thriving cotton port. The economy was booming until the 1920s, when the boll weevil destroyed half of the cotton crop in Georgia.[28] They also noted, however, that blacks were being left behind in this economic boom. They led the founding of a bank to give blacks an anchor in this economy. The Wage Earner's Bank was established near the turn of the century with $102. L. A. Williams was its first president and first depositor. The bank prospered, and "by 1915 the bank complex occupied an entire downtown block." By 1917 it had more than 9,000 depositors, with accounts averaging $25. By 1919, Savannah also had Mechanics Savings Bank and Fidelity Savings Bank.[29]

Other business enterprises developed in Savannah as a result of the black-owned banks and the strong support of black churches. A study of Savannah's black community by John Blassingame showed that in 1870, 66 blacks operated 27 different businesses there. A decade later, 253 people were engaged in 41 different businesses.

Ninety-six blacks owned land in 1870, and in 10 years the number had risen to 648.[30]

Labor Union Organization

Another important economic initiative supported strongly by the churches was the organization of labor unions and their push for what they considered adequate and fair wages. In Georgia, opposition to labor unions was always strong. Still, blacks made valiant efforts to use this approach to contest their economic exploitation.

During the 1867–68 Constitutional Convention, which was held in Albany, black workers there went on strike for higher wages. Philip Joiner of Dougherty County and several other black delegates visited and encouraged them. At about the same time, Jefferson Long, the Rev. Henry McNeal Turner, and J. E. Bryant organized the Negro Labor Union, in Bibb and Dougherty counties. They demanded uniform wages at $15 a month for domestic servants, $30 a month for field hands, and higher wages for mechanics. They organized a small strike in Macon and a larger one in Dougherty County. They found it very difficult, however, to sustain organized labor efforts in these essentially rural areas.[31]

According to Grant, black longshoremen in Savannah were among the best-organized black workers in Georgia before 1900.[32] Maintaining their strength, though, was a constant struggle. In 1867 the Savannah City Council—which would have no Black members throughout Reconstruction—passed an ordinance increasing the stevedore badge fee by $2. At this time the jobs on the docks paid only 25 cents an hour, and the overwhelming majority of dock workers were black. The workers went on strike to protest the proposed increase. The city gave in, but not without a struggle. According to Grant, "Strike leaders were arrested, whipped, fined fifty dollars each, and sent to the chain gang for ninety days."[33] Such labor unrest and suppression were long-lived. In 1881, four blacks were killed in a strike called to demand an increase in their wages. In 1889 they struck again in Savannah when nonunion labor was hired to load and unload a British steamer whose captain refused to use union labor.

The largest 1891 strike by Georgia blacks came when the Savannah Negro Laborer Union responded to threats to cut their pay to 11 cents an hour. The union claimed up to 2,000 members, who formed picket lines in protest but were attacked by well-armed police. To counter this action, strike organizers turned to the churches. They distributed leaflets in all the black churches urging blacks not to help the anti-union forces by being scabs to replace striking workers. This tactic received a measure of success, and port authorities offered the union a 2½-cent-an-hour raise. The union rejected this, their first offer, unaware that it would be their last. "The company brought in private troops," according to Grant, and 1,000 scabs, many of whom were out-of-state blacks, who were paid more than the union had asked for. This broke the strike.

The history of blacks in organized labor in Savannah as elsewhere throughout the South would be spotty at best. But not because in these early years the effort wasn't made. Besides their own families, the labor organizers would find no stronger source of support than the black church.

Political Action

The black church in Savannah became involved in political action soon after emancipation. Political reform was indeed the subject of the very first celebration of Emancipation Day on January 1, 1863. According to historians, Whittington B. Johnson and the Rev. James Simms had secured a copy of President Lincoln's September 1962 preliminary proclamation while he was in Virginia and brought it to Savannah in late 1962. At that time black ministers requested and were granted permission to hold a public dinner on January 1, 1863. Johnson writes:

> The supper was held as scheduled on January 1, 1863 at which [The Rev.] James Porter was reported to have given an excellent address . . . [The Rev.] John Cox, the free black pastor of Second African Baptist Church and (Rev.) Ulysses L. Houston, the nominal slave pastor of Third African Baptist Church, gave prayers.[34]

All four of these activist ministers (Simms, Porter, Cox, and Houston) would be present at the historic meeting of 20 black religious leaders with Gen. Sherman and Secretary of War Stanton on January 12, 1865, and would all become active in Reconstruction politics.

It no doubt gave a special boost to the spirit of blacks when the black soldiers arrived in Savannah to help keep the peace, two months after Sherman departed. "In March, 1865, the 33rd, 54th, and 102nd Massachusetts Negro regiments arrived to assist in garrisoning the city."[35]

Indeed, all the Savannah blacks serving in the Georgia legislature in 1870 were also church officials.[36] Ulysses L. Houston, representative from Bryan County, served as pastor of the Third African Baptist

Church from 1861 to 1880 with only a brief interruption. James M. Simms, representative from Chatham County, was an ordained minister who served as deacon and clerk of the First African Baptist Church from 1858 until he went to Boston in 1861.

Other ministers in the legislature included the Rev. Henry M. Turner, pastor of St. Philip's A.M.E. Church from 1872 to 1876, and the Rev. James Porter of the Episcopal church of Savannah.[37] (Black representation in the 1968 Georgia state legislature is shown in Table 4 in Appendix C.)

The Reconstruction era leaders were especially courageous. They were leading their people into territory that was new and fraught with challenges and dangers. One of these activist ministers was the Rev. James Porter, who was born free in Charleston, South Carolina, and came to Savannah before the war. He was expelled from the state legislature along with all other black members in 1868. When they were all reinstated in 1870, Porter introduced a bill that finally led to the creation of Georgia's first public school system.[38]

Among the most venerated leaders in Savannah was Ulysses L. Houston. His career had its share of ups and downs, though. He won a seat in the assembly in 1868, only to be faced with resentment from some of his parishioners over his absence from church affairs. Others became apprehensive at the hostility his political activity stirred among local whites. Alexander Harris, a church deacon, took advantage of the congregation's discontent and persuaded a majority of the members to elect him as pastor during one of Houston's absences.[39]

When Houston lost his bid for reelection in 1870, he became pastor of another church. Two years later, however, Houston and his supporters, including Baptist minister-politician James Simms, physically occupied Harris's Third African Baptist Church pulpit one Sunday morning, asserting that Harris's activities and election were illegal.

Here was a confrontation of major proportions. Harris called the white city officials who no doubt had encouraged him to seek the pastorate during Houston's service in the legislature in Columbia. The officials swiftly sent in the (white) police, who arrested Houston and Simms and took them to jail. Now Harris had gone too far. The congregation's resentment of Harris spurred it to oust him and reelect Houston as pastor. For this Houston and Simms became heroes. Houston would go on to serve a long and distinguished career at the helm of this historic church. He died in the pastorate in 1888.[40]

Simms, too, was one of the brightest, most able and dedicated of the ministers in political leadership. Baptized by the Rev. Andrew Marshall at First African Baptist Church in 1841, he rose to the post of deacon in 1860. After the Civil War Simms returned triumphantly to Savannah from Boston, rejoined First African Baptist Church, and plunged deeply and successfully into politics. Because of his community leadership, he earned a seat in the state legislature in 1868. But Simms was capable of not a little controversy. In his book *The First African Baptist Church of North America*, written in 1925, the Rev. E. G. Thomas—a former pastor of First African Baptist Church—provides a revealing portrait of Simms:

> He was never very pious, but quite intelligent. He was a fine carpenter and had charge of the wood work in the construction of our present brick edifice (at First African on Franklin Square) which was completed in 1859. This work is executed with great skill and taste. He was *licensed* to preach by the [First African Baptist] church in 1863. During this same year he was fined $50.00 for teaching members of his race to read. During the war, he ran the blockade and got away to Boston and joined the Union army, serving a year before the emancipation.
>
> While in Boston he was ordained to the gospel ministry, and in 1865 returned with a commission from the American Baptist Home Mission Society to labor in these parts among the Negroes. The First African Baptist Church refused to honor the "foreign" *ordination*, and Rev. W. J. Campbell wrote the society and had the commission cancelled.
>
> Rev. Simms then went into politics, where he exhibited great skill and was elected to Georgia Legislature, where he served several terms with marked ability.
>
> Rev. Simms finally got a letter of dismissal (from First African Baptist Church) and united with the First Bryan Church, Rev. U. L. Houston, Pastor. *They recognized his ordination,* and he served several country churches.
>
> Rev. Simms returned (to First African Baptist) with a letter from the First Bryan Church in 1885, *but the (First African Baptist) church refused to honor it.* After assisting Dr. E. K. Love in writing the history of the First (African Baptist) Church, Simms then wrote the history for the First Bryan Church.[41]

The book claimed that First African was not the first but the third black church in Savannah and that First Bryan was not the third but the first. Thus was launched the most divisive controversy in the history of the black church in Savannah. This controversy about which church was prior or first, or a true continuation of the original, raged from 1885 to 1888.

It was more fractious than the decision of 1832 of a small group to leave First African and start a new church which they called Third African for more than 30 years. It was more fractious than the decision by Third African to change its name to First Bryan in 1867, which the court approved.

The issue was settled in 1888. At the request of the Rev. Love and First African, the Sunbury Association, of which both churches were members, appointed a distinguished commission to examine the matter and determine which of the two churches could legitimately be the first. The commission found in favor of First African Baptist. The decision did not sit well with Simms. Most others accepted the verdict.

The Rev. Thomas writes:

> When the report was read, it brought Rev. Simms to his feet with blood in his eye. He said the Committee had been packed in the interest of First African Baptist Church. He referred derisively to Rev. E. K. Love, Pastor of First African and Vice Chair of this Convention as "The ex Bishop of Georgia." Simms spoke for half an hour with great vehemence and was frequently interrupted by indignant members. . . . Calls for order and denials and interruptions flowed thick and fast. In vain the President, and Love appealed to the Convention to hear Rev. Simms, but it howled him down, and the report of the Committee was unanimously adopted.[42]

A hundred years after that decision the acrimony has died out. Only a few people know of the controversy. Fewer still speak of it. The unity among the churches is remarkable. Indeed, the current pastors of these three historic churches—Thurman Tillman at First African Baptist; James H. Cantrell of Second African Baptist; and Edward L. Ellis Jr. of First Bryan, formerly Third African Baptist—are friends and active collaborators in the annual celebration of Emancipation Day, sponsored continually by all the black churches in the city since 1863. As these three men stood shoulder to shoulder at the 1997 celebration, while the Rev. Gerald Durley of Providence Baptist Church in Atlanta urged them all to prepare for another hundred years of political struggle, it was as if the ghost of James Simms and his divisive campaign over "priority" had finally been put to eternal rest.

Of all the black clergy elected to political office in Reconstruction Georgia, by far the most impressive was Henry McNeil Turner, of Macon,

Savannah, and Atlanta.[43] Turner was bright, well trained, articulate, steeped in the Scriptures, and passionately committed to social reform. Moreover, he must have been the bravest man alive during Reconstruction. He was a true forerunner of the late Dr. Martin Luther King Jr.

Turner lived during a very dangerous time. And he changed his times even as he rose above them. He was a preacher, abolitionist, soldier, politician, state legislator, federal officer, educator, author, and much, much more. And above all, he was as fearless as he was devout.

Born of free parents in South Carolina in 1834, Turner joined the white-controlled Methodist Church South at the age of 15. He was licensed to preach at age 19, and in 1855 he was assigned to a pastorate in Macon, Georgia. He joined the A.M.E. church in 1858 and in 1862 moved to Washington, D.C., to be elder at the Israel A.M.E. Church. While in that position he wrote a paper criticizing the Union for refusing to admit blacks into its army. When the policy was changed, Secretary of War Stanton selected Turner to become the first black chaplain in 1863. He served with the First United States Colored Troops. After the war, Gen. O. Otis Howard appointed him a Freedman's Bureau agent in Atlanta. He served only a brief spell before returning to organizing in the A.M.E. church.[44]

Turner developed an early reputation for defying white opposition. He had the habit of speaking plainly and firmly on behalf of black liberation. He was not opposed to the use of firearms by blacks in their own defense.

When Radical Reconstruction emerged, Turner worked hard to get out the black vote. He once wrote, "I first organized the Republican Party in this state . . . and have worked for its maintenance and perpetuity as no other man in the State has. I have put more men in the field, made more speeches, organized more Union Leagues, Political Associations, clubs, and have written more campaign documents that received larger circulation than any other man in the state."[45] He ran successfully for the first Constitutional Convention in 1868 and was elected to the Georgia legislature in 1868 from Macon. He was expelled that same year, along with other blacks, and was reinstated by federal intervention in 1869. He was reelected in 1870 but was refused his seat.

When blacks were expelled from the Georgia legislature, which the votes of blacks for the new Constitution had made possible (while a majority of whites voted against it), black legislators were not permitted to vote on the issue but were allowed to speak on their own behalf. Drago writes:

Henry Turner delivered the most powerful defense of the right of blacks to sit in the legislature. Turner realized that continued deference to whites amounted to political suicide. He refused to plead with whites as some of his black colleagues had because it reminded him of "slaves begging under the lash." Instead, he threatened to "hurl thunderbolts at the men who dare cross the threshold of my manhood," and he accused the white race of treachery and cowardice. Reviewing the legal and constitutional arguments supporting his position, he declared the basic question to be Am I a Man? Moreover, he renounced his earlier efforts to placate the Democrats, including his support of the removal of their voting disabilities. He threatened and promised to "call a colored convention."[46]

Turner would, indeed, play the leading role in organizing such a convention in October 1868.

In 1872 Turner was appointed customs inspector in Savannah by the Republican president. At the same time he served as pastor of St. Philip A.M.E. Church in Savannah from 1872 to 1876. After leaving Savannah in 1876, he was appointed manager of A.M.E. publishing activities in Philadelphia. That same year he was elected vice president of the American Colonization Society. In 1880 he was elected bishop in the A.M.E. Church, and from 1880 to 1892 he served as president of Morris Brown College in Atlanta. Turner amassed a distinguished career in six fields: religion, politics, education, public affairs, journalism, and African colonization. It is fair to say that in each domain he was without peer as he thundered across the landscape of the nation from his birth until his death in Canada in 1915, at the age of 81. He was buried in Atlanta.

Out of his deep disappointment—indeed, disillusionment—over the failures of Reconstruction he threw his enormous intellect and energies into an effort to persuade large numbers of American blacks to repatriate to Africa. Between 1891 and 1898 he made four trips to Africa on behalf of black American colonization, becoming established as a leading advocate of African colonization in the late 19th and early 20th centuries. Turner founded and edited several journals and wrote a history of the A.M.E. church. He was married four times: in 1856 (at age 22), 1893 (at 59), 1900 (at 66), and sometime later. He had several children, only two of whom survived him. In 1973 Turner was chosen as one of three blacks—along with Dr. Martin Luther King Jr. and Lucy Laney—whose portraits were to hang in the Georgia state capitol. Turner Boulevard, in West Savannah, just off Martin Luther King Jr. Boulevard, near the St. Philip Monumental A.M.E. Church, is also a memorial to him.[47]

5

Rev. Ralph Mark Gilbert
and the Civil Rights Movement in Savannah

The evolution of the black church in Savannah as agent of social
reform reached its zenith during the civil rights era. Like past social
movements, this one was led by the pastor of First African Baptist
Church. Indeed, the Rev. Ralph Mark Gilbert, pastor of this church
from 1939 to 1956, is generally considered the father of the civil rights
movement in Savannah.[1]

Gilbert inherited a mantle of activist leadership. The Rev. George
Leile, the founder of the church, actively defied the American authorities in the American Revolution. His legacy spread across five countries. Leile's successor, the Rev. Andrew Bryan, defied the same authorities in 1788. He and his followers would pay a heavy price for such
defiance and ultimately reap the rewards of a strong and growing institution. In 1833, the third pastor of this church, the Rev. Andrew
Marshall, defied and bested the local authorities who sought to dismiss
him. In the agonizing transition from slavery to freedom, the Rev. William J. Campbell had played a leadership role. And, finally, during the
crisis of emancipation and Reconstruction, no voice had been more
eloquent, persistent, or effective in social reform than the pastor of this
church, the Rev. Emanuel King Love.

If these leaders could do what they did under the conditions of
slavery, how much more was required of black leadership in the decade
of the 1940s, when racial segregation held a viselike grip over virtually

every aspect of life in the city? Some say that Ralph Mark Gilbert was sent to Savannah by the Lord of the universe for just such a time as this. And, clearly, as other leaders did before and after him, he rose to the occasion. Church historian Harry James writes, "History will prove that Rev. Ralph Mark Gilbert was one of the most influential individuals that had lived in Georgia since 1900."[2]

Dr. Otis Johnson, who has done an extensive sociological analysis of the role of the black church in Savannah during the civil rights era, concurs with Deacon James's assessment.[3]

Gilbert has been described as "a great gospel preacher, peerless orator, religious dramaturgist, and dauntless leader of all causes and forces which serve an aggrandized mankind."[4] Gilbert reestablished the dormant Savannah branch of the NAACP and served as its president from 1941 to 1950. He also organized an NAACP youth chapter in Savannah. Moreover, he organized and was the first president of the Georgia State Conference of the NAACP from 1942 to 1948. In addition, Gilbert organized the West Broad Street YMCA by calling together 24 men, 12 blacks and 12 nonblacks, and asking them to contribute $50 each to purchase a building which previously had been used by the Army as a USO headquarters. This building became the YMCA center.

Gilbert was instrumental in the creation of Greenbriar Orphanage. He found out that an Adaline Graham, owner of the Graham Apartments, left some money for a black orphanage in her will. Gilbert called a meeting of black ministers for the purpose of organizing the orphanage. He felt that the task was too large for the ministers alone and called for a delegation of three persons from neighboring churches, along with members of Alpha Kappa Alpha sorority, and this diverse group successfully organized Greenbriar, the first orphanage for African American children in Savannah. Today the orphanage is known as Greenbriar Children's Center.

Gilbert was a leader in the political life of blacks in Georgia. As a result of his efforts blacks won the right to vote for the first time in a democratic primary election. Blacks in the state had been allowed to vote only in the general elections, not the primaries. At that time the Democratic party was the controlling party in the state.

Under his leadership the NAACP encouraged the Rev. Dr. Primus King and Dr. T. H. Brewer, of Columbus, to file a suit for blacks to be allowed to vote in the Democratic primary. Dr. Gilbert had a network of NAACP branches all over the state to support the Primus King case, through the state courts to the federal court. His efforts led to the registration of more than 19,000 black voters in 1947. One of the fruits of this effort was the hiring of the first nine black police officers in the state of Georgia in 1948.

Gilbert was also a great builder of the church as a community institution. Under his leadership, the first credit union in a church in Georgia was organized in 1954. He was among the first to organize a Boy Scouts troop. His fight for equalization of teachers' salaries was one of his most progressive civic achievements.

Other pastors of First African Baptist Church were also active leaders during the long, often quiet, phases of the movement. The Rev. Curtis J. Jackson, who served as pastor from 1957 to 1961, led demonstrations at the Board of Education and was in the forefront of the boycott of Savannah merchants in an effort to desegregate public facilities.

The Rev. William Franklin Stokes was pastor from 1963 to 1973, the peak of the civil rights movement, and marched in several demonstrations. He was an eloquent speaker and was well liked by those in the congregation and by fellow ministers.

In some respects Savannah's home-grown civil rights movement was unique in Georgia. It had not been inspired by outside personalities. Rather, local leaders mobilized Savannah and ended up being pushed by their followers.[5]

Building on the groundwork laid under the leadership of the Rev. Gilbert, W. W. Law, the NAACP, and the churches, Savannah blacks were ready for action in 1960 when the student sit-in movement was launched by four black students in North Carolina who sat down at a Greensboro lunch counter.

On March 16, 1960, NAACP Youth Council members, organized by W. W. Law, launched a movement to desegregate lunch counters in the downtown Savannah shopping district. Demonstrators met at the First African Baptist Church and then went to all of the stores with lunch counters.

Most of the stores closed their doors to all customers in order to avoid serving the black youths. At Levy's department store, however, the manager decided to have the youths arrested. The Savannah police dutifully complied, and Carolyn Quillion, Ernest Robinson, and Joan Tyson Bryan were arrested for trespassing. The arrests triggered an economic boycott that lasted for 15 months.

The boycott was led by residents Curtis V. Cooper and Mercedes Wright, and sponsored by the local NAACP. They were given strong backup support by the ministers and the churches.

In an historic pattern of coordination and collaboration, the black churches in Savannah performed in a manner that has been called their finest hour. During the Sunday morning worship services the boycott was a major topic of concern. Notices would be read about the progress and plans of the boycott. Ministers' frequent sermons on the injustices and the boycott were designed to urge their parishioners to participate and to respect the picket lines. Special offerings were collected to provide financial support to the boycott. Members and representatives of the NAACP were usually on hand to underscore the collaboration between the churches and the organization.

In addition, every Sunday afternoon at 4 p.m., well after the morning worship services and the Sunday dinner hour, the black churches in Savannah would take turns hosting the weekly rallies. Churches were often filled to overflowing for these rallies.

In the end, the boycott was nearly 100 percent effective. As a consequence, in July 1961, representatives of all the downtown stores and those from outlying shopping centers as well capitulated. In exchange for an end of the boycott, they agreed to desegregate their lunch counters, remove all signs referring to race from their premises, and desegregate their rest rooms and drinking fountains. Moreover, they agreed to begin hiring blacks as clerks and salespersons. They were, of course, responsive not only to the boycott itself but to the unified determination of the black community, which, after all, constituted nearly half of the population of the city, representing disproportionately high consumer trade.

While the young people were actively engaged in the boycott, the adult chapter of the NAACP, under the leadership of W. W. Law and Curtis Jackson, launched a campaign to desegregate the local schools. The case brought by the NAACP was led by the Rev. L. Scott Snell, pastor of Bethel Baptist Church. Snell was the lead plaintiff, having agreed to sue for admission of his children to the public schools on a desegregated basis. When the "Snell case" went to federal court, the case was dismissed by Judge Frank M. Scarlet on May 13, 1963, on the grounds of "testimony by whites that integrated schools were harmful to both whites and Negroes," according to the *Savannah News* of May 14, 1963. When the case was appealed to the Fifth U.S. Circuit Court of Appeals, however, it was overturned. Judge Scarlet was ordered to instruct the Savannah–Chatham County Board of Public Education to submit a plan to desegregate at least one grade by September 1963. As a consequence, nineteen black youths entered the twelfth grade at Savannah and Grove high schools in September 1963, nearly 10 years after the United States Supreme Court in the *Brown* case outlawed segregation in public schools. Also during the summer of 1963 Armstrong State College in Savannah was desegregated when Otis S. Johnson transferred from Savannah State College. School desegregation moved rapidly and without violence in Savannah. By August 1964 Savannah was the most desegregated city in the South.

In July 1963, the month before the national march on Washington, Dr. Martin Luther King Jr. came to Savannah, while Hosea Williams was still in jail. He addressed an overflow crowd at the same Second African Baptist Church where Gen. Sherman had addressed a crowd nearly 100 years earlier.

It often happens that after a major victory the participants in the movement develop differences that cause a breakup of the successful coalition. This happened in Savannah. In 1963, at the height of the success of the civil rights movement direct action campaign, a major controversy developed among the participants, and the black church was caught in the middle of it all. Hosea Williams had been appointed chair of the NAACP Crusade for Voters, which launched a program of voter registration and political activity. In time, however, Williams and his associates became disenchanted by some of the restrictions placed on them by the NAACP. The controversy came to a head when Williams and his associates, including Ben Clark, Henry Brownlee, Mabelle Dawson, Al Rivers, and Rebecca Jenkins, began leading day and night demonstrations in the downtown area. They received strong support from the black community. More than 300 persons were arrested from June 6 to 10, 1963. Newspapers reported an eight-block-long parade of blacks, 650 persons, leaving the First African Baptist Church one night. Tension mounted. The NAACP dissociated itself from the night marches. Williams was furious at this denunciation but showed no signs of discontinuing. Eventually Williams was suspended by the national office of the NAACP, and he took his Crusade for Voters into independent status. Later he joined the Southern Christian Leadership Conference and appointed himself Dr. Martin Luther King Jr.'s local agent.

The majority of black ministers were solidly behind the NAACP and began refusing permission for Williams to hold meetings of his Crusade for Voters in their churches. The Rev. C. T. Vivian, aide to Dr. King, was dispatched to Savannah to try to resolve the impasse between Williams and the NAACP, but to no avail. Williams's Crusade for Voters began to wither. The NAACP reemerged as the dominant civil rights agency in Savannah with the churches a close ally. Meanwhile, Williams would be arrested and would spend more time in jail than any other civil rights leader in the South.

After winning the public accommodation and school desegregation battles, the NAACP turned to political activity with a vengeance. The local Democratic Party began to respond to the NAACP power by the appointment of blacks to positions and by supporting blacks for political office. Strong belief in the integrity of W. W. Law made the NAACP Political Action Council the dominant political force for blacks in the city of Savannah.

According to Johnson, what emerged during the '60s was an effective coalition between the NAACP and the black church in Savannah that determined the character and direction of the civil rights movement in that city.

Social activism on the part of activist ministers is not without cost, however. Sometimes this results in tension between the congregation and the pastor, especially when congregants don't share the pastor's vision. An excellent example of this is an A.M.E. church in Savannah. The church has a tradition of activist ministers dating back to the Rev. Henry M. Turner, who served as pastor from 1870 to 1874. In 1973, however, in the midst of the civil rights movement, a new pastor was assigned to this church. A faction in the congregation opposed to his leadership successfully petitioned the bishop to replace him.

When the new minister arrived, he led the church into more community projects. He established a number of economic ventures. It was his political activities, however, which caused conflict with substantial elements of the membership. In 1974 he led a group of ministers in support of a political candidate opposed by the NAACP. The ministers' candidate won.

In that year, the Rev. Jesse Blacksheer, a member of the Georgia state assembly, was a candidate for reelection. He had been elected two years earlier with the joint support of the NAACP and the black churches. A young man in his early 30s, highly educated, and motivated for community service, he also had a tendency to think for himself and to act on his own insights from time to time. This brought him into some difficulty with the NAACP. During his first two years, he had attempted to work with all groups in the community and not exclusively with the NAACP. When the time came for his renomination, the NAACP opposed him in favor of his opponent in the Democratic primary. A group of black ministers took issue with the NAACP and organized a campaign of support for Blacksheer through the Ministerial Alliance. Thus were the two strongest forces in black Savannah arrayed against each other. The Democratic Party stood aside to see the outcome of this fratricide.

The Rev. Blacksheer beat the NAACP-endorsed candidate in the primary. Thereafter, the relationship between the NAACP and the churches was strained.

Again during the summer of 1975 this same A.M.E. pastor moved to the forefront of social action. He rose to leadership in the Ministerial Alliance and led in three campaigns for social reform. One was to continue the work of his predecessor to make the alliance an independent political force in the city. A second was to stop a controversial plan to desegregate Savannah State College by merging it with the white Armstrong State College. The third was a selective-buying campaign organized by a group of ministers called The Black Summit, in which he was also a leader.

This selective-buying campaign involved demands for more black employment in the city, the use of black-owned media for advertising, patronage of the local black-owned bank for deposits, and donations to black charities. The NAACP opposed this selective-buying campaign. The Ministerial Alliance invited the bishop of the A.M.E. church, who came to town and endorsed the campaign. Thereafter, the churches got the upper hand, and the campaign was successful.

This activism of the A.M.E. minister, combined with accusations that he neglected church duties, led the same faction of the church to demand that the bishop remove him. In 1979 this minister, too, was assigned to another city. His replacement in Savannah followed a low profile in community affairs and concentrated on unifying the church for a number of years.[6]

Dr. Otis Johnson has said that "The sixties represent one of the most fantastic compressions of political ideas and actions of any decade in American history, especially for the South." He continues, "To go from a caste system of rigid segregation via the Civil Rights movement to cultural revolution (Black Power) to a relatively desegregated society in a ten-year period is almost beyond comprehension. And yet, it was accomplished."[7]

Ralph Mark Gilbert Civil Rights Museum

In August 1996 the city and county officials of Savannah officially opened the Ralph Mark Gilbert Civil Rights Museum at 460 Martin Luther King Jr. Boulevard in Savannah. The opening kicked off a four-day celebration to mark the culmination of this project, which had been long in the making.[8]

The theme of the four-day celebration was "And Still We Rise." Friday featured a dress-up jubilee gala reception as a fund-raiser for the museum. The highlight was an all-day gathering at First African Baptist Church on Saturday, which featured a reenactment of a mass meeting at the church during the height of the civil rights movement and a mass march down Martin Luther King Jr. Boulevard to the museum. Sunday the festivities moved into all Savannah churches with special museum offerings and membership drives.

The museum is housed in the old Guaranty Life Insurance Company building, once one of the city's largest black-owned businesses, located at the corner of Alice Street and Martin Luther King Jr. Boulevard. The building was erected in 1914 and served for a time as headquarters for the African American Wage Earner's Bank and the Savannah NAACP.

When visitors enter the museum the first thing they see is an oversized judge's bench accompanied by an account of injustices that blacks experienced prior to the civil rights victories. A second venue is a lunch counter, similar to the 1950s lunch counters in downtown stores that excluded blacks and were the object of the boycott of 1960–61. On the mezzanine level the visitors find a small sanctuary and a 15-minute film on the civil rights movement as centered in the churches. An exhibit on the second floor, "When West Broad Street was the Main Drag: Martin Luther King, Jr. Boulevard before 1950," features photos of prominent black-owned enterprises.

Another exhibit shows how the education and judicial systems have improved. The museum also houses an audiovisual room and reading room to be used by children using words and music to tell the continuing story of civil rights. A small theater in the basement is a children's theater. A room on the third floor is dedicated to the history of Laurel Grove South Cemetery, a landmark for the black community because in many cases the tombstones and grave markers are the only viable memorial and documented record of black life in Savannah. The oldest section of the cemetery is bounded by First Avenue, Fourth Avenue, George Street, and Booker Street. The cemetery is covered with live oaks and Spanish moss and is set back from shady streets.

A splendid collection of photographs depicts the history of the cemetery from 1852 to the present. The collection has been described by W. W. Law as "a precious treasure that bears witness to a deep and abiding faith in God, pride of race, perseverance and outstanding achievement against the odds."

The oldest marker in the cemetery is the grave site of James Bryan, dated January 23, 1789. Bryan was deacon in the First African Baptist Church, of which his brother, Andrew Bryan, was pastor from 1783 to 1812. The brothers were strong allies. It has been said that James Bryan was to his brother Andrew as Ralph Abernathy was to Dr. Martin Luther King Jr.

Another photograph is of the burial site for Annie Nuttall, who died in 1929 at age 69, and her husband, George Nuttall, who had died in

1893 at age 63. Another is of Dale Monrow, who died December 28, 1882, at the age of 115 years and his brother George Monrow, who died August 28, 1882, at the age of 120 years.

Prominently featured is the crypt that contains the pioneering ministers the Rev. Andrew Bryan, the Rev. Andrew Marshall, and the Rev. Henry Cunningham. For W. W. Law, who is the guardian of the cemetery and the museum and the history they represent, both are invaluable treasures. They are repositories of the African American experience in Savannah for more than 200 years in slavery and freedom.

6

—⚏—

First African Baptist Church, Richmond: Seedbed of Social Reform

In Richmond, emancipation and Reconstruction were played out somewhat differently than in Savannah, but no less dramatically. The Confederacy's capital, Richmond was burned by the Rebels when it became clear they could not stave off a Union attack. And as the Confederates watched their world crumble, blacks in Richmond watched a new world take shape, one in which their longings for freedom and dignity seemed to be on the brink of being satisfied.

But they soon found that the struggle was in some ways just beginning. And the black church, which had been a source of solace and solidarity during slavery, moved to the central position in the struggle, becoming a source of courage and will to resist further oppression and inequity.

The fall of Richmond to Union forces on Sunday, April 2, 1865, signaled the end of the war. And among the many ironies of the war is that this cradle of the Confederacy fell at the hands of black Union troops.[1] In the ensuing crisis, the black churches were called upon to help ease the transition from slavery to freedom. First African Baptist Church was first among these. It was a large and strong institution. It had functioned in that community since 1790 and was a veritable seedbed of social reform. The situation unfolded as follows:

That Sunday, the president of the Confederacy, Jefferson Davis, was worshiping in St. Paul's Church in Richmond. In the midst of the service a messenger brought him a telegram from Gen. Robert E. Lee. The note said simply that Richmond was about to fall. The Confederate forces could hold it no longer. Lee's telegram informed Davis that the last southbound train out of Richmond would be leaving in a matter of hours. The president would be well advised to take that train.[2]

By that Sunday afternoon, the evacuation of Richmond was in full force. Near panic ensued among the white population as people rushed to take the last train out of Richmond, or drove wagons and rode horseback heading south.

One infamous slave broker named Lumpkin owned a jail that was used for the imprisonment of slaves on their way to market. Lumpkin arrived at the train depot with 50 of his prisoners chained together two by two, valued at $50,000, planning to board this last train and take his property south with him. Alas, there was not room enough on the train for him and his cargo. In a spirit of personal survival, Lumpkin cursed his bad luck and unchained his prisoners, and as they wandered aimlessly about the station, he boarded the train alone.[3]

As the Confederates evacuated Richmond, they set the city on fire in an effort to destroy all the resources that might be of immediate value to the conquering federal troops. Shortly after midnight Richmond was in flames.

Here the four black churches in Richmond were called upon by the black community to play a heroic role. The churches responded gallantly. Thomas Morris Chester writes in a dispatch on April 10, 1865: "The colored people being aware that the city would be evacuated on the evening of the 2nd of April, and fearing that the rebels would drive them (the Blacks) before them, passed the night in the Negro Churches, where they remained until they saw the colored soldiers arresting rebel soldiers found in the city."[4]

One of the most extraordinary and underreported events of the Civil War had taken place: On Monday morning, April 3, 1865, a unit of black Union soldiers captured Richmond.

The Fifth Massachusetts Cavalry, a black regiment under command of Colonel Charles Francis Adams, grandson of President John Quincy Adams, was the first to enter the city. They were soon followed by companies C and G of the Twenty-Ninth Connecticut Colored Volunteers, and the Ninth U.S. Colored Troops.[5] Indeed, at least four other reputable historians and observers have reported that black troops took Richmond, but still it has not penetrated the general public's knowledge base.

The historian R.J.M. Blackett writes as follows: "It is one of the ironies of American history that . . . those whose offer to join the Union's defense, four years earlier, had been spurned because they were black, now found themselves in the vanguard as Union forces marched into Richmond."[6]

The black population of Richmond was ecstatic to see black Union troops take charge of the city. Quarles writes:

> Richmond Negroes were beside themselves with joy. Here on horseback and afoot were men of color, in neat blue uniforms, their shoulders erect, their heads high, their eyes confident. The black admirers ran along the sidewalks to keep up with the moving column, not wishing to let this incredible spectacle move out of sight. In acknowledgement of their reception, the Negro cavalrymen rose high in their stirrups and waved their swords. The cheers were deafening.[7]

A Visit From the President

Then in the midst of this celebration, word was whispered through the black community that an event second only to the fall of Richmond in the eyes of local blacks was about to occur. President Lincoln had decided to make a hasty, secret visit to the captured city; he and his party arrived on Tuesday, April 4, one day after the fall of Richmond. Lincoln's arrival was so hurried that there were no security forces awaiting his arrival. When he stepped ashore at Richmond holding his son Todd by the hand, the only people waiting to greet him were about 40 black dock workers.[8]

They recognized him and crowded around him in an almost worshipful manner, blocking him from proceeding. So Lincoln, as was his habit, paused to speak a few words to his audience. Quarles writes, "He urged them to live up to the laws, obey the Commandments, and prove themselves worthy of the boon of liberty."[9] They shouted and cheered their approval. Only then did they make way for him to proceed into the city. In what surely were the sweetest moments of his troubled and triumphant career, Lincoln walked through the streets for a mile and a half surrounded by swarms of blacks till he reached the former Confederate capital.[10]

Black people could not contain themselves. Many of them acted as though they were attending a religious revival, Quarles writes.[11]

Five days later, Gens. Robert E. Lee and Ulysses S. Grant signed the peace accord at Appomattox Courthouse.

Six days after that, on April 15, President Lincoln was dead. The black community was plunged, with most of the North, into a state of severe remorse, loss, and mourning. Indeed, the sense of loss was as deep as the elation had been high on April 4 and 5.

After celebrating the end of the war, after sheltering the frightened blacks on the evacuation of the Rebels, and after leading celebrations for the victory and mourning for the dead president, the black churches of Richmond had major work to do to ease the transition from slavery to freedom. Here, again, a large black church, First African Baptist, would be at the center of this work.

Confrontation at First African Baptist

Members of the First African Baptist Church were eager to realize the benefits of their new freedom after the collapse of the Confederacy. They were not, however, of a mind to treat their white pastor with anything but the courtesies that they had extended to him and that he had justly earned during their 24 years of fellowship. So how to honor a man who still believed in slavery, but had given more than two decades of kindness to them when slavery was the law of the land? Members of First African Baptist Church did not have long to ponder the theoretical fine points of this dilemma. One week after the black federal troops took control of Richmond, a defining moment was presented to these parishioners.

In a dispatch dated April 10, 1865, Civil War correspondent Thomas Morris Chester reported an incident that occurred the previous Sunday.

> The colored churches yesterday were densely crowded with delighted audiences. The First African Baptist, the largest one in Richmond, was densely packed, and to the astonishment of a redeemed people, Rev. Robert Ryland, the white pastor, preached a rebel sermon, so marked in its sentiments that the colored soldiers many of whom happened to be present, abruptly left the building. The speaker emphatically discouraged enlistments in the Union army. He also urged them to stay with their former masters. When the services were over the colored soldiers met Mr. Ryland at the door as he came out and arrested him. Strange as it may seem, notwithstanding the madness of the canting hypocrite, and his desire to continue the perpetration of the wrongs of oppression upon negroes, the (Black) members of his church begged and entreated (with the soldiers) that he be spared the indignity of an arrest, out of respect to his age. He was then required (by the colored soldiers) to report to the provost marshal, to answer the charge of using improper language.[12]

The result, which came too late for Chester's dispatch, was that Alvah Hovey, a member of the Christian Commission of the federal army, was dispatched to First African Baptist Church to settle the difficulty. When Hovey arrived for the afternoon service, a crowd had already gathered before the doors of the church. The black soldiers refused to permit the Rev. Ryland to enter the church for the service.

Hovey, knowing that in Baptist doctrine the congregation has the ultimate authority in all matters of church operations, quickly put this knowledge to good use.

Hovey spoke directly to the black soldiers, his comrades in the struggle for freedom. Since it was the rule in Baptist churches for the congregation to decide such matters, he proposed, why not permit the congregation of First African Church to choose their own speaker for the afternoon service?

The suggestion that this issue be put to a vote of the congregation resolved the issue immediately. The soldiers could not refuse such a democratic suggestion. Everybody knew what the outcome of such a vote would be. Or at least all the black people knew, and Ryland knew. Hovey probably knew the outcome as well.

History records that the matter was put to a vote, and the congregation chose the Rev. Ryland to be their speaker for the afternoon service. The doors of the church were opened by the deacons, and the service proceeded without further incident.[13]

But Ryland, who was nothing if not intelligent and sensitive, must have seen this confrontation as the last straw. Within a few weeks he submitted his resignation as pastor to the congregation he must truly have loved. When the first black pastor of First African Baptist Church was installed, a deacon whom Ryland had groomed for leadership, Ryland would take part as the representative of his white First Baptist Church, which had given birth to the black church. And when the first black college, Virginia Union, was opened in Richmond, Ryland would volunteer to join its teaching staff. But an era had ended amid sadness and joy. And the first black pastor of this historic black church, the Rev. James R. Holmes, would prove as suited to the demands of the new era as the Rev. Robert Ryland was to the old.

In June of 1865, less than two months into freedom and before Holmes was installed as pastor, he exhibited leadership as a senior deacon in this church.[14] Blacks noted absence of legal equality and respect shown to them by white government officials installed by the Union forces. They were being mistreated by the governing body, by the Union army, and by the police. They complained about the brutal enforcement by the police and army of pass and curfew laws, which were designed to expel thousands of blacks from the city. In the face of this mistreatment black leaders conducted a court of inquiry into official misconduct. They reported their findings and recommendations to local authorities. Nothing changed. Failing to win redress from local officials, black leaders called a mass meeting for June 10, 1865, at the First African Baptist Church.

By now five strong black independent churches had emerged from slavery, and all participated in this rally. More than 3,000 blacks showed up to protest. At the meeting they approved a protest petition and selected seven representatives to take their petition to Washington and present it to the president, Andrew Johnson.

The seven-member delegation included a representative from each of the five African American churches in Richmond and was financed by collections taken in these churches. When they arrived in Washington, they were given an audience with President Johnson. They told the president in their petition that the black community in Richmond was a law-abiding community with several thousand literate and propertied members, more than 6,000 regular churchgoers, and a tradition of caring for the sick and the poor. They argued to the president that their proven respectability and past loyalty to the Union had earned them and theirs the right to fair treatment, not the abuse and lowly status the army was according them.[15]

After listening to their grievances, President Johnson promised to take action on their behalf. Then another amazing thing happened. O'Brien writes: "By the time the delegates returned to Richmond and reported back to their constituents, the pass and curfew laws had been repealed, the civilian government removed, and the offending army officers replaced."[16]

The members and leaders of these black antebellum churches stepped up to the challenges history had laid out for them. And, because they acted, they helped to shape the course of history itself.

The Evolution of First African Baptist Church

The First African Baptist Church dates its founding to 1780, for good reason. When the white First Baptist Church of Richmond was formally organized in 1780, it had large numbers of black members.[17]

Meanwhile the black membership in the First Baptist Church continued to grow. By 1828 there were 300 white and 1,000 black members. After 1831, when the self-proclaimed Baptist preacher Nat Turner organized and led his revolt against slavery, which succeeded in killing 64 white men, women, and children, even more severe restrictions were placed on black worshipers. Still, by 1836 there were 400 white and 2,000 black members.

Finally in 1841, black members were provided their long-demanded separate house of worship. In petitioning the Dover Association on behalf of their black members, the white officers wrote, "Our hearts are greatly set on furnishing separate religious instruction for our colored people. Their number calls for a larger place of meeting and their peculiar habits, views, and prejudices demand peculiar instruction."[18] This time the Dover Association granted its permission.

They would build a new church for the white members and sell the old church to the black members. It was done, and First African Baptist Church was established. And, although the church building was appraised at $13,000 in 1841, the whites sold it to the blacks for $6,500. Though whites helped the blacks raise the money, $3,500 was raised by the black congregation itself—a phenomenal sum for people in their circumstances. The First African Baptist Church was neither completely independent financially or organizationally. The governing body was composed of representatives from the white Baptist churches in the city. They insisted on a white minister for the black church, and a constitution for the black church was drawn up by this committee. It did provide, however, for black deacons to approve or reject the white minister appointed by the supervising committee.

In the evolution of the First African Baptist Church of Richmond, its social reform impact would be most dramatically expressed through the lives of its members who took the teaching of the church into the larger society through their roles as change agents. Prominent among these individuals were Lott Carey, the first black missionary to Africa; Jane Richards, a slave who would be executed because of her actions; the Rev. Robert Ryland, the white man who would become first pastor of this black church; the Rev. James H. Holmes, the first black pastor after slavery; Mrs. Maggie Lena Walker, the first black woman to head a bank; and L. Douglass Wilder, the first black person elected governor of Virginia. All these members of this historic church represented and implemented the social reform mission of the church in their various achievements.

I. Lott Carey and Collin Teague: Missionaries to Africa

Despite its limitations and frustrations, the First Baptist Church was a nurturing training ground for black leadership. Born into slavery near Richmond in 1782 to Christian parents, Lott Carey attended the First Baptist Church and, at the age of 25, was converted to Christianity. By then, Carey had acquired a strong desire to learn to read and write. He eagerly attended classes set up expressly for black members in the church by one of the white deacons, William Crane. Classes met three evenings a week. He taught them reading, writing, Bible, and arithmetic. Lott Carey was one of his most ardent students.[19]

Carey had a strong desire to be free, which was heightened by his new learning. After working extra jobs for six years, he was able to purchase his freedom and that of his wife, son, and daughter in 1813 for $850.

His goals and aspirations in life kept expanding with each level of accomplishment. Now he longed not only to be free, but to live as a man and be judged on his merit, not on the color of his skin. He began to read about his ancestral homeland in Africa. He was encouraged and supported in all his interests by his church, and soon he was licensed by the First Baptist Church to preach.

Carey struck up a close friendship with another black member of the church, Collin Teague. Teague had also learned to read and write, and had purchased his freedom and that of his family. Together these two families formed an association. They read and studied about Africa and ultimately were founders of the First Foreign Missionary Society, which was organized in the First Baptist Church in 1815. The first officers were James C. Cram, a white man, as president, and Collin Teague as secretary. It was this society that gave Lott Carry and Collin Teague $700 to support their trip to Africa in 1821. They persuaded the local missionary society, the African Colonization Society, and the First Baptist Church to sponsor them.

Now they were almost ready to sail. But first, Lott Carey and his family, Collin Teague and his family, and Joseph Langford and his wife met at the home of deacon William Crane, their teacher, and formed the First Baptist Church of Liberia. The name would be changed later to Providence Baptist Church, and Lott Carey would become its first pastor.

A most impressive send-off was arranged by the church. And after some 44 days on the high seas, Carey and his family and Teague and his family became the first blacks from this country to establish missionary work in Africa. They landed in Liberia, where Carey would spend the rest of his short life.

Carey's desire to go to Africa was partly humanitarian and partly very personal. "I am an African," he said. "And in this country, however meritorious my conduct and respectable my character, I cannot receive the credit due either."[20]

Carey felt the freedom to give wide expression to his vision of the practical ministry in Africa. He threw himself into his work with a vengeance for the seven years he would serve there before his death. He worked very hard with his associates in the African Colonization Society to form a just government structure in Liberia. He established an African Mission in Monrovia and served as medical officer, soldier, teacher, preacher, and organizer of the First Baptist Church in Monrovia. He also helped to build an education system there.

Finally, in 1826 he was appointed lieutenant governor of Liberia. When the white governor of the colony, Jehudi Ashum, became ill and returned to the United States for treatment, Carey, who had led several revolts of the black colonists against Ashum's dictatorial administration, became acting governor. Ashum died of this illness, and it has been said that on his deathbed, he requested that Carey be appointed governor to succeed him. The governing council did so in 1828, and Carey accepted. Before he could be installed as governor, however, Carey was accidentally killed. He was preparing for an impending attack by organizing the arms cache in a store when a lighted candle accidentally set the place afire. He died in the flames, and the store was destroyed. Still his influence remained.

One of Carey's active campaigns had been against the slave trade. It has been said that after his tragic death, "the shock stirred the people to immediate action. Liberia was freed from slave traffic, and Lott Carey's plans were carried out completely."[21]

Another of Carey's legacies is the Lott Carey Society, a national movement by black Baptists supporting mission work in Africa, India, and the West Indies. The society was established in December 1897, at Shiloh Baptist Church in Washington, D.C. The convention supports more than 130 missionaries in Africa, India, and the West Indies. Most recently the convention has contributed to AIDS research, in light of its devastating effects on Africans.

Thus, the First Baptist Church, by nurturing and supporting Lott Carey and Collin Teague and their families and by launching and supporting them in their mission work in Africa, made an important contribution to social reform even during the time of slavery. It was during its years as a separate black church, after 1841, however, that this church made its greatest contributions to social reform. One of the early actors in this drama was Jane Richards, a black member held in bondage.

II. Jane Richards: Campaign Against Slavery

African American women, both enslaved and free, have often been called upon for extraordinary sacrifice and heroism in the interest of their children, their families, their people, and their conscience, and especially in the interest of social justice. Sometimes they have been called upon to sacrifice their own lives and the lives of their children in the interest of these higher values. Toni Morrison, in her novel *Beloved*, tells of a mother who had escaped from slavery with her children but was caught and was soon to be enslaved again. As a consequence, she decided to take the lives of her children so they would not suffer reenslavement.

Though Morrison's story is fictional, it is based on historical fact; some people facing slavery took their own as well as their children's lives. But sometimes they turned their despair outward. They took the lives of those belonging to the oppressor class.

Jane Richards, a member of the First African Baptist Church, was tried, convicted, and hanged for such an atrocious murder in Richmond in 1853.[22]

One early morning around dawn, Richards crept quietly into the bedroom of the family whom she served. With a hatchet, she murdered the sleeping mother and her infant child, and then struck several blows against the man of the house. He was able to escape with his life, however, and thus provided an irrefutable eyewitness account of the incident at the trial. His testimony was really not necessary, however, because Jane confessed to her deeds. She was remorseful and proud at the same time. As a Christian woman, she abhorred murder. As one held in bondage, she abhorred the slave system even more.

At this trial, the husband not only recounted Richards's deeds, but reported that his puzzlement and anguish were heightened because he felt betrayed by her. He had recently done her an extraordinary kindness. At her request, he had recently purchased Richards's husband, who had been sold by his owner to a man who was planning to take him to another section of the country. This kindness on his part enabled Richards and her husband to remain in close proximity. The aggrieved husband thought that she should have been grateful for that and other kindnesses his family had extended to her. In fact, he said, they had treated her as though she were a member of the family.

Feelings against Richards ran high in the white community. In First African Baptist Church her people prayed for her. On the day of her execution, Jane was driven across the city on display in a four-horse wagon.

Then a remarkable series of events unfolded. Standing by her side along that long journey was the white pastor of her First African Baptist Church, the Rev. Dr. Robert Ryland. When their wagon reached the place where the gallows had been built, Ryland turned and faced the assembly. Almost 6,000 white people had gathered there to witness the execution.

In his address, Ryland said that all creatures are sinners. He exhorted every man and woman present to remember that they, too, needed mercy from a just God. In consequence, he said, every person in the crowd should have mercy for Jane, a fellow creature, "sinful though she might be."

It was written in a Richmond newspaper afterward, "Never before did religious ceremonies fall upon more unwilling ears." The mob wanted vengeance—without further delay. But then Ryland turned to Richards and requested that she kneel. He knelt beside her and offered up fervent prayer in behalf of her immortal soul. Now it could be seen that no longer were the executioners in charge of these ceremonies. Ryland had taken charge, if only for a moment.

When his prayer was concluded, Ryland got up. He signaled to the authorities that he was now ready for them to do their job. But yet another remarkable thing happened. Richards was not ready. She continued to kneel in prayer for several minutes more. When she had finished praying, Jane Richards rose and without a word walked with complete composure to the gallows, to pay with her life for the crimes she had committed. She was ready to meet her Maker.

III. Robert Ryland, White Pastor of a Black Church

Who, then, was this Dr. Robert Ryland?

Ryland was an ordained Baptist minister, a member of First Baptist Church, and president of the local College of Richmond, a Baptist institution of higher learning for white men, when he was selected by the white supervising committee as the first pastor of the First African Baptist Church. Indeed, had it not been for the First African Baptist Church, history would have paid scant attention to Robert Ryland.[23]

Because he continued to serve as president of the college at full salary, he required only $500 a year in salary from the church.

Under the leadership of Ryland and the black deacons the church prospered. Funds to support the church, pay the pastor's salary, purchase the church building, pay the sexton, and so on, came from the black members during Sunday collections. Another source of revenue came from renting the church building to political parties, entertainers, and lecturers. A third source was the popular church choir, which gave concerts periodically to the general public. The church also gave generously to secular humanitarian causes. It joined with other black churches in buying several slaves and setting them free. It donated entire collections to struggling black congregations in other places. It contributed money to aid yellow-fever victims, and to feed famine victims in Ireland.

Ryland allowed the black deacons to pray and speak from the pew. These prayers were often sermons in disguise. A million of these delicate compromises characterized relations between pastor and congregation for a quarter of a century.

One of Ryland's progressive innovations was to establish a mailing system in the church to keep track of members and keep them informed. Once, however, police discovered that black members were using this mailing system to aid and assist runaway slaves, it was abolished.

Ryland was honored to serve as pastor of what he said was the largest Negro Baptist church in the state and the second largest in the nation.[24]

Ryland appreciated the singing talent of his black members: "The singing of the choir was performed with scientific skill and Christian heartiness, but when the vast congregation poured out its full soul in the old-fashioned songs, the long and loud bursts of praise reminded one of the 'sound of many waters.' "

He encouraged discipline. In a remarkable tribute to this congregation, he wrote: "During the twenty-four years of his ministry among them, the Pastor did not see a single instance of a group of persons, young or old, engaged in talking and laughing during public worship."

Soon after the Confederates lost the war, Ryland lost his pulpit. "At the close of the War," he wrote, "the constitution and rules of order were so far modified as to adapt them to the new relations which the colored people sustained to society." (He could not quite bring himself to say "emancipation" or "freedom.") "The Pastor then offered his resignation from a belief that they would naturally and justly prefer a minister of their own color."[25]

Clearly, First African Baptist Church required new leadership. And Ryland by his work with the church deacons had done no small feat in helping to prepare just such leadership.

IV. Rev. James H. Holmes: Pioneer Black Pastor

In 1867, the church elected the Rev. James H. Holmes as its first black pastor. Holmes had been a deacon in the church under Ryland for a decade and had often been permitted to speak and pray, but not from the pulpit. Holmes had been elected assistant pastor at the time of Ryland's resignation and served a two-year apprenticeship under a local white minister. Holmes was pastor of the church even longer than Ryland, serving for 33 years, from 1867 until his death in 1900.[26]

During his tenure the church continued to grow and prosper. In a single year, 1878, 1,100 persons became members of the church. And on his 17th anniversary as pastor in 1884, Rev. Holmes could report that he had baptized 5,800 persons, conducted 1,500 funerals, married 1,400 couples, and ordained 12 ministers. He was not only an inspiring preacher and effective administrator, but a master builder of the church.

It cannot be said, however, that Holmes was born to leadership. He was born December 9, 1826, in King and Queen County, Virginia, some 40 years before the end of slavery. His parents before him, father, Clairborne Holmes, and mother, Delphia, were held in bondage by the same landowner, a Judge James M. Jeffries.

At age nine his erstwhile owner sent him to Richmond and hired him out in a tobacco factory owned by one Samuel S. Myers. Holmes would follow that occupation for 12 years, until he turned 21.[27] Meanwhile, in 1841, at the age of 15, he was married for the first of three times. He was also converted to Christianity that year and became one of the charter members of the new First African Baptist Church; Dr. Robert Ryland would become his lifelong mentor. He and his wife became parents of two children. After seven years of married life, church life, and work life, however, Holmes was sold down the river to New Orleans, away from his wife and family and Richmond.

The fate of his wife and children left behind took a fortuitous turn. In the fervor of the freedom movement, Holmes's wife's own mother and father had run away from slavery via the Underground Railroad and made their way to Massachusetts. There they succeeded in arranging for some abolitionists to purchase their daughter and grandchildren. They were then brought north and set free. Holmes would never see his wife and children again.

So, this strong and ambitious young man of 22, though held in bondage still, now applied himself diligently to his work on the docks of New Orleans. He rose through the ranks of dock workers, acquitting himself well as a worker. In one of several misfortunes to overtake him, an explosion occurred on the wharf that blew him off the boat on which he was working. Falling timber struck his forehead and left a life-long scar. Worse, his arm was dislocated from the shoulder. Holmes was now useless as a dock worker.

In still another turn of misfortune, Holmes's owner in New Orleans suffered economic reverses and committed suicide. This left Holmes adrift; not free, but adrift. Meanwhile, he married for a second time.

Now he and his wife were purchased by the same man. This man, too, failed in business in New Orleans and returned to Richmond, bringing Holmes and his wife with him.

Thus, in 1851, after an absence of four years, Holmes found himself back in his favored Richmond. He was still young, only 26. He would spend the rest of his life in Richmond, rising from servitude to the highest levels of community and national leadership.

His rise, however, was neither swift nor certain. He was again hired out to work in the tobacco factory, where he spent two years. He also reunited with the First African Baptist Church and began his slow rise to the top. His owner bought a general store and put Holmes in charge of running it, a position in which he would remain until the death of the owner. Holmes was then left in the hands of the widow. Holmes soon resolved, however, that the life of bondage was not for him. At the age of 27, Holmes purchased his freedom for $1,800 with money he had saved from his portion of the wages earned in the tobacco factory and in the store. But his wife and children were still being held in bondage.

In 1862, near the outbreak of the Civil War, Holmes's second wife died. The next year he married for the third time. He and his new wife would remain partners nearly 40 years, in slavery and in freedom.

By 1855, the 29-year-old Holmes had risen to the rank of deacon in the First African Baptist Church. He was nominated to this post by Ryland and elected by the black Deacon Board. He served in this position for 10 years, growing in wisdom and strength, and rising in stature as well. In 1867 Holmes was elected the first black pastor of the First African Baptist Church in Richmond. At his installation, Ryland served in the official delegation representing the First Baptist Church of Richmond.

Meanwhile, Holmes's third wife bore several children, making Holmes the father of seven children in all by 1885, when at 59 he had been pastor of First African Baptist for nearly two decades.

Holmes was thus the preeminent leader in guiding this church and the black citizens of Richmond from slavery to freedom. Among his most fateful acts as pastor of this church was baptizing and nurturing Maggie Lena Walker, who would take the church to the highest levels of social, economic, political, and educational influence.

V. Maggie L. Walker: Phenomenal Woman

Maggie L. Walker was a truly extraordinary woman. Her career in the church and in the community were so intertwined as to give real meaning to the concept of the black church as an agent of social reform. For her the relationship between her community leadership and her church were reciprocal. The Rev. Holmes baptized Walker and took her into the church in 1878, when she was 11 years old. She was buried by that same church, by the Rev. H. V. Johnson, Holmes's successor, in 1934, at the age of 67. Daniel Perkins remembers the event as though it were yesterday, in large measure because he could not find a seat in the standing-room-only crowd. But he felt fortunate to be able to stand. "People from all walks of life from all over the state and the nation were there," he said.

In 1928, at the dedication of the new church building, recognition was given to Walker as follows:

> The old historic First African Baptist Church is happy and proud to have on its roster a daughter in the person of Mrs. Maggie L. Walker, who has so distinguished herself by her valuable work in the church, community, and country, that today she is known nationwide for her great accomplishments. Mrs. Walker delights to say, "I owe my success to the influence of my church," of which she has been a communicant, a strong worker and a liberal supporter for the past fifty years, contributing largely to her church and all of its activities.[28]

She amassed this reputation based on the reality of her remarkable accomplishments.[29] And in public and private conversations, she never failed to give credit for her success to the First African Baptist Church of Richmond.

Walker was born July 15, 1867, two years after the Civil War ended and the same year the Rev. James H. Holmes became pastor of First African Baptist Church. Her mother, Elizabeth Draper, was free during slavery and worked as a servant to Elizabeth Van Lew, who was a famous spy for the Union. Elizabeth Draper married William Mitchell in the Van Lew house on May 27, 1868, when Maggie was already a year old. Mitchell was a waiter in the St. Charles Hotel, at that time the city's most prestigious. He therefore was, by that occupation, a man of considerable social standing in the community. In what would be the first of a series of mysterious tragedies in her long life, Maggie's father, disappeared in February 1876, when she was nine years old and her brother John was six. Five days later his body was found in the James River. The official coroner's report indicated that he had committed suicide. Most observers, however, said that he had been murdered. Neither the reason nor the perpetrators were ever identified. Maggie's mother supported the family by working as a laundress from her home, with the assistance of her two children.

At age 11, Maggie was baptized by the Rev. James H. Holmes during the great revival in the summer of 1878. She joined the Sunday school at the church, the first Sunday school organized in a black church in the United States. Her speeches and diaries, as well as the minutes of the church, indicate that this church was central to her life and work.

Early in life, Maggie demonstrated intellectual acumen and qualities of leadership. She attended public school in Richmond, graduating in 1883. Her graduation class made history by demanding to have its graduation ceremonies in the same public facility, the Richmond Theater, that the white graduating class used. They were refused, but the 10 members of the class were declared local heroes for their daring.

After graduation from normal school, Maggie joined a local chapter of the Order of St. Luke, one of many mutual aid charities in Richmond.

Maggie was an active member of the order and frequent attender at its annual conventions. As a delegate to the convention in 1895, when she was 28 years old, she submitted a resolution to create a Juvenile Division with Circles, headed by matrons in each of the local chapters. The resolution passed, the Juvenile Division was established, and Maggie Walker was elected grand matron of the division, a position she held until her death nearly 40 years later. Over the years, tens of thousands of children would become members of this division, including many members of the First African Baptist Church in Richmond.

Maggie's next step was to participate in the formation of the St. Luke Association, formed by 25 local councils for the purpose of purchasing property for a headquarters. Maggie became secretary of the board of this association. Their efforts were enormously successful. In 1903 an impressive three-story brick building was built, a symbol of achievement among blacks in Richmond. It was not only headquarters for the order of St. Luke, but an important place of regalia and printing enterprises and meeting rooms, an auditorium, and a tremendous source of pride for the African American Community.

Her organizing and managerial talents, as well as her public speaking and dramatic talents, were increasingly recognized and rewarded. At the 1899 Convention of the Order, when Maggie was 32 years old, she was elected unanimously as the chief executive officer of this fledgling national movement. For the next 35 years she would build it into a highly successful cluster of business, educational, civic, and social enterprises.

The next milestone for Walker was to become a banker. She prepared for this by spending a few hours a day as a volunteer in a local Richmond bank. When the St. Luke Penny Savings Bank opened in St. Luke Hall in 1903, Maggie Walker became, arguably, the first woman bank president in America. St. Luke's was quite successful. When it later merged with two other black-owned banks, becoming the Consolidated Bank and Trust Company, Walker became chair of the board. The bank is still in existence today, doing an active and successful range of financial enterprises.

A few years after starting the Penny Savings Bank, Maggie Walker and her associates opened a department store in downtown Richmond called the Emporium. This was perhaps their most ambitious and most difficult project. It was also their only conspicuous failure. Situated on Broad Street in a three-story building with an elevator, it promised to provide substantial employment for blacks, especially women. The store met with a hostile reception and boycott by white merchants. That, combined with a pattern of preference on the part of black shoppers for name-brand products, proved too much to overcome. After operating for six years, the Emporium was forced to close in 1911.

Walker was a great example of moving from strength to strength. She would serve a distinguished career in the leadership of the Order of St. Luke. She was consecutively chair of its business, finance, and budget committees, and was a member of its executive committee until her death in 1934. Also, in 1912 she founded and became president of the Richmond Council of Colored Women; she remained president until her death. One of the major projects of this council was raising funds to support the Industrial School for Colored Girls, which served as an alternative to jail for delinquent girls. Other activities of the council included the purchase of a house at 00 Clay Street in Richmond, which served as an office for black organizations and community affairs. When the depression came in the 1930s the building was sold to the city and became the first black public library in Richmond. Today this site is the home of the Black History Museum, which opened in 1991.

From 1923 until her death, Walker served as a board member of the national NAACP.

Her one overt political campaign occurred in 1921 when she was nominated for the office of state superintendent of public instruction, running on the Virginia Lily Black Republican ticket. The ticket did not win. Along the way she earned a master's degree in Education from Virginia Union University.

In all these activities Maggie Walker had the strong support of her congregants at the First African Baptist Church and its minister, the Rev. H. V. Johnson, who succeeded the Rev. James H. Holmes. Yet the church was never more supportive of her than in the two personal tragedies that struck her adult life. The first occurred in 1915. One evening her son Russell heard a noise on the roof of their home. Thinking the noise was made by a burglar, he took a gun, went up to the roof, and shot and killed the person making the noise. It turned out to be his own father. The son's story was hotly disputed and debated all over town. Some said he deliberately killed his father. Some said his mother put him up to it. The son was indicted and tried for murder. He was eventually acquitted, but Maggie Walker's leadership and standing in the community was in question for a number of years. With the strong support of her associates, none stronger than the members and pastor of First African Baptist Church, she was able to surmount this tragedy and continue her work. Reports indicate that she did not abandon or neglect a single one of her many church, local, or national responsibilities.

Meanwhile, Russell continued working for his father's construction firm and at his mother's bank. He died nine years later, predeceasing his mother by ten years and his brother by eleven years. During this time Maggie's adopted daughter, Margaret Anderson, now married to Polly Payne, looked after her mother and the big house on Leigh Street. By all and legendary accounts she devoted herself unstintingly to these assignments, becoming almost inseparable from her mother as companion, assistant, and protector.

Some years after Russell's death another tragedy struck Maggie Walker. In the late 1920s she began to lose the use of her legs, for reasons that were not clear. She still did not give up any of her major responsibilities. And "after several years of trips to Hot Springs, Arkansas, exercise regimens, and braces that constantly broke, one day, with characteristic decisiveness, she customized her automobile to accommodate a wheel chair." She continued to travel all over the country to lecture and conduct business. She continued her active participation in First African Baptist Church.

Trustee Perkins remembers when he was a boy being privileged each Sunday to help bring the wheel chair from her car and carry it up a ramp into the church. Maggie Walker sat in the front row with her customary dignity, dressed in the most tasteful garments, and contributed generously to the church. The pastor often referred to her and her staunch support of the church, her individual stamina, and her capacity to overcome the most devastating of adversities. Perkins remembers today the awe and admiration he felt toward her and how honored he was to be able to help her. It did not diminish his admiration that she also gave him and the other boys a quarter each Sunday for helping her into the church.[30]

Mutual Reinforcement. The social interaction between the business career of Mrs. Walker and the church is both manifest and latent. In 1994,
the First African Baptist Church was in the midst of a $1 million ren-
ovation to provide better space for auxiliary church programs. This included the community-oriented child development center that it runs
with no external funding except low fees paid by parents.

Remembering that black churches often have difficulty getting
large loans from local banks, and knowing that Baptist churches generally do not have large organizations able to subsidize their building
programs, I asked the Rev. Dennis E. Thomas whether he had trouble
getting construction loans. "Not at all," he said. "You see, we borrowed
our money from Maggie Walker's bank. It's the bank where we make
all our deposits, and most other black churches in town do, too. So
none of us have any difficulty when it comes to getting loans."

This was a three-pronged statement that not many black churches
in our study, or in the nation, are able to make. First, that black
churches in a concerted fashion make their deposits in the same bank
is unusual. Second, that black churches in Richmond are able to get
bank loans readily is somewhat unusual. And, finally, that there is a
large, strong, black-owned bank that provides the fulcrum for these
intricate social and economic transactions is even more unusual. As in
Walker's day, several officers and employees of this bank are members
of the First African Baptist Church.

Perkins remembers how as a very young lad he was enrolled by
his parents as a depositor in Maggie Walker's bank. He has continued
to this day and now serves on both the board and the loan committee.

This situation in Richmond does point up the enormous potential
of the black church to support and sustain black-owned enterprises,
which in turn will be helpful not only to the church but to black and
white customers.

This tradition of community service continues to the present time.
It is reflected in the experience and perspective of Gov. L. Douglass
Wilder.

VI. L. Douglass Wilder: The Church and the Community Today

When L. Douglass Wilder announced in 1989 that he would be a candidate for governor of Virginia, becoming the first African American to
do so in the history of the state, there were skeptics all over the state
and the nation. None of these skeptics, however, could be found in the
First African Baptist Church of Richmond. Many had known Wilder
since he was born. Wilder's father and grandfather before him had been

members of this church. Wilder's grandfather, though held in slavery, was among the first of the black deacons of this church as it became separate from its parent white First Baptist Church in 1841. They knew him as a winner. Members of this church had been solidly behind Wilder in all his previous political campaigns. And together he and they had never lost a race. For the members of this historic congregation, the former senator's aspiration for statewide leadership was just "One More River to Cross." It created just one more challenge for this remarkable church as an agent of social reform.[31] And although Wilder is not as active in the church as he once was, his sister still is. Indeed, the church historian says that at no time since before 1841 did the church rolls not include members of Doug Wilder's family.

In 1994, after Wilder had served the constitutional limit of one term as Virginia governor with distinction and national acclaim, with a balanced budget, and without a hint of scandal, his political influence backed up by the black churches in the state would again be on display. When Democratic Sen. Chuck Robb won reelection to a second term by a narrow margin, despite a national sweep of Republican candidates, Wilder could claim credit for Robb's margin of victory. The first thing Wilder did for Robb after endorsing him in the waning weeks of the campaign was to take Robb to church. Introducing Robb at a string of black churches, including an early visit to First African Baptist Church, Wilder was able to translate some of his enormous popularity with African Americans to the Robb campaign—just enough to make the difference.

So how did the church help in his political career? We wanted to get the former governor's own perspective on this, so we went to see him in his law office atop a hill overlooking the city.[32] He is a proud Virginian and a history buff. He pointed the author to the church next door to his office, where one of his distinguished predecessors as governor, Patrick Henry, had delivered his famous speech, "Give me liberty or give me death." Indeed, Wilder seemed almost as proud to call Gov. Thomas Jefferson his predecessor as President William Jefferson Clinton is to bear the great patriot's name.

When we turned to the subject of the impact of the black church on politics and on his career, he was emphatic. First, he said that the basic values of hard work, service, saving, and achievement that he received in his family were strongly reinforced in First African Baptist Church. These values have been essential building blocks for his many achievements in school, in the military, in law, in business, and in politics. Moreover, he repeated the Perkins's statement that in every one of his campaigns, members of this church had been early and active supporters of his efforts. This was true of his very first campaign, and it was true of his most recent short-lived campaign for the U.S. Senate. Indeed, Wilder reported that the group of black ministers who organized to support his senatorial campaign and Sen. Robb's campaign has not disbanded but decided only to become inactive at his request. They stand ready for future service.

Who is this Lawrence Douglass Wilder, the politician? Born January 17, 1931, in Richmond, he was baptized early into First African Baptist Church, having no real choice in the matter. He remembers walking past another church to get to First African and asking his mother why they couldn't go there. He explained that his mother was particularly determined that all family members belonged to First African Baptist to keep the family tradition alive. They walked to church on Sunday even though they could afford to ride, because his father, a frugal and successful businessman, insisted that walking was not only good for them but would save money. He was always very bright, able, and hardworking. He was educated in church-founded private black schools. He earned a bachelor's degree in chemistry in 1951 at Virginia Union University in Richmond, where he earlier entertained the idea of going into medicine. After returning from service in the Korean War, he earned a law degree from Howard University in 1959.

Along the way, Wilder and his wife at that time, Eunice, had three children, Lynn, Lawrence Jr., and Lauren. All have successful careers. Lawrence, an attorney, once served a term in the state legislature.

Wilder remembers in his childhood how he admired the people in the church for their values, their deportment, and their dress—the cutaway jackets worn by the ministers and the careful dress of the officers and ushers impressed him. While he admits to being mischievous, and more than once was removed from the congregation and sent to the basement by his father for misconduct, he learned very early in life to respect the people in this church as being as good as any people anywhere. And they made him feel that he could be so, too. As he grew older, he noted that only in the church and at his father's insurance business, which he also frequented, did he find such role models for achievement and upward mobility.

When he went off to college at Virginia Union, church members not only encouraged him and gave him a great send-off but kept in touch with him during college and insisted that he keep in touch with them. In later years he drifted away somewhat but never severed his ties to the church. As he pursued his profession, his business, and politics, the church has been a reliable and enthusiastic support base.

The basic values he learned in the church, however—strong self-worth, high achievement motivation, strong commitment to community service, education and, above all, willingness to work hard—have served him well over the years.

The Road Ahead

It seems highly likely that the themes and values represented in the lives and works of these pioneers, Lott Carey, Jane Richards, Robert Ryland, Maggie L. Walker, and L. Douglass Wilder, will continue.

The current pastor, the Rev. Dennis E. Thomas, was attractive to this historic church in part because he brought a record of accomplishment both in the basic areas of ministry and in community outreach. And the church was attractive to him because of its history, not only as a center for spiritual development but as a seedbed of social reform.[33]

Thomas, 38, has been the leader of this historic congregation since March 1, 1987. A native of Philadelphia and a third-generation Baptist minister, he graduated from Central High School in that city, then from Eastern College with a double major in sociology and religion and a minor in urban studies. For theological training he graduated from Eastern Baptist Theological Seminary with a master of divinity degree.

His vision for the future of this church includes installing in members a greater appreciation of its illustrious history, and building on that history with more extensive community outreach programs. He considers economic development in the community an area of critical need in which the church can be especially instrumental.

Early in his tenure, Thomas recommended to the church a long-range program. At the October 19, 1992, church conference, he set forth seven ministries of the contemporary church as follows: preaching ministry, worship ministry, Christian education ministry, fellowship ministry, stewardship ministry, leadership ministry, and mission outreach ministry.

Here, speaking boldly as did the prophets of old, Thomas advised his parishioners as follows: "I believe that our missions outreach lacks relevance to the times in which we live. We must seek to extend ourselves and our mission dollars to help heal the growing hurts of today. How prepared are we to adequately respond to the aches and pains of homelessness, AIDS, drug traffic, and teenage crisis?"

All his recommendations were approved by the church conference. This 900-member, 215-year-old church now has a renewed sense of mission and a new set of marching orders. Just as it nurtured Lott Carey and his associates for their mission in Africa, and just as it had supported Jane Richards and Robert Ryland, James Holmes, Maggie Walker, H. V. Johnson, Doug Wilder, and countless others who took the church into the community, this church seems now poised to lead the congregation and the community into a new birth of freedom.

II

THE CONTEMPORARY
BLACK CHURCH REACHES OUT
TO THE COMMUNITY

7

—⚊—

New-Time Religion

We have seen by conducting extensive ethnographic case studies how individual black churches evolved from early antebellum times to the era of the civil rights movement in selected Southern states and how these churches have exhibited both a religious or spiritual function and a social or community outreach function.

Now we move beyond individual case studies to embrace large-scale sample surveys of churches in different regions of the country in order to show how generalized or widespread and how patterned is the community outreach role of the contemporary black church.

Clearly, large numbers of contemporary black churches have heard the same voice enunciated so distinctly by the Rev. Cecil Chip Murray of the First A.M.E. Church, Los Angeles: "The days of coming to church for personal salvation alone are over." Congregations, he said, are actively pursuing "not only personal salvation but social salvation as well."

The *New York Times*, as early as May 23, 1988, called attention to what seemed to be a renewal of community action on the part of black churches. In a prominent editorial, the paper wrote "Increasingly, the black churches have stepped in to try to repair the breaches in Black family life left by social, economic, and political change. Their efforts range from complex, foundation-supported child development programs to simple but sensible adopt-a-family projects."[1]

This social outreach role of the black church was also exhibited in the November 1993 issue of *Ebony Magazine*, the leading publication in black America. This issue featured *Ebony*'s selection of the 15 "Greatest Black Preachers" in America. The list was headed by Gardner Taylor, emeritus pastor of Concord Avenue Baptist Church in Brooklyn, the late Samuel D. Proctor, emeritus pastor of Abyssinian Baptist Church in Harlem, Jeremiah Wright of Trinity United Church of Christ in Detroit, Charles Adams of Harford Memorial Baptist Church in Detroit, and J. Otis Moss of Olivet Institutional Baptist Church, Cleveland.[2] (The complete list of *Ebony*'s top 15 preachers is shown in Table 5 in Appendix C.) Every one of these leaders was a highly educated, community-minded activist, and each of their churches operates extensive community outreach programs. Twelve of these 15 ministers have made some contribution to our research for this book.

Another leading publication, *Black Enterprise Magazine*, also profiled some of the same ministers and churches in its September 1993 edition. All were pastors of churches with extensive economic and community development programs. "All across America," the magazine observed, "the Black church is helping to revitalize inner-city neighborhoods and rural communities."[3] *Emerge Magazine*, an up-and-coming black-oriented magazine, also did a special article on urban churches and social reform.[4] The question we address in this chapter is, How widespread is this outreach by the black church?

On the basis of our surveys, we conclude that there is widespread recognition among contemporary black churches of the duality of their mission, and large numbers, perhaps a majority of large urban churches, are therefore engaged to some degree in community outreach activities.[5]

In all our surveys in various regions we found a majority of black churches surveyed are actively conducting one or more community outreach programs in addition to their primary religious programs. Specifically, we found that among the 315 churches in the Northeast region, spread across 10 communities in New York, New Jersey, Pennsylvania, Massachusetts, and Connecticut, 69 percent are actively engaged in one or more outreach programs. Among 320 churches in the Midwest, embracing 10 communities in Michigan, Illinois, Missouri, Kansas, Ohio and Indiana, 66 percent of them conducted such programs. Among the 80 churches in the Denver Survey the proportion of churches conducting outreach programs reached 75 percent, and in Atlanta 85 percent of the 150 churches surveyed sponsored one or more community outreach programs. Among the 100 churches surveyed in three rural counties of South Carolina, a strong minority are also engaged in community programs.[6] A most instructive aspect of the South Carolina Survey is that the vast majority of pastors of these small rural churches indicated that their churches would conduct such community service programs if funding were available. Lincoln and Mamiya also found that 71 percent of the urban churches in their national sample conducted such programs.[7] In 1980 Dr. Otis Johnson found that a majority of the churches in his sample from Boston and Savannah were actively engaged in some type of community outreach program.[8]

From these surveys we draw two conclusions: First, community outreach activities are much more widespread than is generally believed, especially in urban areas, and more widespread than we expected. This suggests that a majority of contemporary black churches have not abandoned community issues since the civil rights era or withdrawn into their spiritual mission of seeking personal salvation alone. The dual mission posited by Lincoln and Mamiya, which we found in the case studies in Part I, is still alive and widespread.

We also concluded that the nature of that outreach activity is different from the community activity of the civil rights era. During the 1950s and 1960s, black church outreach was more likely to be social action and protests against the oppression from forces external to the black community. Contemporary black church community outreach, on the other hand, is more likely to be social service or community development, addressing problems within the black community. Thus, the external strategies of reform of the earlier era have been supplemented by internal strategies of reform today. The rationale for this change is that the nature of the crisis facing the African American community has shifted dramatically. The earlier problems have not been solved, despite extraordinary progress. But new problems have overtaken the old ones in saliency and immediacy. (For a complete discussion of how we surveyed these churches, see Appendix B.)

Family-Support Programs

We have noted that the most frequent type of community outreach program operated by black churches in our surveys is that designed to strengthen and support families. Elsewhere we have identified two categories of functions that families are expected to meet for their members.[9] Some of these are instrumental functions, which include basic life-sustaining needs, such as food, clothing, and shelter. Others are expressive functions, which include providing for the emotional, intellectual, and spiritual development and well-being of family members. Some functions, such as basic education, child care, and health-related support, incorporate both instrumental and expressive characteristics. Moreover, the two types are mutually enhancing.

When we observe the 635 churches in the 12 states of the two Northern regions, we note that 419 of those churches provide 1,685 specific family-support services. These services fall into six areas of support. Two of these dimensions are expressive in character—counseling and intervention, which account for some 18 percent of programs offered, and social recreation programs, which account for 10 percent. Counseling includes family counseling, aid to incarcerated individuals and their families, women's services, including help for abused spouses, child-welfare services, parenting workshops, and workshops on human sexuality. Two other dimensions are instrumental in character. These are basic-needs assistance, which accounts for 40 percent of programs, and income maintenance, which accounts for only 6 percent. Basic-needs assistance includes food distribution, clothing distribution, emergency financial aid, referral to appropriate services, shelters for the homeless, and various types of home-care services. Finally, two dimensions have been categorized as jointly expressive and instrumental in character. These are education and awareness programs, which account for 19 percent of the total, and health programs, which account for 7 percent.

In both regions, food and clothing support services are by far the most frequently provided services. Programs offered by churches in Denver and Atlanta are similar.

An example of a church-sponsored family-support program is the Couples Ministry at Bethany Baptist Church in Detroit. Bethany Baptist Church is a 50-year-old church with approximately 300 members. It was described as a mostly working-class church, with a salaried senior minister and several paid staff positions. One unpaid minister is also affiliated with the church. The church's senior minister has received seminary training and is currently working on a doctoral degree. The church has 14 community outreach programs, but we selected the Couples Ministry to describe here because of its emphasis on family.

The first lady of the church is the program director for the Couples Ministry, which has been in operation for two years.

The informant explained: There seemed to be a breakdown in the black family, and the church is providing avenues for more communication among couples of various ages to encourage cohesiveness in the family unit.

The Couples Ministry is considered one of the church's most successful programs. It has helped couples strengthen their marriages by bringing to them a strong Christian perspective. The effectiveness of this program, many say, is due to the fact that the younger couples learn from the older, more experienced couples. At weekly meetings, couples exchange ideas and experiences, and do not just rely on the senior minister for guidance. The major aims of this program are to help couples try harder to stay together and to enhance communication between each couple and their children.

A similar couples ministry is conducted by the Ebenezer Baptist Church in Atlanta with a husband/wife team of Ph.D. psychologists, Wayne and Fleda Mask Jackson, conducting the weekly session. The pastor, the Rev. Joseph Roberts, says it is one of the church's most effective programs and is cost-effective as well.

Programs for Youths

In our surveys the second most frequent type of program operated by black churches after family-support programs is children and youth programs. Here we focus specifically on those programs designed for black adolescents.

Our survey of 635 Northern churches found that 176 churches reported having at least one program directed at adolescent members of the community, most of whom are from low-income homes.[10]

Turner and McFate conducted a study of community programs that serve young black males in six major cities: Atlanta, Boston, Cleveland, Oakland, New Orleans, and St. Louis. They found that of 175 such programs in these cities, 27 were sponsored by black churches with a total expenditure of nearly $1.3 million. Six of these church-sponsored programs were exclusively for black males. Programs included mentoring, Afrocentric education, rites of passage, drug-abuse prevention, health education, and tutoring.[11]

Evaluation of these programs shows that they are generally effective. For example, in an evaluation of Project Spirit, an after-school family-support program sponsored by the Congress of National Black Churches in Oakland, California, Atlanta, Indianapolis, Indiana, and Washington, D.C., McAdoo and Crawford reported that parents and children who had participated in the program found the program helpful for strengthening their family relationships.[12]

A major focus of these youth programs has been on efforts to stem adolescent out-of-wedlock births. The Children's Defense Fund (CDF), for example, has a network of more than 100 black churches engaged in its fight against teen pregnancy and childbirth. And the black crusade for children led by Marion Wright Edelman of the CDF has mounted a vigorous program in this regard. Moreover, the Congress of National Black Churches has launched a program among the seven historically black denominations to address this problem. One church, First A.M.E. Church in Los Angeles, has a preventive program in which condoms are dispersed. Still, the efforts are relatively small considering the need.

In our survey of 635 Northern black churches we found that 426 churches (67 percent) sponsored a total of 1,804 community outreach programs. These churches sponsored 566 (31 percent) of programs directed at children and youth.

Children's programs included Head Start and child welfare. When we searched for programs addressed specifically to adolescents, we found that 176 churches reported having a youth-support program. Teen support programs (39 percent) and sports programs (31 percent) were the most frequent types of youth programs. Fifteen percent of the church programs provided parenting/sexuality, counseling, classes/ workshops, pregnancy prevention, seminars, and support for teen parents. Other youth programs conducted by black churches included scouting, mentoring, recreation, drug-abuse counseling, academic support, and basic education. Among the least common programs were youth AIDS support programs (3 percent) and youth health-related services (2 percent). The former consisted of classes/seminars, counseling, and financial support to persons with AIDS. The latter included clinics, seminars, and screenings for specific health problems.

Increasingly, black churches are sponsoring comprehensive programs for at-risk black male youth in low-income communities.

One such program is Project Image, designed to strengthen the image, role, and presence of African American males through church-based programs. Started in 1984 by Gwendolyn Rice and the St. Mark United Methodist Church in Chicago, the project has spread to 12 other Methodist churches and currently embraces some 700 black youths ages 8–18. Workshops are held after school at each church site daily. They cover a variety of topics, including gang involvement, drug awareness, male/female relationships, and sexuality. Four paid staff and 64 African American male volunteers operate the program. It is supported financially by the churches, corporations, foundations, and individuals. The annual budget is $567,000.[13]

The black male youth project at Shiloh Baptist Church in Washington, D.C., was begun in 1986 under the leadership of the pastor, the Rev. Henry C. Gregory III, and a church group called "Men of Shiloh." The project is an after-school mentoring program for males ages 11–17. Co-sponsored by the Washington, D.C., Health Department and supported by grants from the Ford Foundation and others, the project aims to increase the youths' cultural awareness, self-esteem, health knowledge, and knowledge of African American history and culture, as well as their academic competence, through daily workshops, recreation, and mentoring. Teachers, parents, and others work together in the program. A staff of two, plus volunteers, operate the program, which has served more than 300 youths during its first 10 years of operation.

In a pathbreaking approach to helping low-income families care for their children, the Friendship Baptist Church in Columbus, Georgia, conducted a community survey to ascertain the major needs of these families. On the basis of these findings two needs emerged as paramount. These were quality, affordable child care for working parents and after-school care for children 6–13. With considerable investment of its own funds, space, and volunteers, and under the leadership of its pastor, the Rev. Emmett Aniton, the church proceeded to develop programs to meet both these needs. When we visited this church in 1995, the Child Development Center, which involved children, parents, church volunteers, and professional staff, was a vibrant example of how this church functions as a family support system.

Clearly, however, the magnitude of the crisis facing African American youths is greater than black churches or any one segment of society can combat effectively. But, just as in other crises, the black church can lead the way and galvanize others in a concerted attack on the problems black youths face. An outstanding example of how this is being done is in Savannah, Georgia, and will be discussed in Chapter 8.

The Black Church and the Elderly

A third type of outreach program identified in our surveys is service to the elderly. This is important because among African Americans, as other groups, the elderly are more likely to be members and supporters of churches than other age groups.[14]

It is estimated that roughly 78 percent of elderly African Americans belong to a church. A general profile of church functions indicates that they promote contact and social integration among members that contribute to the emotional well-being of the elderly.[15] Further, churches provide concrete help in the form of day centers for older adults and medical screenings for various diseases and conditions.[16] Moreover, churches can establish links to social service agencies as a means of expanding services to the elderly.

In our survey of 635 black churches in the northern portion of the United States we found that 67 percent (n=426) of the churches in this sample sponsor at least one outreach program in the community and, of these, 28 percent, or 120 churches, offer support programs for the elderly. In Denver and Atlanta a similar proportion of outreach programs were focused on the elderly.

Those 120 churches with elderly support programs provide a total of 153 senior services. The most frequently sponsored programs are home-care services (39 percent) that are designed to assist the elderly with household cleaning and related tasks. Fellowship activities account for 18 percent of church-based senior programs and are intended to maintain the seniors' involvement in the community. Daily home delivery of meals is the next most common program offered (10 percent), followed by senior citizen housing (9 percent) and multiservice programs (5 percent).

We noted that churches that have an established working relationship with social agencies in the community tend to offer support programs for the elderly, compared to churches that do not work with community agencies. It is important, however, to recognize that social service agencies have program development expertise that could be very useful for churches that work with the elderly. Even fellowship programs and activities that are primarily social may require some assistance from such resources as the local transportation department or recreational agencies.

Conservative, Moderately Active, and Activist Churches

Throughout this chapter we have seen that large numbers of contemporary black churches have not abandoned the community since the civil rights era. A majority of churches in our study are engaged in community outreach activity. This activity is principally the sponsorship of social services in keeping with "internal strategies of social reform" or building up self-help capabilities within the African American community.

At the same time, however, we noted that a substantial minority of churches in our surveys have chosen not to engage in community outreach programs. This group amounts to 31 percent of churches in the Northeast, 34 percent of those in the Midwest, 25 percent of those in Denver, 15 percent of the Atlanta sample, and a majority of those in the rural South Carolina sample. Why is it that some black churches do not engage in social and community action? To answer this question, we placed the churches into categories.

We found that the number of programs sponsored by each church ranged from none to 25 with a median of three programs. We then organized the churches into three categories. The first group, which we term conservative churches, indicated that they operated no community outreach programs. A second group conducted one or two programs, and we labeled them moderately active. A final group of churches conducted three or more programs and were labeled activist churches.

What distinguishes those three types of churches? Specifically, what distinguishes the activist churches from the others? In Chapter 1 we advanced the proposition that strong and resourceful churches with strong and resourceful pastors were more likely than other churches to respond to the crisis in the community. We found strong support for this proposition in the case studies in Part I. The surveys reported in this chapter allow us to examine the proposition more broadly. Basically, we found that two sets of factors distinguish the activist churches from the others. One set of factors is associated with the church as an organization. The other set is associated with the senior minister as leader.

Characteristics of Activist Churches

We found seven characteristics of the church as an organization that make a difference generally in whether a church does outreach. These are denomination, church age, size, membership composition, ownership of church building, number of clergy, and other paid staff. In sum, churches that are characterized by more of the above resources are much more likely to engage in community outreach programs than churches with fewer of those resources.

Denominational Differences. While a substantial majority of churches in all denominations are actively involved in community outreach programs, some denominations have a higher percentage of churches involved in these pursuits than others do. Overall, Methodist churches (77 percent) are more likely than are Baptist churches (65 percent) or Pentecostal churches (60 percent) to conduct community outreach programs (see Figure 5 in Appendix B). The pattern is similar though not exactly the same in both Northern regions, as well as in Denver and Atlanta.

Indeed, the preeminence of the black Methodist congregations in community outreach is so consistent that I asked a Methodist scholar, Dr. Joseph M. Shopshire of the Wesleyan Theological Seminary in Washington, D.C., to explain this tendency. To quote him,

> The Methodist churches early embraced doctrinal ideas and articles of religion which emphasized the importance of grace, scriptural holiness, free will, justification, sanctification, perfection, and good works as a product of faith. These beliefs predisposed Methodists to an acceptance of outreach ministries as an important aspect of the faith response. Benevolent efforts, mission and service through practical forms of caring for others have from early times been embraced as a necessary response of the life of holiness.
>
> Since theological education for Methodists takes place in many predominantly white seminaries and only a few historically black seminaries, it will be increasingly important to reshape those institutions to be responsive and relevant to the needs and experiences of black families and churches . . . Seminaries have an important obligation to do theological education that takes seriously the actual needs of the people and the values of the "black sacred cosmos."[17]

In further explanation of the primacy of Methodist churches in community outreach programs, the Rev. Ronald Brailsford, then assistant pastor at the Big Bethel A.M.E. Church in Atlanta, pointed out that social reform was the major reason for the founding of the A.M.E. Church and, while there is often some tension among members over the extent of community outreach, it is characteristic of A.M.E. doctrine to grapple with the social problems of the day. This is no doubt why, several years later, as pastor of the Bethel A.M.E. Church in Columbia, South Carolina, the Rev. Brailsford would lead the church in a vigorous program of social outreach dealing with issues of housing, substance abuse, employment, and especially education in an effort not only to revitalize the church but the community as well. "That's what it means," he says, "to be an authentic A.M.E. Church."

When we observed the different Baptist groups separately, we found that churches in the Progressive National Baptist Convention are more likely to be engaged in community outreach programs than are churches in the other Baptist conventions. Altogether 79 percent of the churches in the Progressive National Baptist Convention involved themselves in community efforts, compared with 67 percent of churches in the National Baptist Convention USA Inc., 64 percent of churches in the National Baptist Convention of America, and 52 percent of churches in other Baptist conventions. It is in keeping with the

history of these various Baptist denominations that those churches affiliated with the Progressive Baptists should have a more advanced position in community action. Churches strongly supportive of Dr. King
and civil rights activism broke away from the parent body and formed
the Progressive National Baptist Convention.[18] They have transferred
their external strategies of social reform in the '50s and '60s to the
internal strategies of today.

Finally, while Pentecostal churches in general rank below Methodists and Baptists on community outreach, there are some conspicuous exceptions. The West Angeles Church of God in Christ, under
Bishop Charles E. Blake, and the Church of God in Christ in Brooklyn,
under the Rev. William Dougherty, operate extensive outreach programs. Moreover, the Mason Temple Church of God in Christ in Memphis, where Dr. Martin Luther King Jr. made his last speech, represents
the epitome of activism among Pentecostal churches. All these activist
churches are strong and resourceful, with strong, resourceful, and
highly educated pastors.

We also found that in all denominations and across regions the age
of the church makes a difference. In general, the older, more established churches were more likely than younger churches to be engaged
in community outreach. Approximately 78 percent of the churches
more than 75 years old reported involvement in community outreach,
as compared to 72 percent of those between 41 and 75 years old, and
62 percent of those younger than 41 years old. This is true in the two
Northern regions and in Denver and Atlanta as well.

Social class composition of the local congregations is another dis-
tinguishing feature. Churches with a mixture of middle-and working-
class members, which is the composition of a majority of the churches,
are much more likely to engage in community outreach programs than
those with primarily working-class members. The presence of middle-
class members among the congregation seems to make the difference.
Eighty percent of churches with a majority of members from the middle
class sponsor community outreach programs. This percentage declines
to 71 percent of the churches whose congregations represent a mixture
of members from the working and middle classes, and drops again to
59 percent among churches with congregations composed predomi-
nately of working-class members.

A fourth and major factor that distinguishes activist churches is the
size of the congregation. Smaller churches are less likely than are larger
churches to engage in community outreach. However, although
churches with fewer than 70 members are least likely to engage in
community outreach programs, 40 percent of these churches reported

operating at least one program. By comparison, 63 percent of the churches with 71 to 175 members reported conducting outreach programs. The percentages rose to 78 percent of churches with 176 to 400 members, and to 80 percent of churches with at least 400 members.

Among the more striking findings of this study is that churches that own their building are much more likely than churches that rent to engage in community outreach programs. Overall, 71 percent of churches with paid-off mortgages engage in community outreach programs. This proportion declines slightly to 67 percent among churches that are in the process of purchasing their building. However, among church renters, the rate of participation in community outreach programs drops to 42 percent of churches in this category. This finding highlights the importance of the availability of church resources that help to sustain outreach programs. In addition, rates of ownership relate to black churches' sense of independence and pride, both essential to the continuation of self-help and community outreach. This is a trend among churches in all regions.

An additional church resource that relates to community outreach is the number of paid clergy employed by the church. Churches with more than one paid clergy person are more likely than churches with only one or no paid clergy to engage in community outreach work. Specifically, 62 percent of churches with one or no paid clergy engage in community outreach work. The proportion rises to 75 percent among churches with two or more paid clergy.

A similar finding indicates that, in addition to the senior minister, having other paid staff helps to sustain community outreach programs.

In sum, what we have termed strong, resourceful churches are the ones most likely to engage in community outreach activities. These tend to be older, larger churches with a mixture of several classes, and with substantial other resources.

Characteristics of Senior Ministers

We also noted that in addition to the characteristics of the church as an organization, personal characteristics of the senior minister vary between activist and other churches.

In general, churches with younger senior ministers are more likely to be engaged in outreach programs. And churches whose senior ministers are married also are more likely to operate such programs.

The educational level of the senior minister is a critical factor. This holds for both academic education and professional or theological education. More than half (55 percent) of the senior ministers have at least a college degree. Nearly one-third of those with college degrees have gone on to earn master's degrees or academic doctorates. The more highly educated the minister, the more likely is the church to operate community outreach programs. Thus, among churches headed by pastors with master's degrees or above, some 83 percent conduct outreach programs. This declines to 75 percent for those with one college degree, to 67 percent with some college, and to 52 percent for those with high school only. (Figure 7 shows that this pattern is similar in both Northern regions; see Appendix B.)

Seminary and Bible College Training. An additional impressive characteristic of the ministers in our surveys is that the overwhelming majority (82 percent) of the senior ministers also have specialized professional training in the ministry in addition to backgrounds in academic disciplines. These relatively high levels of education are noteworthy and impressive, particularly, as we acknowledge Dr. Lawrence Jones's observation that the black church generally has no formal education requirements for being called to the pastorate or for ordination. This pattern held across all regions. The Methodist churches, however, reported a higher proportion of highly trained senior ministers than did the Baptist or Pentecostal denominations.

Service Orientation. When senior ministers were questioned about the primary role of the contemporary black church (member service or community service), only 5 percent emphasize serving the members only, and 9 percent indicated that the church's primary responsibility is to the community. However, the overwhelming majority (86 percent) of the senior ministers said that the role of the church was to serve the members and the community. Ministers who hold this "community orientation," which might be consistent with the "prophetic" versus the "priestly" roles, are much more likely to head churches with substantial community programs.

In addition to their institutional leadership roles, a majority (nearly two-thirds) of these ministers are active in their communities on an individual basis, serving as leaders in the National Association for the Advancement of Colored People, National Urban League, on civic, social, and educational boards, as well as in political and economic agencies. The remainder of the ministers restrict their leadership roles to the church organizations.

Churches whose ministers are themselves active in the community are much more likely to sponsor outreach programs. Generally, ministers of activist churches do not have sources of employment outside of the church.

When we subjected these findings to a multivariate analytic procedure, we found that of all these characteristics of the church and the ministry, the two characteristics that make the most difference between conservative churches and activist churches are the size of the congregation and the education and training of the senior ministers.

We interpret these findings to support our proposition advanced at the beginning of this book. That is, strong, resourceful churches, with strong, resourceful leaders, are the ones most likely to move out into the community and, as the Rev. Cecil Murray said, pursue not only personal salvation but social salvation as well.

A Model for Church-Based Social Services

How, then, does a particular large, urban black church go about merging a vital spiritual mission with an extensive display of its communal mission? A new study by Dr. Willie F. Tolliver, associate professor of social work at Hunter College in New York, provides an excellent example of how a church goes through just such transformation. And though Pentecostal churches generally have not been prominent as community activist churches, this church is one of several outstanding exceptions.[19]

First, Tolliver introduces us to the senior minister. Then to the church and the community. Then he discusses the concept of mission and the specific programs operated by the church. The minister meets the criteria we have set forth for activist ministers.

> Six years ago, I met a pastor who grew up in Harlem and had his share of close calls with fate at an early age. As a young man, the would-be pastor was not destroyed by the crime and drugs that threatened his neighborhood. He finished school, went off to the army and returned to Harlem to raise a family. Today he is pastor to a church with over 800 congregants, steward over a sizable budget and involved in developing programs to help his community.

Then Tolliver describes the community in crisis.

> Located in Central Harlem, the church was established in 1917, and the neighborhood where the church is located still contains signs of its once grand status. Today the surrounding area is an odd mixture of the urban scene. Within a block of the church there are prostitutes,

drug addicts, and dealers, decaying and abandoned buildings, vacant lots, and beautifully appointed brownstones and apartment buildings.

Then the church itself:

> The church is housed in what was previously a public school building purchased by the congregation in 1983. The building and its grounds occupy an entire city block. In addition to the main sanctuary, the first floor contains church offices, two gymnasiums, a counseling center, and a day-care center. The upper floors of the building primarily consist of classrooms used for various church ministries. There is a fully operating cafeteria in the basement.

The pastor estimates that 60 percent of the congregation consists of single heads of households, making it very much like the urban setting in which it is situated.

The Harlem church funds its missions work through pledges from the congregation given through a donor system known as "faith promise giving." Congregants pledge an amount of money to their choice of mission, and this amount is contributed weekly, biweekly, or monthly. The system of funding for missions raised $206,000 in 1991.

The missions department links congregants to missions through prayer groups. Every member of the church is assigned to one of 11 prayer groups, each named for the church mission with which it is associated. There are prayer groups for Harlem, Kenya, South Africa, Nigeria, India, Aruba, St. Vincent, and other regions of the world where the Harlem church has an interest. The constant training of attention on the issues and needs brings the prayer group's members to the realization that "I could be the answer to my own prayer."

8

The Black Church and the Male Youth Crisis

Among the many problems that afflict the African American community today, none are more troubling than those involving
youth. In many urban areas, as many as a third of blacks between the
ages of 17 and 21 are now under the jurisdiction of the criminal justice
system. One scholar speaks of black male youths as an "endangered
species."[1]

When the Rev. Dr. Gerald Durley of Providence Baptist Church was
asked in 1996 whether the black church could play a role in the prevention of crime and violence among black youth, his response was an
emphatic yes. The church, he said, not only has a role and an obligation
to deal with wayward youths—it is the *only* institution capable of turning their lives around. And in South Carolina, a decades-long series of
annual statewide conferences by Brookland Baptist Church and Benedict College has identified the black church as a major resource for
curbing criminal behavior among black youths.

This cluster of problems presents a particular challenge to the
church because people in this age range tend to drop out of church.
The problems faced and presented by black male youths were very
much on the mind of the Rev. Thurmond Tillman of First African Baptist Church when we interviewed him in April 1993. Tillman, a 38-
year-old graduate of the International Theological Seminary in Atlanta,
is the son of a distinguished minister, and is a former probation and
parole officer and an apprentice aircraft pilot. Lean and lithe, he looks

more like a high school athletics teacher than a traditional preacher. When he was installed pastor of First African Baptist Church on June 6, 1982, he was the second-youngest minister to pastor the church. While some members may have thought that a 26-year-old recent seminarian was too young for the task, he has proved them wrong. One of Tillman's chief interests is the youth of the church and the community.

When we asked Tillman what the essential mission of the black church is today, he immediately responded: "To meet the needs of the people." Any particular needs? we asked. "All their needs," he said. "Whatever the needs of the people, that they cannot meet by themselves, it is the mission of the church to help them." Can the church do all that? we asked. Tillman continued in the same vein, "The church need not worry that it is not up to the task. We can tackle any problem our people face because the church comes to the problem not bound by its own resources and capacities. The church is God's representative on earth. We have access to all the resources that implies." It was the most expressive conception of the role of the contemporary black church we would encounter in eight years of research.

Though not feeling good that particular day, Tillman, suffering from a cold, nevertheless held forth far beyond our allotted time. "Take the matter of our youth," he said, returning to his favorite subject.

> Many of them have gotten into drugs and other trouble and sometimes seem almost incorrigible in the eyes of other people. But not in our eyes. We should reach out to those young people and try very hard to meet their needs, whatever they are; whether they are members or not; and whether or not they are polite to us as we approach them and offer our help. That is the mission of the contemporary black church. And if we die in the struggle, at the hands of our own youth, it is still what Dr. King would call a redemptive death. So we have nothing to be afraid of.

Earlier in the day, when we first approached Tillman and explained our study about what the church is doing in the community, he looked at his watch and asked, "What are you doing at 3 o'clock?"

"Today?" we asked.

"In 15 minutes," he said.

The other researcher and I looked at each other, and I finally said, "We're going with you."

"Let's go," he said and led us out the door, mounted his minivan, and set out for the local high school. On the way he told us about a recent situation that brought the church into the community in a dramatic way.

Jenkins High School Ten Plus Five

On Thursday, April 15, 1993, a group of black youths in the large racially integrated Jenkins High School got into a fight in the cafeteria. Though no one was hurt, the school was tense. The school had recently adopted a policy of "zero tolerance of violence." The assistant principal summoned the students to a special room. The police were called. The police approached the 15 black youth, placed them under arrest, and booked them for a court appearance the next day. The judge held a hearing but without lawyers representing the youths or their parents. He heard the report of the school authorities and spoke briefly with the youths. Then he released the five juveniles under 16 to the custody of their parents and ordered them to appear at a juvenile court hearing later for sentencing. He sentenced the 10 youths 16 and over on the spot to a month in the local detention center. The media went wild. Local officials vied with each other in denouncing the students. Rumors spread while the students sat in jail.

Naturally, when the parents heard about this, they were quite alarmed. The parents knew what the judge, the police, and the school authorities apparently did not know: When 16-and 17-year-old black male youths spend a month in jail, they will not be able to pass to the next grade. And for these youths a lost grade in school is often the beginning of real trouble. So they organized a meeting to plan how to get their children out of jail and back in school. And, naturally, they held their meeting at the First African Baptist Church. And, just as naturally, when a delegation went to the school, the jail, and the judge to see about these youths, Tillman was at the head of the delegation, which included several other ministers as well. All to no avail. The students continued to sit in jail. The parents recognized that the fighting was wrong but urged the school to punish the students rather than leave them in jail. The superintendent said it was now out of his hands. The court had acted; justice had been done; violence could not be tolerated.

Then Tillman got a new idea. He called the judge and asked to speak with him in his chambers. The judge agreed. After some serious reasoning, Tillman persuaded the judge to release the older youths to his custody. After six days he released them from jail, gave them six months' probation, and ordered them to do community service at the discretion and under the direction of Rev. Tillman.

Every day these youths met at the church to get their assignments. But the school would still not readmit them. So, Dorothy McCain, a schoolteacher and owner of a local gift shop, organized study hall for them in the basement of the church, while the ministers and the parents negotiated with the school authorities.

By the time the students were readmitted to school, they had not only kept pace with their studies, but had become convinced of the errors of their ways and had organized a lecture program whereby they met with groups, classes, and assemblies of students, talking to them about the stupidity and senselessness of the type of behavior they had engaged in. Moreover, they offered to serve as positive examples for other youth. They continued their after-school community service. In time, they organized a private enterprise titled A-MEN Enterprise, which designed and marketed T-shirts honoring Dr. Martin Luther King Jr.

Jenkins Ten Plus Five

Our continued monitoring of the youths is reflected in the field notes of the research assistant after meeting with the Rev. Tillman on June 19, 1993:[2]

> In addition to their community service and their schoolwork, the young men had spoken at Sprague Elementary School and at Ester Garrison Elementary School to fourth-and fifth-graders to encourage young people to avoid violence and other antisocial behavior. Ms. McCain, the teacher who assisted the Rev. Tillman with their educational programs, took the youths to the Youth Leadership Development Institute that was sponsored by the First A.M.E. Church in Hampton, Georgia. They were the special guests on WSOK's Open Line Outreach, a public call-in show.

Our next encounter with these youth when they completed their probation and community service assignment under supervision of the Rev. Tillman.

As a reward for their successful milestone, Tillman called a press conference to allow the youths to announce to the community that they had successfully completed their probation, had learned some valuable lessons, were doing well in school, and were counseling other youths on how to stay out of trouble. But although the newspaper, radio, and TV reporters had swarmed all over the case when the boys were arrested the preceding April, they were nowhere to be found in September when they were called to witness the success of these same youths. When two reporters were asked about this they said simply that the matter was no longer newsworthy.

Tillman had a better response to his second effort to honor these youths. He and Mrs. Tillman took the boys to Atlanta to visit the sights and attend sessions of a regional convention. The boys also visited Morehouse and Spelman, where faculty members talked to them about the advantages and the nature of college. Later the boys attended a mathematics class at Morehouse, where several of them were more active in the question period after the lecture than were the college students in the class.

Our next encounter with these youths occurred in mid-June 1994. At this time six of the Jenkins Ten, having completed their senior year, were graduating from Jenkins High School. These were Samuel Eaddy, Roderick Gardner, John Jones, Curtis Lovett, Nijumo Smith, and Quade Stanley. At the graduation exercises, each time one of the boys walked across the stage to get his diploma, the whole auditorium seemed to erupt with thunderous applause. Way up in the balcony, making as much noise as a proud parent, was the Rev. Tillman, who had done so much to make the boys' graduation possible.

A year later, in June 1995, the three remaining seniors from the Jenkins Ten graduated from Hershel V. Jenkins High School on schedule in the Savannah Civic Center. The Rev. Tillman reports that of the 15 boys who originally got into trouble, 14 were doing well now, more than two years later. They are either in college, have jobs, or are on their way to college. Only one of the juveniles has gotten into repeated trouble. Tillman went to that boy's Juvenile Court hearing in July 1995, where he was given two years in detention for getting into trouble. Tillman wanted this young man to know that when he gets out of detention, Tillman, the church, and other elements in the community will again be there for him.

St. Paul Academy

In Savannah, First African Baptist Church is not alone in reaching into the community to confront the crisis among black youths. Littway Baptist Church, under the Rev. Leonard Smalls, conducts an innovative program that has rescued significant numbers of black youths—male and female—from drug abuse. And St. Paul C.M.E. Church has responded to the specific needs of male at-risk youths with a pioneering program that puts the boys directly under the church's influence. The program succeeds by inserting the church into a context in which these youths' behavior has received singular notoriety: the schools.

By the 1990s, the problems encountered and caused by black boys in the public schools had become a national concern. Among the solutions proposed by a number of black educators was the establishment of special schools exclusively for black boys. The thinking was that this would provide the possibility of concentrating exclusively on the learning potential, learning styles, and the learning and behavioral difficulties of these boys in a more effective manner than can be done in the traditional coeducational interracial settings dominated by white and feminine cultures.

It was an idea, simple and straightforward, that grew out of the best motivations to improve the performance of these boys. It seemed to have a great deal of merit. But the idea was resisted, particularly outside the black community, often by the same forces that originally resisted efforts to the integrate schools.

While public authorities and advocates and opponents were debating the merits, the legality, and the politics of all-black boys schools, a number of black churches put the idea to the test. They could do so in part because of their private status, their independence, their commitment to black progress, the allegiance they hold in the black community, and the claim they can exercise on resources in the larger white society.

St. Paul Academy is an example of what these capacities and aspirations can do. The school was founded by St. Paul C.M.E. Church under the leadership of the Rev. Henry Delaney. The church raised money to purchase an abandoned public school building, hired a small cadre of teachers, and in the fall of 1993 admitted some 35 boys in grades five through eight. All the students had performed poorly in public schools. They were referred to St. Paul Academy by their parents, public-school officials, juvenile authorities, or other concerned adults. The school follows the regular academic curriculum for these grades, but also includes a heavy dose of Bible study and African American history. The school does not yet have a strong athletic or extracurricular program, and counseling services are limited. Faculty members, though few in number and not paid as well as in the public schools, are exceptionally competent and committed.

In June 1994, six boys graduated from the eighth grade and headed for various high schools in the city. Though in a number of communities around the nation in the 1990s fierce controversies had broken out whenever the idea of a school for black boys was introduced, here in Savannah a black church had actually brought it off, taking responsibility and giving leadership to this movement.

A year later, in June 1995, the Rev. Delaney reported that five of the six boys who graduated the year before had completed successfully their first year in high school without getting into any trouble with the authorities. One lad was not able to keep out of trouble and did not stay the course.

At the second graduation exercises at St. Paul Academy, another five boys graduated from eighth grade and headed for high school. Still other measures of achievement include the fact that four students made the honor roll, and six students had perfect attendance for the year. And of the 30 students enrolled this year only one was asked to leave the school, which was simply not equipped with the clinical facilities to handle his personal problems.

Several factors, tangible and intangible, account for the success of this second year of school operations. First, the boys were extraordinarily bright, despite their behavior problems. Second, the teachers were extraordinarily gifted, patient, and creative. Third, the board of the school worked tirelessly to put into place uniform policies. But the chief factor is that the school is a church-based initiative. The Rev. Delaney and the church stood strongly behind the school with an abundance of faith and strong financial support. And because it was operated by the church, the community beyond the church, both black and white, continued to believe in the St. Paul Academy and to give it support and legitimacy.

The Urban Christian Academy

Another church in Savannah has long cooperated with an academic school for black children and youths. The Urban Christian Academy has attained enormous success over its 10 years of operation and is now in a position to teach a few lessons on the ingredients of success in working with largely low-income African American children and youths outside the public-school setting.

The experience of the Urban Christian Academy teaches several keys to success. They include strong discipline; strong academics, including computers and language study early and throughout the curriculum; strong programs in African American history and culture; active extracurricular and sports programs; strong, consistent, and hands-on leadership; strong and committed faculty and staff; continual communication between the families of the students and the school; a strictly businesslike operation and atmosphere all undergirded and overlaid with a strong devotion to spirituality and to the moral development of these young people. No idea of separation of church and state, or of school and community, are allowed to interfere with this set of standards.

Project Success

Still another example of black churches in Savannah that are reaching out beyond their walls and their memberships to confront the crisis among black youth is Project Success. Begun in the 1980s, this is a collaborative effort among a dozen churches under the coordination of the Savannah/Chatham County Youth Futures Authority to provide after-school programs for students from kindergarten through high school. The program is led by the Rev. Walter Farrell, who is surely among the most dedicated and committed ministers in the city. Project Success provides adult supervision, assistance with homework, tutoring, recreation, African American history, and biblical history.

The churches participating in this cooperative venture that host groups of students at their premises are Bethlehem Baptist, Royal Church of Christ, Second Bethlehem Baptist, St. James A.M.E., Bolton Street Church, St. Paul C.M.E., Central Baptist, First Tabernacle, African Baptist, Montgomery Pinpoint Group, First Bryan Baptist, First African Baptist, Holy Spirit Lutheran, and East Savannah.

For the first nine-week marking period during the school year 1992–92, the 14 churches sponsored 182 children in this after-school program. Of these, 150, or more than 82 percent of them, passed all their courses. During the same period some 126 of these students, or nearly 70 percent, had a perfect attendance record; and 35 of the 182, or nearly 20 percent, were on the honor roll.

The Church's Spheres of Influence

This movement of the black church's influence from the crises of the civil rights era to the contemporary crisis among black male youths attests to the resilience and adaptability of this institution. It also shows that the reform spirit ignited long ago by church leaders such as George Leile and the company of his successors who lay buried in Laurel Grove South Cemetery continues even unto this generation. And leaders such as the Rev. Thurmond Tillman of First African Baptist Church, the Rev. Henry Delaney of St. Paul C.M.E., and the Rev. Walter Farrell of Project Success are living symbols of the power of the black church as an agent of social reform.

In the next chapter we see how the spirit of reform evolved among historic black churches in Richmond. We will see some major differences from and some striking similarities to that evolution as it occurred in Savannah.[3]

9

—ᴡ—

The Black Church Confronts
the HIV/AIDS Crisis

When the HIV virus was first discovered in America more than two decades ago, black churches by and large stood aside from the issue. That situation has changed as an increasing number of church members and their relatives suffer from this disease. It is the fastest-growing deadly disease in the community generally, and a disproportionate percentage of its victims are black.[1]

A recent study by the National Cancer Institute reported that one in 33 black men ages 27 to 39 may be infected with the AIDS virus. The study calculated that one out of 98 young black women may be infected. The rates for whites are one out of 139 men and one out of 1,667 women. Maureen Downey, in a November 30, 1995, article in the *Atlanta Journal Constitution* quoted Dr. Stephen Thomas, director of Emory University's Institute for Minority Health Research, as saying, "AIDS has escalated into the civil rights battle of the 1990s."[2]

Downey's article pointed not only to the extensiveness of the HIV/AIDS crisis in the African American community but also to the strategic importance of black churches in confronting this crisis. She called attention to two of Atlanta's black churches that are addressing the problem.

One was Providence Missionary Baptist Church, whose pastor, the Rev. Dr. Gerald Durley, is also president of the citywide organization "Concerned Black Clergy."

"Chilled by the one-in-33 statistic," writes Downey, the Rev. Gerald Durley devoted his Sunday sermon to AIDS. Though those who could directly benefit from his message may not have been in the pews, he said, their mothers and grandmothers were there.

"After the service, a visiting young woman and her brother came up to thank me, saying their brother had died of AIDS three weeks ago, and this was the first time they had heard the disease discussed openly," says Durley.

Some churches are enlightened enough to encourage AIDS victims to join efforts to battle the disease. Moreover, some churches, such as the First A.M.E. Church of Los Angeles, actively promote the use of condoms as part of their prevention programs. Though the use of condoms in the program has been severely criticized by outsiders and other ministers, according to the church's pastor not a single criticism has come from any one of the 9,000 church members.

The personal nature of the HIV/AIDS crisis is further illustrated at the New Birth Missionary Baptist Church in Atlanta, among the largest and fastest-growing churches in the city and nation. Under the dynamic leadership of Bishop Eddie Long, an AIDS Ministry has been established, with a member of the church as director. The ministry engages 400 volunteers who are learning about the disease and teaching awareness and prevention to this large, youthful congregation. In Columbia, South Carolina, the Brookland Baptist Church under pastor Charles B. Jackson operates a pioneering AIDS ministry for the area, with a band of extremely dedicated "angels of mercy," which has been warmly embraced by the pastor and the congregation.

After some initial hesitation, the black church is responding nationwide to the crisis by reaching out to the community, secular agencies, families, and individuals caught up in the epidemic.

The National Black Leadership Commission on AIDS

Debra Frazier-Howze, social worker, administrator, feminist, humanist, and African American leader, knew instinctively that the time had come for a new organization. Why? Because a need had arisen.

She knew that the time had come for action and that she was the chosen agent. The issue of HIV infection and AIDS had, within a decade, moved to the front ranks of the killers of black men and women across multiple generations and two continents, embracing people of all sexual orientations.

So Frazier-Howze, a well-regarded and effective professional with the New York Urban League, gave up her secure job to establish a new movement. With rigor and imagination, she organized The National Black Leadership Commission on AIDS (BLCA) in 1987. By 1995, it was the oldest and largest black organization of its kind in all of North America.[3]

Within seven years the organization could claim outstanding accomplishments:

- It served more than 2,330 institutions, including 750 black churches across the country, with information and technical assistance on the prevention of HIV/AIDS.
- It had helped to raise more than $35 million in AIDS-related direct service funds for black communities.
- It created the first citywide programs for the black clergy and churches in New York City.
- It served as chief consultant on HIV/AIDS-related issues for the National Baptist Ministers Conference, the National Rainbow Coalition, the National Football League, the NAACP, the 100 Black Women and 100 Black Men; and as adviser on AIDS prevention to the federal government.
- It had expanded its prevention, education, and policy services to six communities in New York state and to 17 other cities around the nation. The cities in New York state are Newburgh, Syracuse, Mount Vernon, Buffalo, Hempstead, and Rochester. The other cities are Baltimore, Philadelphia, Washington, D.C., Chicago, Newark, Detroit, Atlanta, Houston, Miami, New Orleans, Memphis, St. Louis, Cincinnati, Los Angeles, Jersey City, Boston, and Indianapolis.

From the outset, the Black Leadership Commission on AIDS has been guided by distinctly African American cultural values. The patented BLCA ribbon is fashioned after the royal African cloth—kente—worn by ancient Africans of renown. It is combined with the ribbon that symbolizes compassion for people living with HIV/AIDS. According to Frazier-Howze, "The royal kente also symbolizes our communities' commitment to preserve life through increased and culturally competent HIV/AIDS prevention and education targeting communities of African American descent."

The organization put together a board of governors consisting of a cross section of clergy, politicians, agency executives, policy experts, and medical and business professionals from each of the five boroughs of New York City. According to Frazier-Howze, "This indigenous leadership has reinvented the Afrocentric model of community reform based on the 'Council of Elders' model used before and during slavery."

Also, since its inception BLCA has sought to incorporate the deepest, most indigenous value within the African American cultural heritage: spirituality, represented by the church.

The meeting of the organizing committee called by Frazier-Howze in 1987 drew upon prominent black clergy from the New York area. The Rev. Calvin Butts III of the Abyssinian Baptist Church, and the Rev. Calvin O. Pressley, leader in the New York City Mission Society, were charter members of the board. Before long, a third of the organization's members were ministers.

The organization early enlisted a group of distinguished black ministers in the New York City area and persuaded them to devote a sermon on the prevention of HIV/AIDS on the same day in all their churches across the city. Videotapes of these sermons were then made available for wide distribution.

In one of the most dramatic recognitions of the power of the spiritual values, BLCA organizes an annual "Choose Life" Benefit Gospel Concert, held each fall in the historic 2,000-seat Abyssinian Baptist Church in New York. This event is a major fund-raiser for the education and prevention program. It is also a stirring call to arms to march out to fight this disease. But, beyond all that, it is an evening of elegance and spiritual and artistic uplift.[4]

Finally, Frazier-Howze and her board of directors organized a Black Ministers Summit on AIDS in April 1995, held on the top floor of the Equitable Life Assurance Company in New York City, courtesy of Darwin N. Davis Sr., chair of the BLCA board and senior executive at Equitable. Forty ministers came from all over the country to be educated about the prevention and treatment of AIDS. Experts presented a wide range of information about AIDS over a three-day conference. One observer remarked that it amounted to a whole college semester course in 72 hours of intense instruction. These church leaders returned to their churches and communities armed with new resolve and new knowledge to attack this problem. Within a few weeks of the conference, the Rev. Joseph Roberts, pastor of Atlanta's historic Ebenezer Baptist Church, hosted a citywide conference, called to alert and inform a cross section of African American leaders. All over the country ministers took similar follow-up action.

Southern Christian Leadership Conference Initiatives

Shortly after the action programs of the Black Leadership Commission on AIDS were launched, the Southern Christian Leadership Conference (SCLC) launched a program on AIDS awareness and prevention called

Reducing AIDS Through Community Education (RACE).[5] It was funded in 1988 by the Centers for Disease Control and Prevention, based in Atlanta. The project was to provide AIDS education in five cities. One of the first acts of SCLC was to commission Dr. Stephen Thomas, a public health researcher, and his associate, Dr. Sandra Crouse Quinn, to conduct an assessment of black church members' knowledge of AIDS in five cities: Atlanta, Charlotte, North Carolina, Kansas City, Missouri, Detroit, and Tuscaloosa, Alabama. The churches were from a wide variety of denominations, including Baptists, United Methodists, Christian Methodist Episcopal, African Methodist Episcopal, African Methodist Episcopal Zion, United Church of Christ, Presbyterian, Catholic, Seventh-Day Adventist, Nation of Islam, Church of God in Christ, and Episcopalian.

The RACE project's objectives were to assess AIDS education needs in the communities, develop culturally appropriate AIDS education materials, disseminate AIDS information throughout the communities, start a trainers program, and provide a standard introductory AIDS education message to church members and surrounding communities. To gather information, researchers surveyed a sample of church members from the five cities. Church members attending Sunday services, church committee meetings, and other activities were asked by site coordinators to participate. Site coordinators assured respondents that participation was voluntary and that their responses would be anonymous. A total of 1,054 completed surveys were analyzed. In addition to the baseline survey, one focus group was conducted in each RACE site during the summer of 1990. Sessions were held in SCLC offices, a restaurant, and a housing project auditorium. Results of the formative research were used to develop various components of the RACE intervention.

Thomas and Quinn found that knowledge about the major modes of transmission was fairly high. Approximately 87 percent knew that a woman infected with HIV could infect her unborn child, and more than 90 percent identified as true the statement, "You increase your chances of getting AIDS by having sex with many different people." Knowledge about causes of the disease was not as high. Thus, 26 percent agreed with the statement, "If someone with AIDS coughs or sneezes in your face, you can get the disease," and another 22 percent agreed with, "You can get AIDS from sitting on a toilet seat." Moreover, 31 percent incorrectly believed that HIV was transmitted through donating blood to the Red Cross.

Knowledge on specific aspects of risk reduction was mixed. While 92 percent knew that "proper use of condoms during sex can help prevent the spread of AIDS," only 47 percent knew that latex condoms are more effective than natural skin condoms to prevent transmission of HIV infection. Finally, 66 percent of church members knew that cleaning intravenous needles with bleach and water could reduce risk of HIV transmission. The researchers found the education level of the respondents to be a key factor. Those with some college education had significantly higher levels of knowledge about AIDS than those with only a high school education or less.

The staff of this project utilized the results of the research to tailor a slide show that was culturally sensitive and that accommodated the knowledge gaps among these church people. The slide show included messages related to civil rights and church activities aimed at stimulating an atmosphere of compassion and support for those affected by AIDS. Scripture was used in the slide show, and the church's message of abstinence and monogamy was incorporated into risk-reduction activities.

The hope is that other black churches will be able and willing to use this AIDS education program developed and sanctioned by the SCLC.

What this initiative by SCLC suggests is that once the church's reluctance is overcome, it will bring the strengths, resilience, and Christian love that have seen black Americans through their painful history to the challenge of this crisis.

Black Churches in Washington

The first reported AIDS case in the District of Columbia was in the early days of the crisis, but the response to the epidemic by the community at large was very slow, mainly because of its perceived links to homosexuals and drug abusers. Also, a number of origin theories about AIDS made the African American community suspicious of information provided by government authorities. By virtue of its frequency and the "sinful" things associated with it, the HIV/AIDS problem was an embarrassment in the black community. So, naturally, the first cry in the church community came from those already infected and affected by HIV/AIDS.[6]

Three major barriers have undercut the constructive Christian response to the epidemic. They are the perceptions of AIDS as a sinner's disease, a sexual disease, and a suffering disease.[7]

Despite these barriers, black churches in Washington, D.C., have begun to show signs of progress in many areas. Efforts are being made to develop AIDS ministries and train people to work in them all over the city. The Congress of National Black Churches and the D.C. Public Health Commission's Office of AIDS Activities have made presentations on the "ABC's of AIDS" at more than 100 churches. In addition, the Office of AIDS Activities has organized an aggressive program called Love in Action, which has trained more than 150 ministers to share the information on HIV/AIDS with their congregations. Also, coalitions of churches are forming to do special projects directed specifically at the issue of AIDS. Prison ministries and home and hospital visit ministries are just a few such projects. Some churches prefer to do their work quietly, while others prefer to be out front and visibly advertise.

The Inner City AIDS Network (ICAN), under the direction of the Rev. Andrea Scott, was developed in response to AIDS as a growing epidemic in the District of Columbia. ICAN is funded by the D.C. Office of AIDS Activities to provide five- and eight-week programs to educate segments of the religious community.

Another organization that has been active in preparing the religious community to work with HIV/AIDS is the Division of AIDS Ministries of the Church Association for Community Services, under the direction of the Rev. Frank Tucker. This consortium of churches provides housing and support to persons living with HIV or AIDS.

There are also a few individual unsung heroes who are doing their work quietly, like the Rev. Anthony Motley, who is presently the liaison between the Office of AIDS Activities and the religious community, and the convener of the Religious Community Roundtable on HIV Prevention. Motley has been instrumental in forming a coalition of three churches in one ward of the city that has donated property to house a number of persons living with HIV/AIDS. Another such hero is the Rev. Albert Gallmon, who is presently the chair of the Clergy Commission on AIDS. This commission, funded by the Lilly Endowment, was formed to bring area ministers to the front lines of this struggle.

Another hero in the movement against AIDS is the Rev. Adora Lee, former chief of the Office of AIDS Activities. Her efforts were instrumental in keeping the religious community abreast of the need for church involvement, and it was during her administration that the Religious Community Roundtable on HIV Prevention was formed. The Very Rev. Dr. Elias Farajeje-Jones, assistant professor of history of religion/sociology of religion at Howard University School of Divinity, who referred to himself as an "AIDS terrorist," is one of the leading authorities on HIV diseases in the black church. He uses his knowledge to help train large numbers of young, newly ordained ministers to appreciate the theological perspective on AIDS.

It is already clear from this vigorous activity in the nation's capital city that the community can indeed be aroused to combat this HIV/AIDS crisis. And these developments support the view that if the black community does become energized in fighting this disease, it will be due in no small measure to the leadership of the black church.

Health Objectives for the Year 2000

In the final analysis, the AIDS crisis must be viewed and treated within the broad context of the health status of black Americans.[8] In 1990, Dr. Louis Sullivan, secretary of Health and Human Services, presented to the nation *Healthy People 2000: National Health Promotion and Disease Prevention Objectives.*[9] These objectives include special population targets for decreasing the disparity in health status and for health promotion and disease prevention activities in the black community. HIV/AIDS is one of eight major diseases taking an enormous toll and causing excessive deaths among African Americans. The others identified in the landmark Heckler report (of 1985), "Health Status of Black Americans," on black and minority health are shown in Table 13, together with their risk factors; see Appendix C.

Healthy People 2000 represents a comprehensive strategic plan designed to focus national health resources on prevention in its broadest sense. It constitutes a recognition that medical care alone will not eliminate the devastating effects of chronic disease, or many of the other health problems that disproportionately afflict black Americans. It is a major accomplishment that gives direction for a rational health policy with three broad goals for the decade: to increase the span of healthy life for Americans, reduce health disparities among Americans, and achieve access to preventive services for all Americans.

It is within this broad context that the fight against AIDS must be waged. Black churches, because of their history and current status, are major sources and potential sources of attack in this crisis.

While the attempt to bring services to blacks under the auspices of the church can contribute to more culturally sensitive approaches and greater access, there is also a potential for the church to be used for unethical purposes. For example, the Tuskegee Study of Untreated Syphilis in the Negro Male, 1932–1972, is the longest nontherapeutic study on human beings in medical history. The purpose of the study was to observe the effects of untreated syphilis on black men, and for the 40 years of the study subjects were effectively denied treatment. The U.S. Public Health Service recruited almost 400 black men in Macon County, Alabama, through such community sites as the church, schools, and plantations. Some medical examinations for the study were conducted in local black churches, and participation was encouraged by black ministers.[10] While caution must be exercised to ensure that the church is never used again in unethical medical research, the value of church-based programs should not be diminished by their association with the Tuskegee Study. In recent years the insensitivity and high-handed pressure tactics used by some government agencies to coerce black churches into participating in the government's "welfare reform" have run the risk of government overkill.

There is, of course, the danger of overload for the churches, as government, private agencies, professionals, and the community itself turn more and more to the churches for leadership in the multitude of crises now engulfing the African American community. No amount of black church action can take the place of enlightened public policies and adequate resources of the larger society.

10

—◊—

A Tale of Two Cities:
Black Churches
in Denver and Atlanta

The tendency for churches and their leaders to attack social problems independently is on prominent display in the role of black activist churches today. Clearly, there are times when collaboration might be more timely and more effective.

In this chapter we show how the potential for collaboration was developed in Denver and Atlanta and how it is proving appropriate and effective for both internal and external strategies of social reform. Denver is a large gateway city to the West. Its black population comprises a third of the population. It has a relatively large black middle class but few historically black institutions other than a wide range of churches. And though Denver does not have the rigid housing segregation known in most Eastern cities, most blacks and most black churches there tend to cluster in contiguous areas.

Atlanta is a large metropolitan gateway to the South. It has a large majority black population with a large middle class. Blacks hold strong positions in government, education, and business, and support a large number of historically black institutions. Both cities have pockets of poverty. Most black churches in both cities are Baptist; 40 percent of them in Denver and 44 percent in Atlanta. Next come the Methodist followed by Church of God in Christ churches.

Membership size of churches in both cities varies widely; many— 49 percent of churches in Denver and 52 percent in Atlanta—have between 100 and 500 members. Denver has a greater number of black churches with memberships of less than 100 (33 percent), while Atlanta has a greater number of large churches with 500 or more members (33 percent). Atlanta also has a substantial number of churches with memberships of more than 1,000 (15 percent), and some with more than 5,000. It even has a few mega churches with memberships over 10,000.

As might be expected, the memberships of churches in both cities are heavily female. In Denver, 90 percent of the churches have a majority of female members, while in Atlanta it is 93 percent. At the same time, the leadership is overwhelmingly male. In both cities fewer than 10 percent of the clergy are women.

Some progress is being made in the appointment of women as assistant or associate pastors. In Denver, for example, the large, predominantly middle-class and historically activist Shorter A.M.E. Church, under the longtime leadership of the highly able and popular Rev. Ramsford Boyd, had two female associate pastors.

In Atlanta, female associate or assistant ministers are increasingly common. All three of the city's large historic churches, Big Bethel A.M.E., Wheat Street Baptist, and Ebenezer Baptist, had female assistants during our study. In both cities and in most black churches the senior officers of the church, the board of deacons or stewards, and trustees or finance committees remain solid bastions of male dominance while sustaining overwhelmingly female memberships, attendance, financial support, and volunteers.

An exception to this pattern is the large, growing, and activist Providence Baptist Church in Atlanta, under the longtime leadership of the Rev. Dr. Gerald Durley, who also holds a professorship in community health at the Morehouse School of Medicine. This church has pioneered in female leadership roles. In addition to female assistant pastors, women occupy prominent roles in many of the church organizations, those devoted to internal church business, including the board of deacons, and the many external community services as well.

The socioeconomic mix of the congregations in both cities is similar. About 49 percent of the churches in Denver have socioeconomically mixed membership from the working class and the middle class. In Atlanta this is true of 80 percent. Perhaps surprisingly, Denver congregations are more likely to have a greater proportion of low-income members; 34 percent compared to Atlanta's 11 percent, while Atlanta has a larger proportion of churches with mostly middle-income members (47 percent) than Denver (18 percent).

We note a strong tendency in both cities for black churches to own their buildings rather than rent them. The percentage is 58 percent in Denver, with another 25 percent holding mortgages on their properties, for a total of 83 percent of the churches in ownership status. At the same time, 51 percent of the Atlanta churches have already paid off their mortgages, while another 44 percent are currently paying off the mortgage, for a total of 95 percent in ownership status.

A majority of churches in both cities conduct at least one nonreligious community outreach program: 75 percent in Denver, 87 percent in Atlanta. So, activist churches constitute the norm in both cities. This is particularly true of the large churches. Perhaps the most activist church in Denver, though, the Agape Christian Church, has less than 100 members. Under leadership of the Rev. Robert Wolfolk, this church considers its extensive community outreach programs to be as essential to the Christian faith as their worship services, maybe even more important.

Metro Denver Black Church Initiative

A small private foundation in Denver, the Piton Foundation, under the leadership of one of its program officers, Grant Jones, launched a program in early 1992 that became known as the Metro Denver Black Church Initiative.[1] The purpose of the initiative was to improve conditions in low-income black neighborhoods through the local churches.

The initiative has evolved in four interrelated phases. Phase I was a research phase. A survey was conducted among the black churches to ascertain the extent to which they were involved in community outreach programs, focusing on the types of programs being undertaken and the attitudes of their senior ministers toward them. The second phase was an implementation phase based on the findings that grew out of Phase I. In Phase II a number of collaborations among churches and between churches and secular agencies occurred as a result of the support of a local foundation to engage in expanded community outreach programming. Phase III focused on technical assistance to these church collaborative efforts. They provided help with management, financial operations, and other barriers to effective functioning, and with raising more money to support a continuation of these community outreach initiatives.

The fourth phase is the evaluation phase. The initiative has retained a nationally rated research and evaluation firm to conduct an assessment of these projects. It is conducting both process and outcome evaluations.

Because of the presence and the interweaving of these four distinct phases, the Metro Denver Black Church Initiative presents an extraordinarily rational, coordinated, and follow-up approach to community action and social reform.[2]

Implementation Phase

In the first phase, 80 black churches of various denominations were surveyed. In addition to studying existing church responses to community needs, the Denver Black Church Initiative instituted a second phase that provided money to help churches expand their service to the community.[3] On the basis of input from the research, two conditions were placed on the availability of this support. First, churches had to apply and compete for funds. Second, preference was given to applications that proposed collaboration among two or more churches or between churches and secular agencies. In this phase churches were not limited to black churches. Collaboration frequently occurred across racial lines.

Through local and national funding partners—the Ford Foundation, Lilly Endowment, and Hunt Alternatives Fund—the Metro Denver Black Church Initiative in 1994 began providing grants of up to $20,000 to promising collaborations on projects to improve nonsectarian services to neighborhood residents.

Among the projects the initiative has supported are a Summer Scholars program, sponsored by the Epworth Methodist Church. Denver's "summer of violence" in 1993 convinced Epworth's minister that youth needed more positive, constructive activities to engage them in the summer. The program for at-risk city children could be a model for any urban neighborhood. At three northeast Denver elementary schools, Summer Scholars—a total of 185 children matched with 13 teachers, seven paraprofessionals, seven student assistants and a host of volunteers—were given the chance to gain lost academic ground over a six-week period during the summer of 1994.

Inspired by its ambitious pastor, N. Jorinda Kiwanuka, the church worked with the school district to find teachers and with the parks and recreation department to provide the afternoon activities. The church also trained six people to visit the children in their homes, gain parental support for the children's learning, encourage parents to read with their children 15 minutes a day, and connect the family to resources like food banks.

Initial financing of this project began with the $20,000 grant from the Metro Denver Black Church Initiative. But as the program grew, Epworth was able to secure additional funding from other foundations and city and federal sources. Epworth plans to expand the highly successful Summer Scholars program in future years.

Nearby, in another northeast Denver neighborhood, the Church of the Holy Redeemer is operating "The Place," a program that offers youths from several of the city's most distressed neighborhoods alternatives to gangs and street life. "Father Greg," as the Rev. Gregory Smith is affectionately known, has joined forces with two other churches to provide a variety of after-school and weekend activities, including Saturday night movies and dances, martial arts classes, arts and crafts, and a summer reading program for preschoolers.

It is Father Greg's dream that The Place will eventually be a real place, a building where young people can come at all hours, not just to attend programs, but to get help when they are in need.

On January 19, 1994, and again in March 1995, the Metro Denver Black Church Initiative, headed by Grant Jones of the Piton Foundation, awarded two-year grants totaling $274,000 to 13 church collaborations in Denver. Here is a list of the 13, and their outreach programs.

• *Agape Christian Church* was awarded $22,000 for the Concerned About You Committee. This collaboration of four churches (Agape, Central Baptist Church, Anchor of Hope Christian Church, and St. Andrews Episcopal Church) operates a youth tutoring project in the Five Points, Whittier, and Curtis Park neighborhoods. It targets 80 elementary school students who are at high risk of becoming dropouts. Each church is a tutoring site with a high school youth coordinator, adult supervisor, and volunteer tutors.

• *Church of the Holy Redeemer* was awarded $35,000 for a collaborative program with Peoples Presbyterian Church and St. Ignatius Loyola Catholic Church to provide neighborhood youth ages seven to 18 with after-school and weekend fun activities as an alternative to gangs and street life. Program activities include Saturday night movies and dances, martial art classes, and arts and crafts.

• *East Denver Church of God* was awarded $22,000 for a collaborative effort with House of Joy Miracle Deliverance Church, House of Prayer Deliverance, and two elementary schools in northeast Denver to provide after-school tutoring and mentoring for 25 latchkey children. The program, called "Children Oriented to Growth," operates three afternoons each week for three hours at the East Denver Church of God, with the House of Joy providing transportation for the children and each church providing volunteer tutors and mentors.

• *Epworth United Methodist Church* was awarded $35,000 for a collaboration with five elementary schools in northeast Denver to provide educational and family support services to 125 elementary school students and their families. The program targets seriously underachieving students and provides them with six weeks of special instruction during the summer, with the goal of bringing them up to grade level. Neighborhood outreach workers also visit the students' homes to help foster parents' support for their children's learning and to refer families to needed resources.

• *Grace and Truth Full Gospel Pentecostal Church* was awarded $27,000 for a program operated with Shiloh Temple to provide tutoring and counseling to 100 adolescent girls "in conflict." Gilliam Youth Services Center refers girls released from the detention center to the tutoring center at the church. At-risk girls are referred to the center from Manual High School as well. Additionally, counseling services and other assistance are provided onsite to girls incarcerated at Gilliam.

• *Greater East Denver Ministerial Alliance*, an alliance of 65 Denver churches, was awarded $27,000 to enhance its services to its members and expand its community involvement through the addition of a staff member.

• *Lighthouse Community Church* was given an award of $8,000 for the first year only to support the Westside Education Enrichment Program (WEEP) in conjunction with Redeeming Love Fellowship Church. The goal of the program is to help 50 children in grades three through six improve their mathematics and language arts skills. The tutoring program operates after school and for six weeks during the summer using church volunteers.

• *Methodist Ministers Fellowship* was awarded $22,000 for a collaborative venture of six northeast Denver churches (Scott United Methodist, Jordan A.M.E., Christ Our Redeemer A.M.E., Shorter A.M.E., Spottswood A.M.E. Zion, and Campbell Chapel A.M.E.) at Scott United Methodist Church. The center provides families that often have no other place to turn with help with alcohol and drug addiction, depression, life traumas, grief and loss, and identity problems. Support groups and independent counseling sessions are offered.

• *New Hope Baptist Church* and Cure D'Ars Catholic Church were awarded $12,000 to provide a safe and educationally stimulating place for latchkey children in northeast Denver. Tutoring and mentoring are provided for students in grades 6–12 using church members, retirees, parents, grandparents, and other people from the neighborhood.

• *Open Door Church of God in Christ* was awarded $22,000 for a collaboration with Rehobath International Baptist, All Nations Pentecostal, and seven secular organizations for an "After School Institute" at Columbine Elementary School. Its two basic components are tutoring assistance to youths using the "Hooked-on-Phonics" model and counseling services focusing on self-esteem, self-discipline, and life skills. The program also targets youths who have been involved in the court system.

• *Park Hill Christian Church* has been awarded $22,000 for a collaboration of three churches in the Park Hill neighborhood (aside from Park Hill Christian, Park Hill United Methodist, and Park Hill Congregational churches) to provide after-school activities to 20 latchkey children attending Smiley Middle School. Church members, along with the American Friends Service Committee, provide tutoring, recreational activities, and transportation to the students at the school building three afternoons each week.

• *Mt. Gilead Baptist Church* has been provided a one-year grant of $10,000 to support a summer youth employment program, Kids Korp. The collaboration involves several local high schools, George Washington, Manual, East, Montbell, West, Central Overland, and Smokey Hills, in the referral process. The program provides summer job orientation, training, and placement for youth ages 14–18. A mentoring component provides one-to-one mentors for up to 50 participating youth. Other support services include tutoring, counseling, computer orientation, and cultural awareness. The senior minister works with the business community in developing job opportunities for program clients.

• *First Christian Assembly of God Montbello* has been provided a one-year grant of $10,000 to support collaboration between Montbello Church and a local elementary school for a tutoring and mentoring program during the school year. A six-week summer program of recreational activities, parent groups, and field trips is offered to as many as 40 participating youth.

These 13 funded projects involve collaboration across denominational and racial lines and collaboration with secular service agencies as well. Note that these projects deliver social services directly to individual families and groups within the community. They focus on internal strategies of social reform, using education, counseling, recreation, and alcohol-and-drug-abuse counseling, as well as other social services to children, youth, and families.

Technical Assistance Phase

In addition, the Metro Denver Black Church Initiative, with assistance from the Piton, Ford, Lilly, and Hunt foundations, provides training and technical assistance to area African American churches.[4] This aspect of the program is considered as essential to the potential of the initiative as are the grants.

The training and technical assistance provided by staff and consultants focus on understanding community issues, enhancing organizational capacity, networking, evaluation, and strategic planning for future funding. The goal is to encourage more, and more effective, work in the community.

As part of the technical assistance component, the initiative has sponsored workshops for ministers on topics ranging from collaboration to youth violence. It also has provided the churches with the services of a certified public accountant to help with fiscal management issues, which often are a deterrent to churches' winning grants.

In addition, the Black Church Initiative has arranged for national experts to come to Denver to provide training on urban ministry and church administration and management topics including strategic planning, time management, fiscal accountability, and fund-raising. It also has sponsored ministers to attend training programs in other cities.

Evaluation Phase

A fourth phase of this Denver black church's program is the evaluation phase. The initiative has retained a nationally noted research and evaluation team headed by Dr. Walter V. Collier.[5] It is in the process of conducting both outcome and process evaluation. In a preliminary report this firm has reported that the overall initiative and its various components are quite successful in meeting the objectives established at the outset. It has made some suggestions for improved performance.

Specifically, the purpose of the evaluation phase was to examine the operation of the project and the outcome effects of the second and third phases above and to make such recommendations as might improve the operation. In general, the researchers found the project to be effective in strengthening the organization and the capacity of the churches to assist the needy within their communities. The collaborative aspects of the project were cited as particularly noteworthy.

The participants and grant holders expressed a great deal of satisfaction with the workshops, which grew out of their expressed needs. In their evaluation of the workshops they also expressed need for some additional technical assistance, which the foundation has agreed to provide.

The churches, according to the evaluation report, encountered no major problems in collaborating with other churches of the same or different denominations or with secular agencies. The evaluation report observed,

The only obstacles encountered in implementing the collaboration had to do with internal program matters, i.e., unfamiliarity of church staff with collaboration, insufficient financial resources of smaller churches, problems of recruiting program volunteer staff, and the needs of project staff for further technical assistance and resource development.

The participants reported that they learned several lessons that might be helpful to other churches anticipating collaborative outreach programs. First, collaboration takes committed leadership. It requires both the desire and the courage to be a partner with others, sharing both the joys and the agonies of this work. Participants must be willing to give information about their churches and to share decision-making responsibility. Interfaith and interracial confidence and cooperation are essential. Hands-on management was found to be important.

Finally, the necessity for trained and prepared staff and volunteers was paramount. Projects did not proceed as well when the minister was looked to as the expert in all endeavors.

Outreach to the Community in Atlanta

We sought in a variety of ways to ascertain the extent and type of outreach to the community undertaken by Atlanta churches.[6] In a survey of some 150 black churches we found that 87 percent, 131 local congregations, are actively engaged in extending themselves into the various forms of protest. A slight majority report participating in such community protest activity during the past three to four years.

We found numerous Atlanta congregations actively engaged in community service and community action. One of the best known locally is the Antioch Baptist Church—North. Another is St. Philip's A.M.E. Church, which owns a shopping center and has 47 staff members and 1,000 volunteers in its outreach programs. Still another is the Martin Street Church of God, which has an extensive "recovery program." One of the most extensive examples of community development is provided by the Shrine of the Black Madonna. This black Christian Nationalist church operates successful African American bookstores in the city, a Community Service Center, an academic school, an industrial training center, and a child-care center, and has extensive economic, self-help ventures, including a farm.

Located on the same block is the historic St. Agnes Catholic Church, a source of education and uplift to the community beyond its membership. Mt. Ephraim Baptist Church has an extensive program for the homeless. And St. Paul A.M.E. Church has extensive programs, and once mounted a successful effort to prevent a medical incinerator from being built in the community.

A local temple associated with the Nation of Islam continues to rescue young black men from the streets, the jails, and the drug scene and turn them into self-reporting, self-supporting, law-abiding citizens. It was an extraordinary challenge for women at Spelman College enrolled in a course on the sociology of the black church to gain access to this temple. When they finally did so, with the aid of some young male members, they received a very warm reception and gained extensive information about the impressive achievements of this group. Despite the recruitment of members from the more vulnerable black populations, my students found that no members were unemployed, on welfare, or on drugs, and none were fathers failing to support their children. The students found, however, that the strict discipline and gender distinctions that the Nation of Islam requires may serve as barriers to many youth.

An even larger program of youth outreach is provided by the New Birth Baptist Church. This church sponsors "Project Impact," where first-offending youth are diverted from the criminal justice system and given the opportunity for counseling, personal development, and referral assistance. The city's most famous church, Ebenezer Baptist Church, under the dynamic and inspired leadership of the Rev. Joseph Roberts, is without peer as a national symbol of social reform. One of the most recent projects of the church is a house it purchased and operates as a combination center for elderly activities and child care. The elderly help with child care, which provides both age groups with an immense source of nurturing. So, too, the city's oldest black church, the Big Bethel A.M.E. Church, continues an extensive community outreach program. And, of course, the Wheat Street Baptist Church, under the Rev. Michael Harris, has continued its historic economic and community development programs.

Although these programs by individual churches are impressive, by far the most extensive example of community outreach representing the collective, sustained action of Atlanta churches is provided by the Vine City Housing Ministry.

The Vine City community is more than 100 years old. Located on the western edge of downtown Atlanta, it is across from the Georgia Dome Stadium completed in 1992 near the Atlanta University Center, a cluster of six historically black private colleges and universities. Vine City was once a thriving black middle-class cultural and business community, but in recent years the community has fallen on hard times, due, in part, to downturns in the national and local economies. Ironically, Vine City has also been hurt by a series of developments meant to economically benefit the larger Atlanta community. First among these was construction of the Metropolitan Atlanta Rapid Transit Authority (MARTA) rail line in the 1970s. Another was the planned construction of a state office building in the area. Still a third development was planned expansion of the Georgia World Congress Center, and a fourth was building the Georgia Dome Stadium. All of these contributed to the decline of the Vine City community, because they destroyed homes, churches, stores, and other institutions.

The crisis that produced the Vine City Housing Ministry was a project to build a state office building on a nine-acre parcel designated for redevelopment in Vine City at Northside Drive and Martin Luther King Jr. Drive. Plans called for demolishing vast acres of residential housing, stores, and churches to make way for this newest example of urban renewal. Coming in the wake of other improvements, such as the rapid transit system and world trade center, this new incursion stimulated ministers and other community leaders and residents to form a collective community action strategy. For several months they organized demonstrations and public hearings, which eventually defeated the office building project and substituted a proposed mixed land-use designation for the parcel. This substitution of plans was accepted by the city of Atlanta and was a major victory for collaboration. Today a visitor who passes by the corner of Northside Drive and Martin Luther King Jr. Drive will see a cluster of beautiful pastel-colored town houses instead of an office building.

While at the height of the protest a large number of churches and pastors were active in the movement to "Save Vine City," afterward many of them withdrew from community action and returned to their primary spiritual missions. Eleven of these churches, however, led by their pastors, joined together to form the "Vine City Housing Ministry."

The mission of this ministry was "building and renovating affordable housing for Vine City and surrounding community residents and members of the respective congregations."

The Rev. W. L. Cottrell, pastor of the Beulah Baptist Church, who had been a leading spokesman for the action against the state office building, and whose church had major community programs, was elected chairman of the board of the Vine City Housing Ministry. (Other ministers and their churches are represented in Table 17.)

In 1989 Vine City witnessed the demolition of a neighboring community for the expansion of the World Trade Center. Homes, businesses, and churches were destroyed. So when plans were announced for the building of the Georgia Dome, leaders of the Vine City Housing

Ministry were again catapulted into protest action. Not only was this another encroachment that would destroy houses, churches, and small stores, but there had been no community input into this project. The city officials had approved the Georgia Dome project for the same reasons they had approved the previous "improvements"—it would bring new jobs, new customers, and new tax revenues to the city.

In collaboration with the Atlanta Economic Development Corporation, the Vine City Housing Ministry began negotiations with the city's Department of Community Development and the Urban Residential Authority. Their position was to urge a scaling back of the dome project, to spare more homes and churches, and to have money set aside from the proceeds to support housing and community development projects in the neighborhood. Because the churches were united in this collaborative effort and because they had the aggressive leadership of the ministers, the authorities were forced to restructure the dome project. The ministers confronted the mayor, Maynard Jackson, reminding him that his own father was a minister in this community and would be sorely disappointed that the mayor was supporting this destruction of the neighborhood. The mayor lent his considerable support and prestige to the Vine City Housing Ministry efforts. As a result, though the dome project could not be defeated, it was sharply curtailed.

Another result is that a $10.5 million Housing Trust Fund has been set aside from revenues from dome fees to be made available to non-profit and private groups for housing and redevelopment near the dome. A share of that money was explicitly earmarked for the Vine City Housing Ministry. By 1995 the ministry had built 28 houses for purchase at low mortgage rates and engaged in the renovation of a 12-unit apartment in Vine City. The ministry also began an Employment Resource Center in an effort to find full-time and part-time employment for neighborhood residents at the Georgia Dome Stadium. This case study illustrates how black churches' collaboration not only with other churches but with private and public agencies has helped to preserve an African American community.

Meanwhile, other commercial and civic agencies of the city have also been able to use some of these trust funds for building additional housing in this community. Cottrell gives credit to the churches: "The success of the funding efforts to date has depended greatly upon the church leaders' effectiveness in relationship building and in using the moral and political force of the churches to attract attention and resources to the venture."[7]

The work of the Vine City Housing Ministry was also instrumental in the city's successful competition for one of the Federal Empowerment Zone grants of $250 million in 1994. This zone comprises a 9.3-square-mile area containing 30 of Atlanta's poorest neighborhoods, including Vine City.[8]

The work of the Vine City Housing Ministry shows that the 11 black churches involved had a substantial impact on the promise of redevelopment of their community. And one might speculate that if some of the other churches in this area had maintained active involvement, the results might have been even more impressive. By working in collaboration and by calling upon the rich history of activism, these churches have been able to move out beyond their religious services to play a major role in social reform and community development. This required imaginative, bold, and able leadership. It also required an amazing ability to suspend their individual wills to a more collective effort. Their success has also depended heavily on the cooperation and participation of these established churches with their numbers and political and economic influence. Finally, the success of the Vine City Housing Ministry has required the collaboration between these churches and other political, commercial, educational, and civic agencies in the city. This work so far could not have proceeded to such a level without the cooperation of public and private agencies, which, of course, came in part because of the vision, the organization, and the persistence of the ministers.

This was not the only time black churches in Atlanta have demonstrated awareness of their enormous economic potential. A few years back the *Atlanta Journal/Constitution* did an extensive study in the city of redlining, the practice of banks and other financial institutions refusing to lend money for home building in black neighborhoods. After reading this series of articles, concerned black clergy organized a civil-rights-style march downtown. This time they marched down to the banks that had been identified as redliners, withdrew their deposits, and marched over and deposited these funds in the several black-and white-owned banks that had made loans in the black community. Practices of these offending banks changed dramatically. The bankers know better than most members of the black community that the economic resources of the churches are powerful tools for change if used wisely. They know that one church alone, such as Ebenezer Baptist Church, can deposit as much as $13,000 weekly and has a $1 million annual operating budget. Moreover, the bankers in Atlanta have no doubt that with its international reputation and standing-room-only weekly attendance, the church will be able to raise the $10 million it needs for a new building. Such economic resources, when properly utilized, especially in collaboration, can work miracles.

11

—ɱ—

Often Seen, Seldom Called:
The Legacy of Jerena Lee

When the Rev. Vashti Murphy McKenzie addressed the Democratic National Convention in 1996, she made history as the first black woman preacher to do so. This event brought to national attention the presence of black women preachers. But for the Rev. McKenzie, it was just one more pioneering role in what has become a pattern of breaking down barriers. She was also the first black woman appointed pastor of a large A.M.E. congregation, the Daniel A. Payne Memorial A.M.E. Church in Baltimore.

A graduate of the Howard University School of Divinity, McKenzie seems to bring to her ministry the passion for excellence in community service derived from growing up in the famous Murphy family of Baltimore, owners of the African American newspaper chain. This spirited woman is a spellbinding speaker.

The church has experienced phenomenal growth in its membership since her arrival in the early 1990s. The church has had a substantial increase in male members, as well as growth in its community outreach programs and financial stability.

McKenzie has now risen in national stature. She has become a much sought-after speaker. In A.M.E. circles, she quickly became a prime candidate for early elevation to the office of bishop, a position no woman has yet risen to.

But the Rev. McKenzie's story is exceedingly rare. The number of black women pastors is so small—less than 10 percent in the mainline denominations. So black women can be truly said to be often seen in the pews but seldom called to the pulpit. The struggle of black women for the priesthood today is still reflective of the legacy of the legendary Jerena Lee, first black woman ordained to the ministry.

The Story of Jerena Lee

Jerena Lee worked as a live-in domestic for various families in the Philadelphia area from the time she was seven years old.[1] Born in 1783 to free black parents in Cape May, New Jersey, she received little guidance from her parents. "My parents, being wholly ignorant of the knowledge of God, had not, therefore, instructed me in any degree in this great matter."

Once, while working for a family in Philadelphia, her employer gave her a task to do. Later, when asked if she had done it, Jerena answered yes, but she was lying. The guilt and remorse she felt were so tremendous that she would later credit the experience for her conversion.

"At this awful point, in my early history, the spirit of God moved in power through my conscience and told me I was a wretched sinner. On this account so great was the impression, and so strong were the feelings of guilt, that I promised in my heart that I would not tell another lie."

Jerena attended a series of revivals being held in the area. Once a neighbor invited her to attend the Bethel A.M.E. Church, where the Rev. Richard Allen was the minister. After hearing him preach, she became a convert to Methodism that same day.

"During the labors of this man that afternoon I had come to the conclusion that this is the people to which my heart unites, and it so happened, that as soon as the service closed he invited such as felt a desire to flee the wrath to come, to unite on trial with them. I embraced the opportunity."

Three weeks later, she became so moved during Allen's sermon that she interrupted it. "That moment, though hundreds were present, I did leap to my feet, and declare that God, for Christ's sake, had pardoned the sins of my soul. Great was the ecstasy of my mind." Richard Allen waited patiently until she had finished and then recognized her conversion. She was 21 years old.

Five years later Jerena had a third fateful encounter with Richard Allen. Jerena Lee went through ups and downs in her faith for a number of years after her conversion. Then in 1809, at the age of 26, she received a call to preach. It was a frightening experience, for she had never heard of a woman preacher.

> An impressive silence fell upon me, and I stood as if someone was about to speak to me, yet I had no such thought in my heart. But to my utter surprise there seemed to sound a voice which I thought I distinctly heard, and most certainly understood, which said to me, "Go preach the Gospel!" I immediately replied aloud, "No one will believe me." Again I listened and again the same voice seemed to say, "Preach the Gospel; I will put words in your mouth, and will turn your enemies to become your friends."

At first she thought it must be the devil speaking to her. She had heard that Satan was capable of all sorts of tricks. "Immediately I went into a secret place, and called upon the Lord to know if he had called me to preach, and whether I was deceived or not; when there appeared to my view the form and figure of a pulpit, with a Bible lying thereon, the back of which was presented to me as plainly as if it had been a literal fact."

Almost, but not quite, convinced of her calling, Jerena Lee decided to sleep on this matter.

> During the night following, I took a text and preached in my sleep. I thought there stood before me a great multitude, while I expounded to them the things of religion. So violent were my exertions, and so loud were my exclamations, that I awoke from the sound of my own voice, which also woke the family of the house where I resided.

Now being assured in her own mind that, despite being a woman, she was truly called to preach, she set out to meet again the Rev. Richard Allen, who was by now the bishop of the A.M.E. Church in America. She found him at his home, and he welcomed her into his study. She told him her story.

Allen was receptive and responsive and even sympathetic to her cause. He gave her some limited rights to conduct meetings and prayer services, and to speak before unorganized gatherings, but would not ordain her to preach in the church from the pulpit.

"But as to women preaching, he said that our Discipline knew nothing at all about it—that it did not call for women preachers."

At first she accepted Allen's ruling and felt relieved of the burden of becoming a preacher as a woman. But not for long. After further reflection, she reasoned that, the conclusions of her minister notwithstanding, she had been called to preach by a higher authority. So at the age of 26 she decided to become a preacher and to preach wherever she could raise an audience. She proceeded to do so with amazing success and a wide following, converting black and white alike to Methodism.

Two years later she married an A.M.E. minister named Joseph Lee, leaving her beloved Philadelphia to be with him in Snow Hill, New Jersey. They had two children. She continued to preach, but outside the church. When her husband died, leaving her a widow at a young age, she decided to go into preaching in a big way. And, while her own mother took care of her two children, Jerena traveled far and wide evangelizing. She served as a Methodist preacher for eight years without being officially recognized by the Church. In one year alone she traveled more than 2,000 miles and delivered some 178 sermons. But she did not do so out of simple defiance of church authorities. She had the highest regard and personal affection for Bishop Allen. After all, it was Allen's preaching that had started her on her own spiritual journey.

In contemporary times the rationale for black women to preach might be simply stated: Women wish to preach. They are called to preach. And so it should be. But in the early 19th century, Jerena Lee needed more. In a pattern of logical reasoning, this untutored young woman, not yet 30 years old, almost 200 years ago, set forth in her own mind, and later in print, the ultimate rationale for female ministry. What she says on the subject recommends itself to black women, scholars, and theologians today. Gently chastising the Methodist church for its rules barring women preachers, and Bishop Allen for feeling constrained by them, she reasoned as follows:

> O how careful ought we to be, lest through our bylaws of church government and discipline, we bring into disrepute even the work of life. For as unseemly as it may appear nowadays for a woman to preach, it should be remembered that nothing is impossible with God. And why should it be thought impossible, heterodox, or improper for a woman to preach, seeing the Savior died for the woman as well as the man?

Simply and eloquently she answered the question that had confounded Richard Allen and all the established black and white church hierarchies to that time. After Jerena Lee, the doctrinal, intellectual and social rationale that prevented black women from being fully accepted in the ministry was swept away. Why shouldn't women be allowed to preach?

> If the man may preach, because the Savior died for him, why not the woman, seeing he died for her also? Is he not a whole savior, instead

of a half one, as those who hold it wrong for a woman to preach would seem to make it appear?

We may indeed marvel at how a young black person could arrive at such insight, which had escaped devoted scholars and theologians of all races and in all major religions to that time. Yet, for this lady inspired by the calling of the Lord, there was now no turning back. This conviction fortified her for a fourth life-changing encounter with Richard Allen.

She was at Bishop Allen's church. A guest minister was preaching. After taking his text, the guest preacher faltered. He seemed unable to continue. He lost his place. He lost his voice. He looked distraught. And, finally, he took his seat. At that moment Jerena Lee vaulted from the pews, took to the rostrum, repeated the text taken by the preacher, and completed the sermon on the same text he had set forth. It was a masterful performance. All the while, Bishop Allen sat on the platform. The audience seemed spellbound.

After completing her sermon, Jerena went back to her seat in the audience. She was certainly not permitted to sit on the platform; that was reserved for ordained ministers. Only when she returned to her seat did she begin reflecting on the matter. She knew she had violated the rules and regulations of the church and had usurped the pulpit while Bishop Allen himself was sitting there. After all, while encouraging her to exhort, he had expressly forbidden her to preach in the church. She expected to be harshly disciplined and possibly expelled from the Methodist Church. Then Bishop Allen rose and took the rostrum. For the first time he publicly recognized Jerena's genuine calling to preach. He recalled to the congregation that she had indeed petitioned him for ordination, some eight years before, and he had refused. He then praised her for the work she had been doing since that time and for the quality of her sermon that day, And then, in a manner that would do honor to black bishops today, he ordained her on the spot, saying he had come to believe that she was as much called to preach as any of the (male) preachers present. Bishop Allen then assigned her to preach in his church and invited her to participate in the meetings he held with other A.M.E. ministers. It would be nearly a century before this happened again.

Bishop Turner's Folly

As to the official sanctioning of black women to preach throughout the 19th century, the mainline black denominations remained as closed to women preachers as the white denominations were. Jualynne Dodson has observed that the office of "stewardess" was created in 1869 and the office of "deaconess" in 1900 as vehicles to give a partial response to the demand of A.M.E. women to preach. Even so, they were limited to the subordinate position of "evangelist" and not appointed as senior ministers of congregations.[2]

In 1888, the legendary Bishop Henry McNeal Turner, another progressive bishop in the tradition of Richard Allen, ordained a woman to preach. Here was the leading cleric of his time, a bishop, hero of Reconstruction politics, builder of the A.M.E. Church in Georgia, president of Morris Brown College, author of a history of the A.M.E. Church and a Methodist catechism, who surely knew the Scriptures as well as any. Nevertheless, he was silenced by lesser men, other bishops who severely reprimanded him for his "irresponsible act." The General Conference in its 1888 session overwhelmingly passed the following resolution:

> Whereas Bishop H. M. Turner has seen fit to ordain a woman to the order of a deacon; and whereas said act is contrary to the usage of our church, and without precedent in any other body of Christians in the known world; and as it cannot be proved by the scriptures that a woman has ever been ordained to the order of the ministry; therefore be it enacted, that the bishops of the African Methodist Episcopal Church be and hereby are forbidden to ordain a woman to the order of deacon or elder in our church.[3]

The African Methodist Episcopal Zion Church was the first to officially ordain women. In a remarkable and remarkably late burst of insight, Bishop James Walker Hood declared at the annual conference in 1891 that "there is one Methodist Episcopal Church that guarantees to women all rights in common with men."[4] On May 20, 1894, Bishop Hood ordained the first woman in the A.M.E. Zion Church, Julia A. Foote. A year later Mary J. Small, wife of Bishop Small, was ordained by Bishop Alexander Walters.

These two became the first two women to be officially ordained to the ministry by any Methodist denomination, black or white.[5] It would be a half-century, however, before other Methodist churches would follow this example of leadership.[6] It occurred in the A.M.E. Church in 1948, in the C.M.E. Church in 1954, in the three Baptist denominations much later, and in the Pentecostal churches later still. Indeed, in the largest of the black Pentecostal denominations, the rapidly growing Church of God in Christ, there is still a policy opposed to the ordination of women.

Another unsung heroine of the black church is Biddy Mason, founder of First A.M.E., the oldest black church in Los Angeles.[7] Mason was born into slavery in Georgia and escaped to Missouri, where she married an Indian chief and bore three daughters. When she was about to be reenslaved and her children enslaved, she again escaped and went to California. She made her way by caring for sheep at the end of a 300-unit caravan of covered wagons.

In California she was jailed as a runaway slave. She fought the case through the courts until she and her daughters won their freedom in 1856. She then took a job as midwife and nurse for $2.50 per day, saved her money, and acquired some property by taking land instead of money from some of her customers. She entered the real estate field, buying and selling property, and eventually became a wealthy landowner. It is said that at the time of her death she owned the entire city block from Spring Street to Broadway and from Third Street to Fourth Street in Los Angeles. She founded First A.M.E. church in her home at 331 Spring Street.[8]

As a consequence of the reluctance of mainline black churches to ordain women fully, a number of black women founded their own independent churches affiliated with the Holiness or Pentecostal traditions. Elder Lucy Smith established the All Nations Pentecostal Church in Chicago in the 1930s, and Bishop Ida Robinson established the Mount Sinai Holy Church of Philadelphia in 1924. Both are now large churches.

Two outstanding contemporary examples of black women ministers of large churches are the Rev. Dr. Barbara King of the Hillside International Truth Center in Atlanta, and the Rev. Johnnie Coleman of the huge Christ Universal Temple in Chicago.

The case of King and her Hillside International Truth Center and Chapel is especially instructive of this independent church movement among women preachers. King holds a B.A. degree in sociology from Texas Southern University and a master's degree in social work from Atlanta University. After graduating, she accepted a supervisory position at the Newberry Avenue Center in Chicago, Illinois. She rose to the top of her profession as a social worker and community organizer there, but work and worldly acclaim were not enough to satisfy the longings of her spirit. She had begun to attend Christ Universal Temple, where she was introduced to the "New Thought" concept of Dr. Johnnie Coleman. Ultimately, she entered the Unity School of Christianity, where she was ordained a New Thought minister.

She had a young son and moved with him to Atlanta in 1969 to accept a teaching position at Spelman College. She later became the dean of students at Spelman. It was during her tenure as dean that she began a ministry in her living room at home. The president of Spelman at that time, Albert E. Manly, called her into his office to say that being a minister and the dean of students were incompatible, even though her ministry was taking place in her own home. So she left Spelman and took a leap of faith. Hillside Chapel and Truth Center was born.

This ministry began September 6, 1971, with 12 people sitting in the round in King's living room. By 1996 the center was one of the largest churches in the city, with more than 4,000 members, mostly young professionals, mostly black women and men, with a generous sprinkling of whites and international visitors. The beautiful new sanctuary, located on a hillside in the southwest section of the city, is a veritable studio in the round. Photographs of achieving black women are mounted on the walls.

One of the most successful economic ventures of the church is a bookstore that sells a wide range of religious and secular books and sometimes arranges book signings for authors. The center also has its own credit union, and sponsors, supports, and encourages an organized group of business owners called "Top Level Entrepreneurs." In addition, at least once a month the second service is turned into a showcase for local black entrepreneurs to market their wares.

Thus, by incorporating economic and business development into its regular program of worship and community intervention, the Hillside center gives strong support to the economic development of one community.

When *Ebony* magazine published the results of its search for the 15 Greatest Black Preachers in 1993, all 15 were male. Only when the magazine compiled a second tier of 46 black preachers did it find room for six black women: the Rev. Carolyn Ann Knight of the Philadelphia Church of Christ in Harlem, the Rev. Vashti Murphy McKenzie of Payne A.M.E. Church in Baltimore, the Rev. Prathia Hall Wynn of Mt. Sharon Baptist Church in Philadelphia, the Rev. Katie Geneva Cannon of Temple University, and the Rev. Delores Carpenter of Michigan Park Christian Church, Washington, D.C. Conspicuously absent was the Rev. Susan Johnson, pastor of Temple Baptist in New York City. By 1997, however, *Ebony* would correct this oversight of black women preachers (see Tables 18 and 19 in Appendix C). In addition to the top 15, the magazine featured 20 other black women preachers as runners up.

Lincoln and Mamiya found that, "All of the seven mainline Black denominations are characterized by a predominantly female membership and a largely male leadership, despite the fact that the major programs of the Black church in politics, economics, or music depend heavily upon women for their promotion and success."[9]

The reasons for this are several. They are partly doctrinal, with black churches following the lead of white churches in finding a biblical mandate for male leadership. They are partly historical in the sense that the precedent was set in slavery of male ministers, and it has continued with an ironclad hold ever since. Also, the great religions of Africa were patriarchal. The reasons also are partly contemporary, social, and beyond gender in the sense that both black men and black women in the church prefer male ministers. Few women currently are trained and experienced for leadership in the pastorate. This situation is changing rapidly, however, because seminaries are increasingly training women to be ministers. But changes will come more rapidly if the forces behind their exclusion—are recognized.

It is, of course, little comfort to the cause of social justice to be reminded that as slow as progress has been for women in ministry in the black churches, it is still far ahead of a similar movement in the white churches.[10]

The enormity of this situation can be appreciated by reflecting on the fact that virtually without exception the major established religious bodies—whether Catholic, Protestant, Jewish, Muslim, or otherwise—are exceedingly patriarchal in their leadership structures. A breakthrough by black women in the black church in the United States in the years ahead will have universal significance.

Today a number of brilliant young women theologians and scholars have helped to generate a strong scholarly attack on the exclusion of women from the ministry. Principal among these are Jacquelyn Grant, Katie Cannon, Delores Williams, Kelly Brown, Cheryl Sanders, Cheryl Gilkes, Jualynne Dodson, and Delores Carpenter.[11] A few male scholars and theologians have also joined this movement. In her study of the place of women in the ministry, Jacquelyn Grant provides even greater clarity to the prophetic and perhaps unique role of women.

Having learned from her professor, James Cone, that Jesus is black (*A Black Theology of Liberation*), Grant has gone further to discover that Jesus is a black woman. Observing that the reality of Jesus grows out of the experiences of true believers, she argues that, "For (Jerena) Lee, this meant that women could preach; for Sojourner (Truth) it meant that women could possibly save the world; for me, it means today that Christ, found in the experience of Black Women, is a Black Woman."[12]

Considerable attention has been focused on the black male ministry as the major gatekeepers, who would presumably have most to lose from a major infusion of black women ministers and who, therefore, are seen as barriers to such progress toward equality and social justice. It is a peculiar role assigned to the black male ministry. For surely the most far-reaching movements for social justice in this nation over the past two centuries have been spearheaded by black male preachers.

How, then, is it possible that the black male ministry finds itself accused of systematic sexism and discrimination against aspiring black female ministers?

The evidence is beginning to accumulate to support this charge. In their study of 2,150 black churches in the seven mainline black denominations, Lincoln and Mamiya found that black male ministers in general disapproved of black women as pastors.[13] Only 15 percent of these men strongly approved of women pastors, while another 35.8 percent approved. The other half split equally between strong disapproval and disapproval. There was, however, a striking age disparity. Among younger black male ministers a total of 69 percent approved or strongly approved, while 31 percent disapproved of female pastors. Older ministers were less likely to approve. There was also a difference by education level. Among those black male pastors with less than high school education only 43 percent approved, while among the college educated ones a full 67 percent approved of women pastors.

What is also striking, however, is that black male ministers are not all of one mind and that their position on the matter of women pastors is influenced by their particular denomination.[14] Thus, the Lincoln and Mamiya study showed that black male ministers of the Methodist faith tradition were much more open to women pastors, followed by those of the Baptist persuasion, with the Pentecostal ministers most opposed.

Even more specifically, the denominations within these three broad-faith traditions may be ranked in terms of the strength of their approval of female pastors. This study found that the A.M.E. Zion ministers are the most supportive, registering a substantial 94 percent in favor, followed by the C.M.E. ministers, with 92 percent. The A.M.E.'s bring up the rear of these historically black Methodists. Among the Baptist only the Progressive National Convention ministers give any substantial support to black women ministers, and that is a minority of 43 percent. The other Baptists and the Pentecostals are far behind.

In her pioneering study of black female seminary graduates, Dr. Delores Carpenter found that these women found greater opportunities for pastorates in the white-controlled denominations.[15] Five years later, however, she found that this advantage had dissipated, as the white denominations filled up the vacancies they had in their black congregations.

Carpenter also found a certain degree of loneliness among these female professionals. "Two-thirds of them are single and lack the support that male clergy receive from traditional married family contexts." She finds, however, two bases for encouragement. First, younger men who study with these women in seminaries seem to have a genuine appreciation for their gifts. The second basis for hope is even stronger. She finds an emerging "sisterhood" among women seminary graduates and others. "Women are forming close relationships of trust and are learning how to depend on one another."

The situation is increasingly embarrassing to black male church leaders, theologians, and scholars. Indeed, a leading black scholar in this field, the Rev. James Cone, has gone so far as to confess his own past sexism in not recognizing and promoting a greater receptivity to Black women in the ministry and has renounced his past attitudes. He is strongly critical of black male clergy for not following his lead. He has written that he now considers sexism an evil of similar magnitude to racism and has called to task black male ministers, theologians, and other black male church leaders for perpetuating and enjoying the unjust privileges of their sexism in keeping black women ministers down. Others have joined Cone in admitting to and denouncing sexism among black male ministers.

Moreover, Cone has strongly criticized the two leading black ministers of our time in this respect. In his groundbreaking book, *Martin and Malcolm and America*, Cone accuses both Martin Luther King Jr. and Malcolm X of blatant sexism. Both exhibited gross insensitivity to women in leadership roles in the movement and the pulpit, according to Cone.[16]

While Cone is essentially correct, his criticism is a bit harsh, perhaps allowing a certain insensitivity to context to creep into his otherwise trenchant analysis. The time, the place, the circumstance, and the experience of the leader help to shape the leader's perspectives. Just as Martin would not have been the same leader, for example, if he had lived 10 years earlier or 10 years later, if he had lived in Philadelphia or New York in 1956 instead of Montgomery, Alabama, so it is that his views on gender disparities and injustices might well have been more enlightened if he had lived in the enlightened era of the 1970s, which benefited from the revolution he helped to create in the 1950s and 1960s. Dr. Vincent Harding, in his book on Dr. King, has reminded us of King's enormous capacity to grow in insight, wisdom, and courage as events unfolded around him.[17] He did not always speak out against the Vietnam War, but he came to do so before lots of other preachers. So, too, his insight into poverty grew far beyond that of his earlier years and led him to the Poor People's Campaign. Indeed, it is probable that both Martin and Malcolm would have converted to gender neutrality, or gender equality, or women's empowerment a few years ahead of Cone and others had they not been cut down; such was their talent for being just ahead of others in their time.

No, James Cone had it right the first time. Racism is the major problem affecting black people.[18] It is systemic and endemic in our society, as Andrew Hacker and Toni Morrison and Derrick Bell have shown so eloquently. The same is true of sexism. Black men simply do not have the power—even if they had the will—to inflict on black women the massive pain they suffer because of their race and their gender. At best or at worst, black men of whatever status are pawns in the game of life masterminded by others.

The task, then, would seem to be for black men and women to see their common predicament more clearly, to cling to each other more dearly and fight the common foe more fiercely together.

12

—⚊—

Twelve Gates to the City

The idea of black churches using their enormous economic and financial resources as leverage for building programs that benefit not just individuals and families but the entire community is an idea whose time has come. In a large-scale survey of more than 1,000 churches in all regions of the country we found that in addition to providing direct services to individuals and families, some 20 percent of churches provide some form of communitywide economic or institutional development. Indeed, *Black Enterprise Magazine* profiled a number of the largest black churches in 1993, portraying them as economic enterprises.[1]

In his book on the economic potential of the black church, Gregory Reed designed materials whose aim is "to perpetuate and uplift the community, to aid churches in taking the lead by stabilizing communities in both urban and rural settings."[2] Moreover, in capturing the essence and the enormous potential of Reed's work, C. Eric Lincoln has written:

> The time for looking to others to do for us what we can do for ourselves is past. It will not return. The strategies for economic empowerment are not included in the seminary courses but are included in this text . . . a blueprint for progressive community development.[3]

An even bolder statement of the potential of the black church to revitalize whole communities has been set forth by Dr. Walter Malone

144

Jr., pastor of the Canaan Missionary Baptist Church in Louisville, Kentucky. In a book titled *From Holy Power to Holy Profits: The Black Church and Community Economic Empowerment,* he has set forth a blueprint, based on his own experience, for how other black churches can also develop economically sound community development programs.[4]

In Malone's view, many of the social problems faced by individuals and families can be traced to economic deprivation in the black community, which he firmly believes the black church can remedy.

According to Malone, the black community and black leadership today should place at least as much emphasis on economic empowerment as on electoral politics. He draws a strong analogy to black church activism of the past. Citing the success of the 381-day Montgomery bus boycott of 1955–56, he raises the following questions: "Are we satisfied with sitting on the front of the bus, or do we want to own our own bus company?" "How does economic development take its appropriate mission?" Recognizing that some may consider economic development "radical and out of place" for the church, Malone concludes instead, "The Christ of the Gospels has a concern for the disinherited and dispossessed." The economic, social, and political potential of the large churches, referred to as megachurches, is particularly strong (see Table 20 in Appendix C).

In this chapter we profile 12 great black urban churches with outstanding programs on a scale grand enough to make their cities more livable (see Table 21). That is, they have used their financial resources to influence services, facilities, and institutions that benefit not just particular individuals but large sectors of the community.

For example, the St. John Community Development Corporation was created by St. John Baptist Church to revitalize Miami's Overtown—a low-income community that was devastated by periodic waves of rioting during the 1980s.

The United House of Prayer for All People, which was founded by Bishop C. M. ("Daddy") Grace during the 1930s Depression, continues to revitalize inner-city areas. With 146 churches in 22 states, it has invested $20 million of its own money in building low-to moderate-income housing in Washington, D.C., and 10 other cities.

Similarly, under leadership of the Rev. Johnny Ray Youngblood and his St. Paul Community Baptist Church, 55 churches in the devastated East New York section of Brooklyn have joined forces to build the Nehemiah Houses (named after the biblical prophet who rebuilt Jerusalem), 5,000 owner-occupied row houses, over a 10-year period. This initiative has captured the attention of federal housing officials, and Congress has enacted legislation supporting Nehemiah housing construction by churches and other community-based groups across the nation.

Baltimore United in Leadership Development (BUILD) is another church consortium, comprising 32 churches, that was established for economic development of inner-city neighborhoods.

The 12 churches selected here represent the combined characteristics revealed by our surveys of those churches most active in their communities. They are older, larger, more established institutions than most with large and growing memberships that draw from a wide cross section of socioeconomic classes. They also are led by highly educated, visionary, and community-oriented ministers whose fabled ability to deliver a sermon is matched by their commitment to building strong African American communities.

A further characteristic of these 12 churches is that they all have dynamic worship programs. Indeed, we have found in our studies and observations that churches without dynamic and spirit-filled worship programs are not likely to sustain active community building activities. The two seem to reinforce each other.

Three Gates in the East

In the East, we have selected the following three churches: the Concord Baptist Church in Brooklyn, the Abyssinian Baptist Church in Harlem, and the Allen A.M.E. Church in Queens. These boroughs represent, respectively, the largest, second-largest, and third-largest concentrations of African Americans in the nation's largest city.

Concord Baptist Church, Brooklyn

The Concord Baptist Church is not alone among Brooklyn churches in exercising a major influence in its community. Among others with outstanding programs are the Church of God in Christ, under the leadership of the Rev. Herbert Daugherty; the St. Paul Community Baptist Church, under the leadership of the Rev. Johnny Ray Youngblood; and the Bridge Street A.M.E. Church, under leadership of the husband-wife co-pastors, the Revs. Lawrence and Barbara Lucas.[5] Still, Concord Baptist Church is distinctive.

Many would say that the strongest feature of Concord Baptist Church is the legacy of leadership established by its pastor for more than 40 years, the Rev. Gardner C. Taylor, who headed Concord from 1948 until his retirement in 1990.

Concord dates its beginning to 1848. It is a "megachurch," with more than 10,000 members. And since it has a large representation of working-class, middle-class, and upper-class members, the economic resources of this church are substantial.[6]

By 1986, the church already sponsored an extensive array of community outreach programs, and church-run operations covered an entire city block. Among these facilities and programs was an academic school, a 31-apartment senior citizens housing development, a 123-bed nursing home with an annual operating budget of 4.5 million dollars, a clothing exchange that provides free clothing to some 200 families in the community per month, a publishing house, a housing office purchasing substandard properties nearby and converting them into livable quarters, a credit union with assets of $1.5 million, and dozens of other programs.

Taylor persuaded the church to use its surplus income—income above that required for the operation of church programs—as an investment that would benefit the community. By 1986 the church had an investment portfolio of some $700,000.

The minister then asked the congregation to establish its own foundation and set a goal of $1 million to start this endowment. He asked members to support this goal without any outside help or fundraising campaigns. And in addition to tithing and regular offerings, he asked them to make an annual contribution to the church in memory of a deceased loved one. Through these means, the church had raised $1 million by January 1988.

Called the Concord Baptist Church Christ Fund, the endowment has been established as a separate subsidiary of the church. A deacon in the church, Henry S. Snead, serves as chair of the board of directors, which includes church members and nonchurch members. The annual income from this endowment is used to support a wide range of community programs in addition to the ones conducted, owned, and operated by the church itself. In 1988, the first year of operations, the fund earned and distributed $64,000 to various community groups. These annual contributions were $78,000 in 1989, $66,000 in 1990, $56,000 in 1991, and $56,000 in 1992.[7]

In launching the Christ Fund in 1988, the Rev. Taylor clearly saw it as an example that would be followed by other churches. He said: "We believe that this endowment fund concept will be emulated by Black congregations in all our great urban communities as one means of rescuing ourselves."[8] He also hoped that the wider New York community would take note and applaud this example of black self-help.

We note with regret that the establishment of an independent endowment fund by an independent black church was not seen as newsworthy or praiseworthy by the larger society. The church made this discovery as it publicly unveiled the existence and aims of this fund.

March 20, 1988, was clearly a banner headline day at Concord Church and in its Brooklyn neighborhood and elsewhere. The Rev. Gardner Taylor presided at the ceremony. Vernon Jordan, former executive of the National Urban League, was the keynote speaker. Franklin Thomas, president of the Ford Foundation and a former member of the Boy Scouts troop at Concord Church, was an invited guest. (The Ford Foundation made a generous gift to the endowment, once the members had reached their $1 million goal.)

The church was filled to capacity. The choirs were at their best. The ushers strutted to and fro. Eager to spread the word about such a positive development, the church had sent out news releases to all the media of New York City, which has been called the largest media market in the world. The ushers reserved a large space for reporters. Alas, of all the nonblack city news media, only the *New York Newsday*, a local newspaper, covered this event. No television stations responded. One observer remarked that if the pastor had been accused of stealing $1 million of church funds the news media would certainly have shown more interest.

When the Rev. Gary V. Simpson, then the associate minister of the church, was asked how was it possible for the church to do so much, he said, "Two things. First we do it because Reverend Taylor inspires us to do it. Every one of these programs you have seen was first an item in one of Dr. Taylor's sermons. The second factor is this: Most of our members are tithers. And with more than 10,000 members, most of whom are employed, that gives us the resources to do the work which Dr. Taylor inspires us to do."

Since then the Rev. Simpson has succeeded Taylor as pastor, and he is carrying on this work.

Abyssinian Baptist Church, Harlem

Abyssinian Baptist's 2,000-seat sanctuary at 129th Street is still among the largest and most beautiful sanctuaries in black America. Founded in the early 18th century by immigrants from Ethiopia, the church was first located in lower Manhattan. Abyssinian Baptist Church moved to its Harlem location after the turn of the century under the able, inspired, and dynamic leadership of the first Rev. Adam Clayton Powell, father to the former congressman by the same name.

Congressman Powell was succeeded as pastor of Abyssinian by the late Rev. Dr. Samuel Proctor. Proctor had served with distinction as president of Virginia Union University, president of North Carolina Agricultural and Technical State University, associate director of the U.S. Peace Corps, and, as Martin Luther King Jr., distinguished professor of education at Rutgers University, before coming to this church.

When Proctor retired as pastor of Abyssinian he was succeeded by the young Rev. Calvin Butts, who had been associate minister under both Powell and Proctor.

Butts is an outstanding preacher and leader. A graduate of Morehouse College in Atlanta, with seminary training, he has taken the church back into the local political arena in ways that Powell did, but Proctor did not.

Under the inspiration and leadership of Dr. Samuel Proctor, the church launched a program to meet the housing needs of the neighborhood.

By 1987, with the Rev. Butts at the helm, the time had come for putting the housing programs of the church into a more stable and comprehensive framework. Butts has said that he envisioned the development corporation "as a vehicle to become actively involved in the physical as well as the spiritual redevelopment of Harlem on a continuing basis."[9]

The results of this new community development initiative has already been impressive. Within its first five years of operation the Abyssinian Development Corporation could point to substantial improvements in two targeted neighborhoods near the church. Five development projects produced a total of 260 units of housing, and new units have been developed since that time.

The first project of the development corporation was a $9 million, 100-unit apartment building for the elderly, called The Abyssinian Towers. Funded in 1987, the project was completed in November 1990. The towers are managed by a local property management firm, which reports to the board of the Abyssinian Housing and Development Finance Corporation.

While the Abyssinian Development Corporation may serve as a model for other black churches, Karen Phillips, executive director of the program, says there are also some cautions and lessons that should be learned from this experience.

First, this community development program required talented church members as volunteers and co-planners. Second, the program benefited from the availability of underused properties, which the city authorities were cooperative in helping the church acquire. Third, the commitment must be to meet not only the housing needs of a limited area, but the spiritual, social service, and commercial needs as well.

Allen A.M.E. Church, Queens

The Allen A.M.E. church has substantially improved the economic well-being of its surrounding community. The church dates its founding to the early 1830s. When we visited Allen A.M.E. in 1988, the dynamic young Rev. Floyd H. Flake was its minister. Flake had been elected to the U.S. Congress the year before, after 10 years as pastor of Allen, the first black congressman ever elected from the Queens borough of New York City.[10]

I asked Flake, during my visit in 1988, whether there was any conflict between the religious aspects of the church and the community outreach aspects. He responded, "Quite the contrary. You see, the two parts of the church mission reinforce each other. Some people come to the church precisely because of the community outreach programs. And some church members get involved in outreach programs because it is the church that is sponsoring them."

In a most impressive economic venture, the church has bought out a run-down one-block commercial district. Today, these storefronts house a travel agency, medical and legal professional offices, a barber shop, a restaurant, a drug store, a home-care agency, and a preschool. Income from these commercial enterprises is plowed back into the total outreach ministry of this church.

Today, Allen Church continues to set aside one-third of the $3 million it collects annually from its members for development projects. Flake has observed, "If our churches ever learn the power that they have, we can turn the urban communities of America around and have control of them."

By 1998, when he retired from Congress, membership in the church had exceeded 10,000, and the annual budget totaled $6.6 million. The church owned property valued at $50 million and provided employment for more than 1,500 people.

Three Gates in the West

In the western part of the nation, hundreds of black activist churches successfully combine their privatistic and communal functions. In California we have visited several of these churches. Here we will profile three of them, the First A.M.E. Church and the Second Baptist Church, both of Los Angeles, and Allen Temple Baptist Church of Oakland.

Among the other outstanding social activist churches in California are the West Angeles Church of God in Christ, under the leadership of Bishop Charles Blake, and the Homans United Methodist Church in

Los Angeles, led by the Rev. James Lawson, who was both a teacher and follower of Dr. Martin Luther King Jr.

First A.M.E. Church, Los Angeles

First A.M.E. is best known nationally for its extensive community outreach work.[11] In recognition for this work, the church was designated by President Bush as one of his 1,000 Points of Light in June 1990. The church received special attention for its work with gangs and for its community work during the aftermath of the Rodney King and Reginald Denny trials. After the destruction following the verdict in the Rodney King beating case, entertainer Barbra Streisand contributed $100,000 in cash to the First A.M.E. Church to help the church program to rebuild the city.[12] In January 1992, one of the church's members, the television talk show host, actor, and comedian Arsenio Hall, contributed a house worth $165,000 to the church, rescuing it from crack cocaine traffic. The church renovated the house and turned it into a youth center named for Hall's mother.[13] Former Mayor Tom Bradley is also a member of this church.

First A.M.E. is the oldest black church in Los Angeles. It was founded by a woman, Biddy Mason, in her home on Spring Street in 1872.[14]

The current minister of First A.M.E. Church in Los Angeles, the Rev. Cecil L. "Chip" Murray, is the 26th pastor of this historic church. He has served as pastor since 1977, already eclipsing the longevity of his 25 predecessors. Murray was born in the South and received his bachelor's degree from the historically black Florida Agriculture and Mechanical University and a doctor of religion degree from the School of Theology at Claremont College in California. Before entering the ministry, Murray had a distinguished military career. He served for 10 years in the U.S. Air Force, rising to the rank of captain. He served as a jet radar intercept officer and navigator. He was decorated for valor in 1958. He miraculously survived a plane crash in which his co-pilot was killed. He made a determination to give himself completely to the Lord's work. He subsequently entered seminary at Claremont College.

From his appointment in 1977 to 1995, the membership of the church grew from 300 to some 9,500. The membership is a broad cross section of working-class, middle-class, and upper-class black parishioners. Each Sunday about 4,000 people attend church, and about 25 new members join. The average age of the congregation has moved down considerably since Murray's pastorate and now ranges between 25 and 45.

One of the most impressive features about this membership is that of the 9,500 members some 4,000 of them are black men. When asked how he manages to have so many black men in his congregation, the Rev. Murray said, "Because I don't just ask them to come and listen to me preach. We put them to work." The church has an extensive array of task forces for work both within the church and within the community. Many of these task forces are of special appeal to men.

In 1986, the church paid off its mortgage and began a program of physical expansion. The gross valuation of its holdings rose from $1.5 million in 1977 to $13 million by 1991 and to $33 million by 1993. According to *Black Enterprise Magazine* the church launched some major new initiatives after the 1992 uprisings in Los Angeles.[15]

Church officials won a $1 million grant from the Walt Disney Co., which they used to create a Micro Loan Program to supply low-interest rate loans of $2,000 to $20,000 to minority entrepreneurs in the area. "We deal with people who won't qualify for a bank loan," explains Mark Whitlock, executive director of the program. "We don't mind if you have a couple of bad nicks on your credit. We don't mind if you're a brand-new business that has never received a business loan before. But we do mind late payments."

As part of making the loan, the church provides moral and practical support to the new enterprise. "Our membership base has some 300 attorneys, 200 CPAs and 700 business owners," Whitlock says. Each new entrepreneur is assigned a member from the church. Finally, "We suggest to the congregation that they do business with the company owner we just made a loan to.

"Ultimately, the church hopes to raise $10 million from corporations to fund as many as 1,000 businesses."

The church has retained Peggy Graham-Hill to head up this massive extension of its community work. After 10 years as a successful stockbroker, during which time she worked on several church acquisitions, she now works full time for the church (even though she is not a member). She has helped to organize six nonprofit corporations through which the church expresses its community development programs.

Clearly, First A.M.E Church is a city within a city. Its commitment to "moving beyond the walls" and humanizing the city is ambitious beyond measure.

Second Baptist Church, Los Angeles

A second gateway to the city of Los Angeles is the Second Baptist Church of Los Angeles, currently under the leadership of the Rev. William S. Epps. This church demonstrates that a church does not have to be huge in order to make a substantial impact on the lives of its parishioners and the surrounding community.[16]

The 1991 annual report of Second Baptist Church shows a membership of some 1,100 with an annual operating budget of $800,000. Within this budget the church supports the following:

- Canaan Housing Corporation: a nonprofit corporation that has taken the lead in the rehabilitation of two single-room-occupancy hotels in the Skid Row area of Los Angeles.
- Griffith Gardens: a garden apartment complex of 32 units for senior citizens
- Kilgore Manor: an apartment complex of 52 one-bedroom units for senior citizens and the handicapped.
- Second Baptist Credit Union: a full-service credit union for members and staff of Second Baptist Church and its auxiliary agencies.

The Canaan Housing Corporation grew out of comments that the Rev. Epps made to his congregation in the summer of 1988 about the need for permanent and affordable housing in the Skid Row area of Los Angeles. A special committee was formed to explore possible solutions.

The committee unanimously approved the concept of the church providing housing for the poor, and an in-depth feasibility study was undertaken. In March 1989, a church meeting was called to present to the congregation more information on the project. The congregation voted to proceed with the project.

In 1990 Canaan Housing Corporation was formed as a separate, nonprofit 501c (3) corporation, and it began renovations to the two single-room-occupancy hotels. The work was completed early in August 1991. Financial support for the hotels was provided by city, county, and federal agencies, as well as the church.

The church continues to build on the outstanding legacy of all its previous ministers and especially the 25-year leadership of the legendary Dr. Thomas Kilgore Jr., Epps's immediate predecessor. Kilgore, a distinguished educator and preacher, brought this church into community service in a major way.

Allen Temple Baptist Church, Oakland

Northern California is the home of a few churches that must be acknowledged among activist churches who are examples of wise use of economic principles. Glide Memorial U.M.C., pastored by the Rev. C.

Williams, is probably best known. But it is the acclaimed Allen Temple Baptist Church that we will focus on here.

Allen Temple Baptist Church in Oakland is led by father/son co-pastors, the Rev. J. Alfred Smith Sr., past president of the Progressive National Baptist Convention, and the Rev. J. Alfred Smith Jr. The church has two services on Sunday and much religious activity spread throughout the week. The music at services is enlivened by a nine-piece orchestra with Smith Jr. leading the saxophone section when he is not preaching. The congregation is a broad cross section of social classes and ages.

The church operates a 75-unit housing development for low-income and elderly citizens, and a 51-unit housing project. Additional programs include the Allen Temple Federal Credit Union with assets of more than $1 million, a Mini-Mart discount food center, and a Job Information Center for all unemployed persons. Moreover, under the Neighborhood Revitalization Programs the church owns 150 units of elderly housing, and a $1.5 million youth center.

In addition, the church has a long-range committee on economic development of the neighborhood and has purchased commercial property for economic development.[17]

Here we have a strong and resourceful church, led by two strong, highly educated, community-oriented ministers, which features both a dynamic worship program and an extensive community outreach program.

Three Gates in the North

The North is the home of some of the most inventive church-related economic development programs in the country. Here we look at three.

Zion Baptist Church, Philadelphia

One of the most innovative economic development programs created by an individual church in the North was the formation of the Zion Investment Corporation (ZIC), which grew out of investments from members of Zion Baptist Church in Philadelphia.

In 1962, the Rev. Leon Sullivan initiated a "10/36" plan in which 200 parishioners agreed to contribute $10 each month for 36 months to go into investment funds. The money contributed during the first 16 months would go into a nonprofit charitable trust, and its investment income would be used mainly for the education of children and to provide college scholarships for young people. But the money contributed during the final 20 months would be placed into an investment corporation to promote profit-making ventures, with each participant receiving one common share of stock in all of the 10/36 enterprises. By the end of the 1980s, membership in the 10/36 plan had expanded to more than 5,000 investors from about 400 black churches.

One of the first ventures launched by ZIC was the construction in 1965 of Zion Gardens, a $1 million garden apartment development, one of the first housing complexes developed and owned by black people in Philadelphia. By 1967, Zion Gardens was completely occupied with 400 families on the waiting list. The second major ZIC venture was the establishment in 1967 of Progress Plaza, a $1.7 million shopping center with 16 stores, 10 of them owned by blacks.

When the A & P food-store chain signed a $1 million, 20-year lease in Progress Plaza, it was the largest such agreement ever made with a black organization in this country. ZIC launched Progress Aerospace Enterprises, the first black-owned business in the aerospace industry in 1968, and opened Progress Garment Manufacturing Enterprises. Its purpose was to produce a steady supply of women's garments. The organization Opportunities Industrialization Centers (OIC) was founded by Zion Baptist Church in Philadelphia under the leadership of the Rev. Leon Sullivan in the early 1960s.

In 1964, OIC opened its first training center in an abandoned jail using outmoded equipment that was contributed by businesses. However, within five years, OIC had expanded to 70 cities as a result of a large infusion of funds from the federal government, foundations, and private industry. At its height in 1980, OIC operated in about 160 cities and several foreign countries and had trained close to 700,000 people. However, OIC and other community-based job-training programs have not yet recovered from the effects of the sharp budget cuts of the Reagan Administration during the 1980s.[18]

In the 1980s the Rev. Sullivan elevated his social reform to the international arena. As a board member of General Motors Corp., he pioneered a plan to urge American corporations to redirect their investments in South Africa in protest of apartheid. What became known as the Sullivan Principles were widely adopted by U.S. corporations. In the late 1980s, Sullivan retired as pastor of Zion and proceeded to devote himself to a number of national and international ventures.

I was present at Zion on the Sunday in 1991 when he returned as guest speaker. Though he was getting on in age and had suffered severe health problems, he electrified the congregation with descriptions of his newest undertaking. He has organized a dialogue between African American leaders and African leaders. The leaders have already met three times in different countries in Africa. One of the outcomes of that dialogue has been a program led by Sullivan to have massive numbers of African American educators at all levels go to African villages to assist with raising the level of education.

Hartford Memorial Baptist Church, Detroit

Another black church which has established a gateway to the city, through economic development programs, is the Hartford Memorial Baptist Church in Detroit under the leadership of the Rev. Charles Adams. A few years ago one of the deacons in the church noted that women who took their cars to the shop for repairs were often cheated by repairmen. This was especially common among single women, largely because they didn't know enough about cars to know exactly which parts were broken and roughly how much it should cost. So he started an informal course to teach these women about their cars. Over the years this program has evolved into a highly successful auto-repair school whose students get good jobs or start their own businesses.[19]

These programs are led by Adams, who is among the most learned and accomplished religious leaders in the nation, with degrees from Morehouse College and Harvard University.

Many of Hartford Memorial's projects are managed by Agape House, an independent nonprofit agency the church established in 1982 "to bring the spirit of social services and maximum involvement to the community."

The church leaders developed a comprehensive plan in 1985 to revitalize the local community. Ten years later, African American entrepreneurs at the church operated McDonald's and Kentucky Fried Chicken franchises, and in August 1993 they launched a $17 million, 80,000-square-foot shopping center that includes a supermarket, drugstore, and restaurant.

The church plans to build a 40,000-square-foot auto-care and commercial center, growing out of its pioneer program for women. Other plans include a multimillion-dollar housing project to be built on land the church bought for $500,000. This land has increased in value to more than $5 million.

As in most church-based economic development programs, the key to success is the vision and leadership abilities of the minister. "The church needs to concentrate on the business of creating economic institutions," declares the Rev. Adams. "The issue is jobs. People being laid off through all this corporate downsizing is affecting every black community in this country. The church finds itself in a situation where it is the best continuing, organized entity in the black community for the acquisition and redevelopment of land, the building of business enterprises and the employment of people."[20]

Certainly this one church cannot revitalize Detroit all by itself. But in 1996, when government and private studies began to report that Detroit's economic decline had been halted and the city had turned the corner toward economic viability, people who worship at or live near Hartford Memorial Baptist Church could feel a certain pride in knowing that this church had made a substantial contribution to that "miracle."

Olivet Institutional Baptist Church, Cleveland

Ebony magazine rated the Rev. T. Otis Moss among the 15 top black preachers in the nation in 1993. Moss, a Morehouse College graduate with seminary training and a former associate of Dr. Martin Luther King Jr., has become a national leader in social reform. But to see him in operation at Olivet Baptist Church is a marvel to behold. He presides with grace, administers the many programs of the church with finesse, counsels with empathy, and preaches like fire and brimstone. And the people love him.

At Olivet, the Rev. Moss practices a brand of ministry that honors the African American heritage, grounds itself in Christian doctrine, and extends itself into the community for leadership in secular affairs. From the artwork in the church to the teaching methods used, the African American heritage is in evidence.

He has been leader of this congregation since 1975.

By 1997 this church had grown to more than 3,000 members with an annual operating budget of $1.5 million, up from $1.3 million the year before and $1.2 million in 1995. This rate of growth suggested that the church would have very little difficulty meeting its projected budgets of $1.7 million, $2 million, and $2.2 million for the years 1998, 1999, and 2,000. The dual mission of the church as a spiritual and a social resource for the community is in clear evidence through its 40-plus separate ministries. Assisted now by two full-time Associate ministers and one part-time, Rev. Moss continued to set forth a vision of service before his congregation and the wider Cleveland community.[21]

Saturday, November 15, 1997, was a red letter day in the life of the church and the community. On this date the Otis Moss Jr.–University Hospitals Medical Center was dedicated. Heading the list of dignitaries at this ceremony was Cleveland Mayor, Michael R. White, Congressman Louis Stokes, guest speaker Andrew Young, university officials and church officials and officers of the Cleveland Foundation, all of whom had been instrumental in putting together this Health care facility dedicated to "excellence in patient care and education in spiritually supportive environment."

The medical center is a partnership between Olivet Institutional Baptist Church and the University Hospitals of Cleveland affiliated with Western Reserve University. It specializes in high quality pediatric, teen, and adult medical care, offering a full range of women's health care, including obstetrics and gynecology, as well as adult and pediatric health screenings and preventive care including childhood and adult immunizations. This venture in church and community collaboration at all levels offers a possible model for other communities, whose black populations are in dire need of improved health care. The medical center is housed in a three-story building comprising 15,000 square feet. Rev. Moss says that the church insisted on a thoroughly modern facility that is never referred to as a "clinic" because of the negative connotation of this word in the black community. The church owns the land which it acquired over time for $100,000. The University Hospitals constructed the building at a cost of $1.5 million. The staff is predominantly black yet distinctly interracial.

The genesis of this facility dates back to 1975. In that year, Rev. Moss led the church in establishing the Olivet Housing Corporation. By 1982, the pastor was ready with another vision. He proposed at the annual meeting of the church "that we endeavor to build a Medical Center and develop in our community, A Center of Excellence for the private practice of medicine."

By 1985, when the church sponsored a national conference on the African American family, the medical center concept was a major focus of that conference. Developing and maintaining healthy families has been a constant theme in the outreach ministries of the church. Rev. Moss negotiated a memorandum of understanding with the University Hospitals, which continues to guide the medical center operation.

Situated within the hospital is the Olivet Health and Education Institute, pursuing a program of prevention, education, and referral. Headed by Rev. Mark C. Olds as administrative director, with Dr. Daisy Alford-Smith serving as associate director for education and research, with the Rev. Dr. Margaret Mitchell as associate director for supportive care and Terrikay Davis as administrative assistant, Rev. Moss is chair of the board of directors for the Institute. The mission of the Institute is "to promote individual, family and community health, healing and wholeness in a spiritually supportive environment." A hard-won assortment of church, city, private, and state and federal funds made possible the realization of the dream set forth by Rev. Moss more than two decades earlier. It is a monument to bold vision, careful planning, financial sacrifice of members, and expert political collaboration at all levels. And although it may be difficult to duplicate this facility in today's political and racial climate, it stands as an outstanding example for other communities around the nation. For program planning in the years ahead, the church has acquired a half million dollar federal HUD grant with the assistance of Congressman Stokes and a $300,000 planning grant from the Cleveland Foundation. The medical center includes a prayer chapel and a recognition by the entire medical and health education and research team that spirituality can be a major ingredient of healthy life styles and the physical healing practices.

Three Gates in the South

The three churches we profile in the South as gates to the city because of new economic development programs are Third Shiloh Missionary Baptist Church in New Orleans, under the leadership of Rev. Herman C. Forte, Wheat Street Baptist Church in Atlanta, under the leadership of the Rev. Michael Harris, and Canaan Missionary Baptist Church in Louisville, Kentucky, under the leadership of the Rev. Dr. Walter Malone Jr.

Third Shiloh Missionary Baptist Church, New Orleans

It would be difficult to find a more prophetic gate to the city of New Orleans than the 30-year-old, 200-member Third Shiloh Missionary Baptist Church, under the leadership of the Rev. Herman C. Forte. Several other black churches in this city are blazing trails in social reform, but, clearly, Third Shiloh is in a leadership position among them.[22]

The smallest of 15 Baptist churches in the neighborhood, Third Shiloh, on Piety Street in New Orleans, is a block away from Desire, a 97-acre public housing project that 8,000 low-income people call home.

The neighborhood became overrun with drugs about five years ago, when crack dealers set up shop in two abandoned houses across the street from the church.

One day burglars tore off the front doors of the church, stole typewriters, air conditioners, and the public address system. Church officials called the police to no avail. The third time the church was broken into, the thieves got so comfortable that they stayed to take a nap. Soon the church found itself facing higher insurance rates.

The drug traffic "hurt us financially as well as spiritually," said Benjamin Edwards Sr., then chairman of the church deacon board.

Many members and a few officers felt it was time to move. After all, the church had been saving for 20 years to build a new church. It had accumulated a building fund of $35,000. But Deacon Edwards, a successful businessman, had grown up in the nearby project and in this church, and he had a better idea. He persuaded the board to use its building fund to purchase the crack houses across the street and transform them into low-income housing.

So in April 1988 the church agreed to pay $35,000 for the two crack houses and five other houses nearby. The 20-year-old dream of a new church building was put on hold. Now when they called the police to evict the drug dealers from their property, police responded promptly. Then church members marched out the front door, across the street, and went to work. They tackled the old crack houses, clearing out five truckloads of trash from the weeds around them. They boarded up windows and threw out syringes. And in a community with a 61 percent unemployment rate, the church got lots of volunteer help, but hired neighborhood youths to help as well.

This time the government made an investment in the community. The church received federal funds of $61,000 as a share of the $150,341 renovation cost. The government would also subsidize the monthly rental cost of $300 to $400 for each unit.

This project became a family affair. When the researchers went to visit this church, they found Benjamin Edwards Sr., chair of the deacon board, heading up the work crew. One son, Benjamin Jr., who has since replaced his father as chair of the deacon board, was a head foreman on the work crew. Another son was the carpenter. Mrs. Edwards led the crew making and selling dinners to raise money for the project. Some of her other 13 children, all raised in this community, would also come back to volunteer their services.

The church funnels much of the income it receives from the rental units into outreach programs. One fund supports a tutoring program for neighborhood children. Another supports a scholarship fund so neighborhood children can go to college. A third portion of the profits is set aside in a building fund to start saving all over again to build a new church.

When the researchers visited this church in the spring of 1993, they saw a whole neighborhood undergoing transformation because one church had dared to step out on faith and invest its building fund, its heart, and its soul in its community.

The Rev. Herman C. Forte and Deacon Benjamin L. Edwards Sr. wrote to me shortly after a field visit to update me on the status of their "Community Revitalization Housing Project," which had by then been in operation for some six years. The letter said, in part:

The Mission of Third Shiloh "Community Revitalization Project," simply put is to stimulate economic development in the Desire area through the reduction of crime and community fears, the provision of job opportunities, and decent, affordable housing.

Third Shiloh accomplishes this mission through purchasing and renovating abandoned "crack houses" and providing on-the-job training in the construction trade for community residents. Third Shiloh contributed seed money which eventually totaled $175,000 of its own funds.

During its first five years under this project Third Shiloh accomplished the following:

- Eleven (11) abandoned houses were purchased for $53,000.00 which now have a fair market value of $550,000.00.
- Nine (9) crack houses were eliminated, thereby decreasing the sale of drugs and crime in the neighborhood.
- Fifty-three (53) community residents were provided with decent, affordable housing.
- Forty-three (43) community residents were given on-the-job training in electrical, plumbing and mechanical fields, accounting for a hefty 39% of project expenditures.
- Thirteen (13) other homes were assisted in qualifying for HUD's homeowner rehabilitation programs, providing an additional $220,000.00 for renovation in this area.
- Eleven (11) more homes were targeted to receive HUD grants in 1993.
- Third Shiloh scheduled four (4) additional crack houses for renovation beginning in January, 1993, thus increasing the fair market value upon completion from $38,000.00 to approximately $180,000.00

Inspired and assisted by the Church

- Twelve (12) additional homeowners undertook property renovations which resulted in approximately $160,000.00 of increased fair market value.
- Fear has decreased, [and] community residents are again attending night services.
- Long-term employment opportunities are now available for 43 formerly unskilled, unemployed community residents.

Additionally, once the 40 apartment units for elderly housing are completed, safe, decent, affordable housing will also be available for elderly and handicapped individuals. Thus, one hundred, seventy-five thousand dollars ($175,000.00) seed money invested by the church resulted in $917,000.00 of increased value to community residents in salaries and housing improvement.

The letter concluded: "Perhaps, the most encouraging thing about our Community Revitalization Housing Project is that it helps the people in the Desire community to help themselves."[23]

What a remarkable set of achievements for one relatively small church over six short years. It is almost breathtaking. Of course, the church did not do all this alone. But, just as clearly, if the church had not taken the initiative, none of this community revitalization would have been accomplished. Moreover, inspired by this example, the federal and local governments made a major commitment to the reclamation and revitalization of this public housing project, which had been long neglected and the people virtually abandoned.

Wheat Street Baptist Church, Atlanta

In the area of economic development, Wheat Street Baptist Church in Atlanta is in a class by itself. It is the grandparent of all black church economic development. It has been doing it longer than most churches and has a more extensive array and volume of economic initiatives than most other churches.[24]

The minister at Wheat Street Baptist Church in Atlanta, the Rev. Michael Harris, stated the guiding philosophy of the church's economic development program: "Before we can think in terms of heaven by and by, we've got to live here on earth. And Wheat Street, through its economic development projects, wants to make sure life on earth is as good as it can be."

So, with the help of his partner and business manager, Eugene Jackson, Harris and Wheat Street Church are changing the face of their Atlanta neighborhood.

The church's nonprofit corporation, the Wheat Street Charitable Foundation, owns and manages two housing developments, several single-family dwellings, and an office building. The foundation also owns Wheat Street Plaza North and South, two shopping centers in the heart of the Martin Luther King Jr. historic district. They were built in 1969 on land purchased with church money and bank loans and are currently getting a $120,000 facelift, thanks to an interest-free loan from the city of Atlanta.

Indeed, building on the legacy left by the legendary William Holmes Borders, longtime pastor, the church now has some $33 million in real estate holdings, making it one of the wealthiest black churches in the nation.[25]

The centerpiece of Wheat Street's economic development program is its federally chartered credit union, one of the first in a church in the nation. It was organized March 7, 1956, under the pastorate of the Rev. Dr. William Holmes Borders Sr. Harris explains: "The credit union was born one night after a church meeting when the pastor engaged nine members to contribute $5 each to the effort. For the next few Sundays following this meeting, the sermons at Wheat Street Baptist Church became a strange mixture of Gospel passages dealing with stewardship and the practical knowledge of the difference between simple and compound interest." These same ideas encouraged new workers of the Bronner Brothers establishment to join the credit union. Indeed, the large and highly successful Bronner Brothers Cosmetic enterprises grew directly out of this church.

During his time, Borders was asked if he believed that a church could conduct a business and remain Christian in character. He is said to have responded, "In my judgment, education, economic opportunity, and the vote are of equal importance. These gains must be harmonized with religion, with the love of man for his fellows, and his obedience to God."[26]

Canaan Missionary Baptist Church, Louisville, Kentucky

In the Upper South city of Louisville, Kentucky, the Canaan Missionary Baptist Church is making a noticeable difference in the life of the city through its community development programs. At the center of this innovative cluster of housing, business, job preparation, educational, and cultural enterprises is pastor of the church, the Rev. Dr. Walter Malone Jr.

Malone studied at Fisk University, American Baptist College, and Southern Baptist Theological Seminary in Louisville, where he received as master's degree in religious studies. In 1983 he had become the founding pastor of Canaan Missionary Baptist Church. Over the next 13 years the church grew from fewer than 100 members to more than 2,000, which Malone attributes to the church's outreach in the community. When Malone decided that the church should move more vigorously into community reform efforts, he took steps to prepare himself for leadership in this endeavor. He enrolled at United Theological Seminary in Cleveland, under the joint tutelage of two of the nation's leading social reform preachers, Dr. Samuel D. Proctor and Dr. Otis Moss Jr. His dissertation for his doctor of ministry degree was on economic development. It would be published in book form under the title *From Holy Power to Holy Profits*. Armed with this new knowledge, Dr. Malone returned to Canaan Church and injected new vigor into its long-standing outreach programs to the community. In a few years he became nationally recognized as a specialist on the mission of the black church in changing the conditions in the surrounding community.

"We believe that our churches have an obligation to do some things that will strengthen the economic standing of the black community," he told a researcher. "There are some things that black people have to do for themselves, or they will never be done."[27]

Malone's economic philosophy is reminiscent of that of Gardner C. Taylor: "We're not just going out asking for grants or for private persons to give us something for one thing or another. We're builders, not beggars. We want to have capital in the bank. Then when we sit down at the table, we want to be able to speak of what we are doing for ourselves."

In 1992, Dr. Malone persuaded his congregation members to each donate $5 per week to the economic development program. And, in usual Baptist church tradition, the $5 was a general target, with those able to give more encouraged to do so, and those able to do less made to feel they were valuable participants as well.

In addition to his strong belief in self-help, Dr. Malone believes in leadership by teamwork. He recognizes that he cannot do everything himself. He has developed and inspired a small cadre of leaders to work with him, the church, and the community. He recruited as his right-hand man an experienced manager in private industry with a degree in engineering, Robert Eugene McCormick, in 1992. McCormick's initial major mission was the empowerment of people in the community beyond the church to maximize their human potential. He also is chairman of the board of the Christian education program. Dr. Malone also recruited another highly experienced executive from private industry, Sandra Calvin, to be executive director of the church's community development corporation. Calvin has a degree in business administration and experience in private and government affairs. A longtime member of the church, she is also a Sunday school teacher. A third member of the leadership team is the youth minister, the Rev. Bobby Hugely, who had a budget in 1997–98 of $6,000 to direct the large and expanding Rites of Passage program for young men and young women.

The outreach mission of the church is well organized, coordinated, and led, and is supported by the church members. The major structures for outreach are the Family Life Center and the community development corporation.

The Community Development Corporation, a nonprofit entity separate from the church, has in place a number of programs. These include the Computer Literacy and Education program, Employment

Empowering program, Housing program, Performing Arts Center, and Child Development Center. The corporation's major goal is to foster economic, housing, and social empowerment in economically deprived communities. It does so by providing education and training for adults, designing and developing private business enterprises, promoting entrepreneurial and housing initiatives, and providing training and cultural programs. The theme of the corporation is "Lifting Others as We Lift Ourselves."

The Computer Literacy program is operated by Michelle Jones, the director, and has an annual budget of $60,000, which comes from church general funds. The program provides market-demand training to meet the needs of most employers. More than 250 persons have participated in this program.

The Employment Empowering program is operated by Joe Lee Phillips and Gene Bankston, director. It had a budget in 1997–98 of $10,000, which also comes from church general funds. The hands-on program is conducted in cooperation with area employers. It also focuses on self-employment. "We believe that ownership is a very important aspect of economic empowerment. Owning business and properties becomes a must for leveraging talent and resources for economic gains and growth," Phillips stated.

The Performing Arts program, under the direction of Sandra Lafayette, operates a full-scale dance training program from elementary school through high school grades. It has ambitions of becoming the outstanding training and performing resource in the city for disadvantaged but talented youth. Its 1997–98 budget of $105,000 was raised from enrollment fees. Lafayette has performed with the American Ballet Theater of New York, the Alvin Ailey Dance Workshop, and several other professional groups.

The Child Development Center had a 1997–98 budget of $159,900, which came from enrollment fees, supplemented by church funds. Providing a comprehensive early childhood development curriculum, the center places strong emphasis on reading, math, language skills, and cultural awareness, as well as mental, social, and physical development of the children. Parents are strongly urged to become a part of the leadership team. The 50 or so children in the program range in age from 18 months to five years.

The signature program of the Community Development Corporation is its affordable housing for low- and moderate-income families. Begun in June 1994, the CDC established collaboration with a local bank, a building corporation, an architectural firm, and others to launch a home-building program in the Russell area of the city.

The Louisville Housing and Urban Development Agency has made large tracts of land available on the west corridor of 15th Street, near Chestnut and Broadway, in the midst of this historic African American neighborhood, which once was a network of successful businesses, institutes, and housing.

At the time of our visit in 1997, three houses had been completed—beautiful, two-story, three-bedroom homes with one and one-half baths. The homes are priced from $63,000, with generous financing terms provided by cooperating banks. Five more houses are in the process of construction. The aim is to eventually build a whole community of modern affordable housing.

The Canaan Family Life Center is the other major umbrella agency for community outreach programs. The philosophy guiding this center, the director said, is "Through practical ministries, enrichment seminars, and other wholesome activities that address the spiritual, mental, social, emotional, and physical needs of people, we seek to strengthen and set at liberty those that are bruised by destructive forces that hold them captive in this world."

The center is modeled closely on the pioneering church-based Family Life Center at Shiloh Baptist Church in Washington, D.C. Its largest and oldest program is the family recreation center, which offers activities for all ages and for groups. Another program is the Imani Fellowship program, geared toward but not restricted to children of single-parent families. The focus is on building self-esteem, physical growth, educational achievement, and cultural awareness, and "to foster a sense of responsibility in the home and community." Another is the drama ministry, which seeks through this medium to bring out the creativity, self-expression, and self-confidence of young people. Still another is the library ministry, which aims to encourage reading, studying, and listening. The large, well-stocked library is used frequently by members and visitors.

The signature program of the Canaan Family Life Center has become the new, large, expanding, and highly successful Rites of Passage, an intense 10-month program of instruction, attitude, and skill development.

Under the direction of the youth minister, the Rev. Bobby Hugely, the Rites of Passage program has more than 500 participants from ages three to 17 in an intensive, 10-month program of instruction and preparation for adulthood. Like a similar program at the Trinity United Church of Christ in Chicago, this program is frankly inspired by the Jewish cultural program. The Rev. Hugely has stated as a sort of preamble to this program as follows:

The Jewish community has strengthened and given direction to the lives of their youth through what is known as rites of passage. When a Jewish child reaches the age of 13, the family has a ceremony known as "Bar Mitzvah" for boys and "Bat Mitzvah" for girls. The immediate family and the extended family come together and declare that the child has moved into young adulthood with more responsibilities. In the context of this rite of passage, the Jewish child is taught their history and faith. These two aspects of learning enable the child to move from one age level to the next with a sense of discipline, maturity, and values.

He also gives credit to Alex Haley for introducing him to the rites-of-passage concept in his book *Roots*.

At Canaan, the Rites of Passage program communicates its goals through the acronym A.L.I.V.E., for Affirming, Leadership, Integrity, Virtue, and Excellence. The program helps young people to prepare themselves physically, socially, emotionally, intellectually, and culturally for passage into manhood and womanhood.

Major activities are focused around education, community service, entrepreneurial initiatives, personal development, cultural awareness, and career development. Extensive field trips accompany the church-based activities. Parents are urged to participate in the Parent Action Council. The youth meet all morning Saturdays twice a month at the church. Other activities are scheduled throughout the year. The director and 35 adult volunteers help the youths make connections with various community agencies and institutions.

Rural Economic Development

Though economic development is most often played out in urban contexts, its principles can, under special conditions, apply in rural areas as well.

The nondenominational Mendenhall Bible Church, formed in the early 1970s in Mendenhall, Mississippi, is an outstanding example. The Rev. Dorcus Weary and other church leaders knew that if they didn't provide jobs for their members, nobody would. So, they created Mendenhall Ministries, a nonprofit corporation, and built a business complex that today includes a health clinic, law office, elementary school, thrift store, and recreation center. The projects were funded by private and public grants and a few bank loans.[28]

Another example is Greater Christ Temple Church in Meridian, Mississippi. Bishop Luke Edwards founded the Pentecostal church in

1974 with 35 members, 96 percent of whom were on welfare. He got them to pool their food stamps and buy wholesale. Four months later, church members were selling food to community members out of a makeshift grocery store set up in the church auditorium.

Four years later they were able to purchase a supermarket, which they ran for several years, then sold. Today, under its REACH Inc. (Research Education and Community Hope) nonprofit corporation, Greater Christ Temple owns three restaurants, a bakery, an auto-repair shop, and a 4,000-acre farm with 700 head of cattle and two meat processing plants.

Now the church has 200 members who have "delivered themselves from welfare by pooling their resources," says Edwards. "Being black, it's very difficult to get loans. We realized we had to turn to one another. We just had to work together."[29]

In a survey conducted in South Carolina during 1997 by the University of South Carolina Institute for Families in Society, through its Neighbors Helping Neighbors program, a predominantly black group of ministers in three rural counties evidenced strong concern for social problems in the community and a willingness to undertake community programs if money and technical assistance were available. The group identified major social problems in these countries to include drug abuse, teen pregnancy, unemployment, lack of after-school resources, and racism, then was asked about church engagement in community programs. Altogether 12 of these churches currently operate child development programs open to the community. At the same time a majority of 66 indicated that they would offer such programs if they had the necessary money and technical help. A similar pattern of responses was found with respect to after-school programs, drug and alcohol education, and tutorial and literacy programs. Thus in some rural areas, the church remains a major potential resource for leadership in the development of community programs.

The Church as a Power Base

We have seen that in all the four regions of the country—East, West, North, and South—black churches of various denominations and sizes have successfully launched programs of economic development to benefit their local communities. Building homes, schools, credit unions, small business enterprises, and other institutions, they have made a difference in their communities.

While most of these developments are launched by individual

churches, some of the most successful ventures have been those in which churches pooled their resources.

Clearly, such efforts would increase significantly if the clergy and church lay leadership were provided with the appropriate training in finance and business management in seminary or afterward.

We are persuaded by the writing of the urbanologist Jane Jacobs, who wrote passionately during the 1960s, that the way to build strong cities is to build strong neighborhoods. We add to her views the proposition that the key to building strong African American neighborhoods is the strong black activist church.

According to Wyatt Tee Walker, minister of Canaan Baptist Church in New York City, the black church is an institution of primary influence in the African American community in large part because it is a citadel of faith, a self-help economic force, a political power base, an employment service, a vehicle for cultural expression, and a reservoir for leadership.

13

—‧‧‧—

Unashamedly Black
and Unapologetically Christian

Visitors to the Trinity United Church of Christ in Chicago for the first time are likely to be struck by the appearance of a beautiful oil painting that hangs in the vestibule. It is an image of a family—husband, wife, and two children—with an image of Jesus hovering over them. All of the subjects of the painting are black. The sign underneath the printing reads, "We Are Unashamedly Black and Unapologetically Christian."

The painting, the slogan, and their prominent placement in the church suggests that this church has boldly confronted one of the four major challenges confronting the church today, namely, how to be authentically black and authentically Christian at the same time.

The challenge is how to move resolutely into recognition, celebration, teaching, and learning of the African American cultural heritage while maintaining and expanding the understanding and practice of the concepts of Christianity that have made the black church the strong institution it is today.

More than one aspiring young black Christian has been prompted to ask:"Reverend, if we are made in the image of God, and if Jesus Christ is the son of God, why is it that all the pictures of Jesus in our church show him as a white man?"

A second challenge is how to move the church resolutely into the community, confronting the major social, economic, and political problems, while maintaining and strengthening its primary spiritual mission. The Rev. Harris Travis of the historic Zion Baptist Church in Marietta, Georgia, put the matter this way: "You see, Doc," he said, "the black church has two missions: a spiritual mission and a social mission. We do fairly well by our spiritual mission. I believe we are called now to expand our social mission." For this minister and this church the social mission requires establishing programs with youth in the community and with the elderly, even though they may not be members of the church.

The third challenge is as contemporary as the morning news, and as ancient as the church itself. How can the black church move resolutely into the acceptance of women as fully equal to men with all the rights and obligations of church stewardship, including the highest offices available? The issue is not, of course, whether every black church should be required to have a black woman pastor. It is that black woman preachers should have equal access to the pulpit.

How can a church pursue effectively the first three objectives while maintaining its institutional viability? More simply put, how can the church expand its role without the minister getting fired, or the church splitting up, or the building fund efforts failing? That is the fourth challenge and the most taxing of all. More than one minister has lost his or her pulpit, and more than one church has lost its vitality because a schism developed while in the midst of coping with a crisis.

As difficult as these challenges are, the future of the black church depends heavily on their resolution. The good news is that a number of churches are grappling effectively with these four issues. Preeminent among them is Trinity United Church of Christ in Chicago, under the leadership of the Rev. Jeremiah A. Wright Jr.

Since 1970 Trinity United has vigorously confronted each of the four major challenges stated above. And for the most part the church has been amazingly successful. The vitality of this church, once exceedingly precarious, is now distinctly robust. With more than 6,000 members already overflowing their beautiful new building in 1997, Trinity has long since become the largest congregation in the United Church of Christ denomination, black or white.

Trinity United Church of Christ is relatively new, as far as black churches go. Founded in 1961, formed from several existing small black congregations, it grew steadily over the next five years under the leadership of a recent seminary graduate, the Rev. Kenneth B. Smith, to about 200 members. Dr. Smith left to take a position with the Community Renewal Society of Chicago and eventually became president of Chicago Theological Seminary. When we interviewed Dr. Smith at the seminary in 1990 in connection with this study, he pointed with pride to Trinity, not, he hastened to add, because of developments during his five years but because of the extraordinary developments since that time under the dynamic leadership of the Rev. Wright.

After the assassination of Dr. Martin Luther King Jr. in April 1968, the congregation quickly dwindled to only 87 members. Many sought to abandon what they considered a "white-oriented" church.

In a sense, this small group of members at Trinity constituted a basic core, pregnant with potential for revival. They performed as such. Determined to establish a beachhead in the new black consciousness movement, the Pulpit Committee, under the leadership of Vallmer E. Jordan, drew up a statement of purpose for the church. That statement was original and contemporary, in the sense that it departed from the traditional and historic creed of the white United Church of Christ. It was at the same time respectful of those traditions and definitely Christian in its context. They hoped that it would guide them in selecting a new minister and would guide the new minister in building up a strong, black-oriented congregation. Their three-paragraph statement of purpose was shown to each of the candidates for pastor of the church in 1971 and early 1972. Each was asked if he would feel able to lead the congregation in the direction of that statement. The statement of purpose read, in part:

> To become an assembly of the faithful involved in a dynamic modern ministry that minimizes dogma and maximizes love . . . To support a minister that operates on the creative edge of individual growth and personality development through teaching and informing and guiding . . .
> [T]o serve as instruments of God and church in our eliminating those things in our culture that lead to the dehumanization of persons and tend to perpetuate their psychological enslavement.[1]

The Rev. Wright gave an affirmative and persuasive response to this conception of Christian ministry. He was elected pastor.

A Black Value System

Then, after 10 years of working together, the next step for the pastor and the congregation was the adoption in 1980 of an explicitly black value system.

The following 10 elements of a black value system were adopted by the congregation with the admonition, "These Black Ethics must be taught and demonstrated in homes, churches, nurseries and schools wherever Blacks are gathered":

1. Commitment to God
2. Commitment to the Black Community
3. Commitment to the Black Family
4. Dedication to the Pursuit of Education
5. Dedication to the Pursuit of Excellence
6. Adherence to the Black Work Ethic
7. Commitment to Self-Discipline and Self-Respect
8. Disavowal of the Pursuit of Middle-classness
9. Pledges of Community Spirit
10. Personal Commitment to the Black Value System

Each principle was elaborated in this document, which was read and discussed by the congregation in large and small groups.[2]

By 1986, Trinity was ready to take another giant step toward becoming a truly black church. In that same year, under the inspired and intellectually advanced leadership of the pastor, the church adopted a new creed to express the already well-developed program of worship, study, and service.

The creed states "We Are Unashamedly Black and Unapologetically Christian." It and the painting that appears above it at Trinity United have become nationwide symbols of the movement toward a truly black Christian church.

The painting and a booklet describing it, produced and distributed by the church, sets the tone of what the church is about. First it contains an introductory statement from the pastor.

Following in the tradition of the millions of blacks who were Christian long before the African Slave Trade began . . . Following in the Biblical tradition of Africans who were called and claimed by the Christ centuries before there was a "Christendom" headquartered in Rome . . .

Following in the footsteps of those who were neither ashamed of their color or their Christ (Sojourner Truth, Martin Delaney, Harriet Tubman, Henry McNeil Turner, Ida B. Wells, Richard Allen, Jarena Lee, George Leile, and Martin Luther King) . . .

The members of this congregation have affirmed who they are and Whose they are by declaring and vowing to live out a creed that says we are . . . "UNASHAMEDLY BLACK AND UNAPOLOGETICALLY CHRISTIAN!"

Then there is a statement from the artist, Joseph W. Evans. He describes his painting in unusual detail:

The composition is a triangle (the Trinity) with three horizontal arcs superimposed. The upper arc is light; it will overcome the vertical arc that represents the conflict descending on South Africa. The center arc is the family, and CHRIST is painted as the fifth member of the family. The bottom arc is our heritage, extending from Africa into this country.

Members of the family have differing complexions, representing the rainbow that is the Black race. They are the rainbow, the promise of our future. They look the viewer in the eye, unashamedly . . . unapologetically.[3]

The Eight Elements of a Dynamic Black Worship Program

What is most responsible for the viability and growth of this church and enriches and builds upon its dual Christian and African American heritage is a dynamic worship program.[4]

We have identified eight specific elements of a dynamic black worship program. Each of these elements makes a contribution to the challenges and goals set forth above. What makes the worship program at Trinity so dynamic is that it features all these elements. And the basic goals and challenges of the church are reflected in the worship program. These eight elements are:

1. Bringing the Message
2. Making a Joyful Noise
3. Experiencing the Holy Ghost
4. Spirited Prayer Life
5. Engaging Christian Education
6. Faithful Set of Auxiliaries, Especially Usher Boards
7. Sustained Pattern of Financial Giving
8. Expanding Program of Benevolence

Bringing the Message

The most important element in a dynamic black worship program is great preaching on the part of the pastor. Preaching to a black Christian congregation must be based at least in part on the Bible. It must tell stories that touch the everyday lives of the people. It must be filled with lessons to live by and with a spirit of optimism. And it must be delivered in a manner that stirs the intellect as well as the emotions.

The Rev. Jeremiah A. Wright ranked no. 2 in *Ebony Magazine's* list of the 15 greatest black preachers. It may be said that he comes by this gift honestly: His father and mother were outstanding preachers.

Ebony writes of the Rev. Wright:

"Wright, 52 . . . represents," one respondent said, "the first of a new generation of African American preachers who blend Pentecostal flavor with social concerns in their pulpit discourse." A fellow preacher said, "He gives a contemporary, African-American, Afrocentric flavor to the traditional Black shout." A religious scholar said, "A Wright sermon is a four-course meal: Spiritual, biblical, cultural, prophetic."[5]

Though he has three associate ministers, including one woman as chief deputy, the Rev. Barbara Allen, Dr. Wright does most of the preaching. In 1990 he preached 106 sermons in his church and 142 sermons in other churches around the nation.

He is also an active teacher. In 1990, he taught a course for deacons in training, a seminar for ministers in training, a regular weekly class on spirituality, plus a monthly series on Afrocentricity and Christocentricity.

In this regard, Wright had been the mentor to numerous budding young preachers. By 1986 he had groomed some 13 "sons and daughters" in the ministry, with some 17 others still enrolled in the seminary. Of the 13 ministers who had completed their training, almost half, six, are women.

The minister as teacher is reflected in Wright's annual report, which shows the seriousness with which Afrocentric materials are integrated into the Christian training. "During African American History Month we brought Dr. Cain Hope Feldler, the author of *Troubling Biblical Waters*, into our congregation . . . and the seminarians under the leadership of Sister Carmen Cates put together a workbook and study guide that is now in print, on sale and in use from Oakland, California, to New England down to Florida."

His instruction to the deacons is similar to the above.

In the Deacons-In-Training course, the history of the church from Abraham in Genesis 12 to the Black Theology Project of 1991 is covered. The African origins of the faith are taught and the awful impact the African slave trade had on shaping the North American church traditions is covered. The ordinations and the ordinances of the Protestant church, the founding of the United Church of Christ and the role Africans and African Americans have in their denomination are taught along with the responsibilities of the office of deacon.

On still another aspect of his teaching role Wright wrote:

In the Seminary Consortium class there are 40 contact hours for seminarians and pastors around North America. Heavy emphasis is placed on the preaching and music traditions of Africans in North America in order to follow the paradigm established by W.E.B. Du Bois 90 years ago. Du Bois said that in order to understand the church of Africans in diaspora, one has to understand Black preaching, Black music and the Black expression of the Holy Ghost."

Making a Joyful Noise

If preaching is the paramount element of a dynamic black worship service, music is a close second. The black church could not exist or long endure without excellently performed music of various types. The black church has given birth to all the forms of music associated with African American culture, including spirituals, gospel, blues, jazz, and hip-hop. Marian Anderson, Aretha Franklin, Gladys Knight, Roberta Flack, Whitney Houston, and Tony Braxton, to name a few, all owe their early start to the black church. Large music programs in recent years have featured not only the senior, gospel, youth, and children's choirs, and men's and women's choruses, but other specializations as well. Moreover, musical instruments beyond the piano and the organ are increasingly brought into play.

We have observed that the 16th Street Baptist Church in Birmingham, the Shorter A.M.E. Church in Denver, and the Allen Temple Baptist Church in Oakland are among a number of black churches that have moved beyond a rhythm section of percussion instruments and guitar to a small orchestra, including woodwinds, reeds, and strings. The music program at Trinity not only reflects Christian and Afrocentric influences but makes a special appeal to young people.

The pastor is an accomplished musician who frequently plays the piano during services. One of the associate ministers, the Rev. Ozzie Smith, is an accomplished saxophone player.

One of several music organizations of the church is the choir for high-school-age youths, called the "Imani Ya Watume," which is Swahili for "The Messengers of Faith." About 40 male and female voices carry the full 8 a.m. service of worship on the second Sunday of each month. Choir members and the pastor wear African garb, and other members of the church are encouraged to do so.

Another musical unit is "The Little Warriors for Christ," made up of children from preschool through eighth grade.

The Women's Chorus, of 125 women, most of whom are not in the Sanctuary Choir, constitutes another. The Men's Chorus, made up of 90 "Mighty Men of Trinity," sing once a month at the 8 A.M. service.

Clearly, though, the gem of the music program is the Sanctuary Choir, which some churches call the senior choir or the chancel choir. Fifty-two weeks a year the Sanctuary Choir provides the music for the

11 A.M. worship service as well as for all special services. It is made up of persons ages 19 through 78 and is said to be "one of the hardest-working ministries in the church."

The music for worship services at Trinity is not confined to the choirs and accompanists. "On Easter Sunday, the jazz musicians Wynton Marsalis and Stanley Turrentine came by our service and 'jammed for Jesus,' " the pastor wrote in his 1990 annual report. He continued: "Members are still talking about the way Wynton Marsalis came to worship with us on Easter Sunday, 1990, and brought his entire quintet to play during the 11:00 service.

"No one will ever forget Kirk Whalun, who brought his quintet to both services and played 'GLOW'. Every time Kirk is in town he brings his sax to service and plays for us."

It was Stanley Turrentine who provided the church with extra special moments.

> Stanley . . . got surprised on his first of two visits to Trinity this year. Our Ozzie Smith (Associate Pastor, saxophonist) joined in with him. I sent Ozzie over to the mike in the middle of the choir stand, and Stanley could hear Ozzie but he couldn't see him. The more Ozzie played in contrapuntal accompaniment to the song Stanley was playing, the more excited Stanley got. Finally, Stanley stopped playing and turned to me grinning and asked, "Where is he?" I showed him where Ozzie was, and then he turned to face Reverend Ozzie Smith, and they proceeded to wear us out.

The church has shown a special gift for integrating visiting singers into the service as well. "The Thompson Community Singers came into our sanctuary on Palm Sunday and proceeded to sing our souls happy with songs (and moves) like we had never seen before," read the 1991 annual report. Other visiting singers included Vickie Winans.

"Our own member, Mavis Staples, sang along with BeBe and CeCe Winans on their *Different Lifestyles* album and the Word of God as heard sung at Trinity is now heard on every continent in God's world."

At Trinity, then, making a joyful noise embraces both the traditional and the newer expressions of black music in all its variety. Not every black church has been able to duplicate this experience, but almost every one has the potential to.

One of the newest additions to the music program of the church is the Dance Ministry. This ministry is about teaching young people the African roots of dance and the biblical basis for praising God through dance.

Thus, while the music program at Trinity is certainly more elaborate than what was visualized by Du Bois, it is still within the framework of the social scientist's remarkable insight into the significance of music to the black church enunciated nearly 100 years ago.

Experiencing the Holy Ghost

The third element in a dynamic worship program is the emotional fervor which was identified by Du Bois variously as "frenzy," or "shouting," or "feeling the spirit." He also noted the infinite variety in the gradations of such expressions. Sometimes the feeling of an encounter with the Holy Ghost comes on quietly and remains so. At other times it demands more visible expression.

Spirited Prayer Life

A fourth element of a dynamic worship program is prayer. This is a frequent, sustained invocation to God spread throughout the service from beginning to end. Prayers add to the flavor of the worship service and to the solemnity of the occasion. Prayers said out loud can also educate and inform. Moreover we have seen in this research and in life that well delivered prayer can often undergird the first three essentials of black worship.

At Trinity, in addition to the usual United Church of Christ prayer services, the congregation has adopted a black prayer, written by Vallmer E. Jordan, who also wrote the original statement of purpose in 1971. It reads, in part:

A Black Prayer

Father God,
Creator of me, Black in your own image,
Having breathed into me
Your own divine substance, Life
Out of that which you are, Love.
Help me to understand your love and to know
That my destiny, indeed my salvation,
Is to love you in return with all my heart,
    soul and mind.
And this love unavoidably must encompass my
    own Black self
And must include my Black brothers and sisters and the community
we comprise.
O God!

Strengthen . . . prepare . . . and gird me for the
long dark struggle toward freedom.
Help me to live this precious Black life as
if the future and freedom of all Black
people depended on me . . . alone.
And please, God, guide me into those ways
that will best utilize the talents that
you have given me in order that I can
contribute to the best of my ability to
bring my people closer . . . to freedom.
Amen.

Each Sunday, and following the Wednesday prayer services, persons who have participated in a series of sessions conducted by a medical doctor and the pastor stand in the sanctuary, before the altar, inviting "whosoever will" to come for prayer and the laying on of hands.

According to the pastor, this ministry is based on a book written by Dr. Elaine Ferguson, a member of the church, "and the book which is at the center of our faith—the Bible!"

Auxiliaries

A fifth element of a dynamic worship service is the auxiliaries, which come out on display on Sundays. The most impressive of these is the usher board. Ushers are essential. They seat the congregation, keep order, help members in distress, including those who get the Holy Ghost and cannot keep their composure, and lift the offering. A special feature of Trinity is the Youth Usher Board.

Christian Education

The sixth element of a dynamic black worship program is Christian education, or Sunday school or Bible study. No black church can be "vital," as defined by Bishop Roy Nichols, without these programs. At Trinity, religious education programs have been redefined in keeping with their Afrocentric/Christocentric creed.

Courses are taught on: biblical faith and the black American, the religion of the Africans during chattel slavery, Gayraud Wilmore's *Black Religion and Black Radicalism*, and Cain Hope Felder's *Troubling Biblical Waters*, Races, Class, and Family.

The pastor says, "For 17 years we have been trying to do Christian education from the black perspective. . . . We have used the curriculum put together by Reverend Barbara Allen and Dr. Yvonne Delk. We have used the curriculum put together by our former assistant director of Christian Education, Mrs. Julia Speller; and now we are using the curriculum being developed by Dr. Colleen Birchett. It combines the Afrocentric and Christocentric perspective or foci, giving our young people a weekly infusion of the Bible and a weekly infusion of African American perspectives on biblical themes. It is based on Nguzo Saba, the seven principles of Kwanzaa developed by Maulama Karenga: unity, self-determination, collective work and responsibility, cooperative economics, purpose, creativity, and faith."

Finally, we note that critical to a dynamic black worship program is financial stewardship as represented in part by lifting the offering.

Financial Giving

How long would the black church last, how strong and independent would it be, how vital would the worship be, and how could it possibly sustain an extensive community outreach program were it not for the strong traditions of "passing the collection plate"? Indeed, the black church would hardy be recognized without this essential element of financial stewardship. And while Du Bois did not include this financial element in his list of essential elements of a black church, he was a perceptive sociologist and enough historian to appreciate it. We have seen above that even during slavery, black churches gave strong and creative expression to this essential element.

At Trinity, this practice of lifting the offering has resulted in a pattern of substantial financial growth. In 1971 Trinity had an annual operating budget of $39,000. Twenty years later it had reached some $2.38 million. Some 77 percent of this money comes from pledges and tithes of the members.

Altogether Trinity United Church had total assets in 1990 totaling $8.3 million.

Nor did the Afrocentric/Christocentric perspective prevent financial growth as some ministers and church officers might suspect.

"The congregation's commitment to Afrocentricity and Christocentricity has given me much encouragement during a time when many 'Negro' churches are pulling back to the safe harbors of 'soul-saving' and 'colorless Christianity.' The faithful stewardship of the members, giving in excess of $3 million, is a humbling reality," Wright observed in his annual report. Though some people in the black community are wary of and offended by any move toward an Afrocentric view of their world or the adoption of a black-oriented style, these obviously didn't stifle the growth of this church.

Quite the contrary. Afrocentricity seemed to be a major factor enhancing the phenomenal growth of the church. Within 11 years after Wright's appointment as pastor, the membership of Trinity United had grown from 87 members to more than 4,000 members! Such phenomenal growth, along with the Black Value System, catapulted Trinity and Wright into the forefront of national leadership. By 1996, with more than 4,500 members, Trinity was the largest congregation in the United Church of Christ denomination, still a largely white organization. Moreover, the church completed a new $14 million building only to discover that it still has to conduct three Sunday services.[6] All of these factors bear strong testimony to the viability of this church even as it seeks to successfully integrate its Christian heritage with its African American heritage.

Benevolence

How, then, is this church using its enormous resources of preaching, singing, shouting, praying, auxiliaries, Christian education, and financial growth to live out its commitment to community service "in the heart of the community, striving to reach the community's heart"?

This church uses several vehicles to meet its community obligations. One is the sermons and addresses of the minister. Another is the activities conducted by the various church organizations. Still a third is the availability of the church buildings for use by community groups. A fourth vehicle is the financial contributions the church makes to community programs. A sixth is the extent to which the church inspires and encourages volunteers from the church to participate in community programs. On all these measures Trinity Church excels. Finally, a most impressive vehicle used by this church to accomplish its social mission is the direct operation of extensive community outreach programs.

Some of these programs may be categorized as educational programs, others as individual and gender development programs, and others as family development programs, social service programs, employment and economic/community development programs, cultural awareness programs, and diaspora programs.

In education, Trinity operates a Head Start Child Development Center, a scouting program, a high school counseling ministry, and a tutorial program.

Moreover, in 1990 Trinity church had some 200 members who were studying in college out of town, and another 100 who were studying at colleges in Chicago. In addition to providing scholarship assistance, encouragement, and special recognition, the church has an "adopt a student" program, through which members and organizations of the church keep in touch with students at out-of-town colleges. This initiative seeks to ameliorate the extraordinarily high dropout rate for black college students, especially males.

While all the programs of the church are infused with an Afrocentric perspective as a concomitant of the Christocentric perspective, the church has also launched a special cultural awareness program as a daily after-school activity for members and nonmembers as well. The Sojourner Truth Cultural Awareness Institute is frankly inspired by programs in cultural awareness often operated by Jewish synagogues. The pastor said, "As Jewish children go to Hebrew school to learn what the public school systems are not teaching them about their history and their heritage, our children from the church and from the community came three days a week to learn about . . . the great heroes and heroines of Africa who have made us what we are as a people."

Other programs include a rites-of-passage program for men and one for women.

Another category of outreach programs is marriage and family enhancement. This includes: counseling ministry, marriage enrichment ministry, married couples ministry, legal counseling ministry, and foster care ministry.

Services to the needy include: Helping Hands Ministry, drug and alcohol abuse recovery, and the prison ministry.

A final category of community outreach is Employment and Economic/Community Development. This includes an employment ministry, housing ministry, and Outreach to the Diaspora, including special initiatives on the Caribbean.

Even before the new building was completed in 1994, this church was a virtual beehive of activity. Unlike some institutions, all these activities are focused on and informed by a persistent effort to solve the three basic challenges confronting the activist or would-be activist church: how to develop a vital program of Christian worship, how to celebrate and teach the African American cultural heritage, and how to use the enormous resources of these large urban churches to confront the major social, economic, educational, and political problems plaguing the African American community. While Trinity is far from an ideal African Christian community, it is certainly far advanced in that direction and is a model for other black churches to emulate.

Building on its history of resilience, independence, and service, Trinity has faced squarely the challenge of mixing its Christian traditions and its African American heritage. It is far from alone in this regard. We have seen several activist churches in our studies struggling to face up to this challenge. Preeminent among them are the New Bethel A.M.E. Church in Baltimore under the Rev. Frank Madison Reed, and the Payne A.M.E. Church in the same city under the Rev. Vashti Murphy McKenzie. In Washington, D.C., we have seen Union Baptist Church under leadership of the Rev. Willie Wilson make giant strides. So, too, the Emani Temple African American Catholic Congregation under Bishop Stallings, and the shrines of the Black Madonna in Atlanta, Detroit, and Houston, founded by the former Rev. Albert Cleage in Detroit.

It is not an easy matter to introduce change in such a tradition-bound institution. The Rev. Cecil Murray says that before he introduced an Afrocentric painting into First A.M.E. Church, he waited until he had been pastor for a number of years and until a majority of church members had joined under his pastorate. Then he contacted a reputable artist whom he knew and the church janitor. The three of them went into the sanctuary on Friday evening after all programs had finished. They locked all the church doors, with only the three of them inside. When they exited the church late Saturday night, they had removed the most prominent European-oriented Christian painting and in its place the artist had created a magnificent Afrocentric Christian mural. On Sunday morning, when the congregation saw the new artwork, not a single complaint was lodged. A few years later it was much easier to create the current African American history mural that adorns the back of the pulpit as well as other African American art in the church.

Trinity, too, has done all this with a remarkable appreciation for and integration of the role of women at all levels.

In merging what Lincoln and Mamiya call its privatistic (spiritual) and communal (social) missions, Trinity has few peers. It is on every national roster of community-oriented activist churches while maintaining an active spiritual mission as well.

Finally, Trinity manages to do all this not always easily, or without setback, but with amazing success and integrity, and without splitting apart. It is as if the people of Trinity have discovered yet another secret taught by their ancestors: The way to move from strength to strength is to recognize that the work is never finished. There is always one more river to cross.

14

---ↀↀ---

One More River to Cross:
The Black Church Faces the Future

R ivers carry strong symbolism in African American culture. As Vincent Harding suggested in his book *There Is a River*, the whole history of the African American people is like one: infinitely twisting and
turning, ebbing and flowing, and more than occasionally flooding.[1] But
just as the ancient Egyptians did with the Nile, the African American
people have learned to respect the overflowing, to step back and then
return to the hallowed ground once the flood has receded. They knew
that when they did begin to replant and rebuilt, the ground would be
even more fertile for them. The early Africans in America sang of "One
More River to Cross," and of "Jordan River, chilly and cold, chills the
body, not the soul." Then Langston Hughes told the world through his
poetry that the African people have known rivers "ancient as the world
and older than the flow of human blood in human veins." Always in
African American life, and always in our own sociohistorical perspective, there is just one more obstacle to overcome, one more call to the
barricades.

One More River to Cross

It is against this cultural background that this book has sought to
set forth a few propositions and to amass some evidence in support of
them.

At the heart of our view is the idea that if we are to understand the sources and resources of the survival, achievements, and regeneration of the African American people and their communities, we would do well to consider the churches. They stand to represent the deep well of spirituality that keeps these people going. They are enormously resourceful and potent agents of social reform. Their contributions to past, present, and future are not well understood or appreciated by many black and white Americans and others as well. They are misunderstood not only among the skeptics but among believers as well; not only among the laity but among the priestly class as well; and not only among scholars and leaders and professionals but among laypeople as well. This book has tried to make some contribution to closing this gap.

Building on the insights of the elders in black scholarship, particularly Du Bois, Frazier, and Lincoln, this book sets forth a "sociohistorical proposition."

In times of extreme and sustained crisis, the African American community will turn to the churches and their ministers for comfort, support, leadership, and guidance. These are secular crises, and not all, but many churches, will offer leadership and guidance. Those churches so inclined will respond to the extent that they are strong, independent, and resourceful, and to the extent that they are led by strong, independent, and resourceful ministers.

Under these circumstances three types of black churches emerge. Some churches will tend to be conservative, confining themselves to their basic spiritual and religious work, thus ignoring, or seeming to ignore, the social crisis around them. There is plenty of biblical support for following this course. Other churches will reach out just a little bit to embrace social or community issues. They will have discussions about these issues. They may invite guest speakers to address these issues or open their doors for community meetings. They will certainly feed the hungry and clothe the naked on special and irregular occasions. Saving souls must take priority over social action. The third category comprises the activist churches, headed usually by activist ministers. They move with vigor into the community to confront the secular crises engulfing the people. Often, indeed, these churches do not distinguish between sacred and secular issues. They focus instead on their calling to minister to the whole person and the whole community.

This is what has happened in the past. It is what is happening now. It is what can happen in the future.

Not consistently, perhaps, but persistently. This was so in the crisis caused by the British evacuation of Savannah in 1782, which would see the near martyrdom of Leile's hand-picked successor, the Rev. Andrew Bryan. It was so in the crisis of 1832 that saw elevated the Rev. Andrew Marshall to heroic status. It happened again in the crisis caused by Sherman's capture of Savannah in 1864, which saw 20 black religious leaders undertake a remarkable role as social reformers. It happened in the crisis of emancipation, which catapulted all the black ministers in town into the fray. It happened in the civil rights era all over the South and occasionally in other parts of the nation as well. And it happened in Savannah, during the crisis that engulfed black male youths in the 1990s. In all these secular crises, black churches stepped to the head of the line in the struggle for social justice. And they wrote a chapter in history that has seldom been equaled.

As social scientists, we are constrained to note that such bold action has consequences seen and unseen, positive and not.

The answer is that for today and tomorrow, both the internal and the external strategies are essential. Whether one church or one community of churches can or should pursue both strategies is a matter for serious analysis and serious reflection, and as Marion Wright Edelman, of the Children's Defense Fund, and James M. Washington, author of a book on this subject, would remind us, some serious prayer might also be called for, and some singing as well, according to Bernice Reagon and Derrick Bell. The Rev. Cecil L. "Chip" Murray had it right: "The days of coming to church for personal salvation alone are over." The time has come, or come again, for changing the community, for social reform. C. Eric Lincoln would remind us that the African American people must take the lead on their own behalf, and further, that for historical and other reasons the black churches must be at the center of that reform. We have seen throughout this book that there are churches and leaders prepared for this challenge. And we believe, with Lincoln, that "what these churches have done others can do."

Finally, personal belief in the efficacy of social reform is required of leaders and followers alike in order to sustain such effort. And while there are millions of ways to express this imperative, Leon Sullivan, the Martin Luther King Jr. of the North, has come close to Du Bois in setting forth his belief system, with which religious and nonreligious people alike can find common cause. He writes:

> I believe in God. I believe God is working now in the nation and in the world in an extraordinary way. I believe that God can do anything. I believe God wants me to help men (women and children) to live better on earth. I believe not only in milk and honey in heaven but in ham and eggs on earth besides.

I believe in the future. For though we grope through the maze of dark passages, I see the light. And I know the light will conquer the darkness.

I believe in the Black man (woman and child). I believe that he has the brain power, the heart power, the soul power, to equal in every enterprise or activity any other man on the face of the globe, and to match him accomplishment for accomplishment and ability for ability. All the Black man needs is the opportunity to prove fully and freely, and without obstacles and restraint, what he can do.

Indeed, I believe in America. I am, in many ways, a patriot. I am proud of my Americanism. America, with all her faults, is still our country and the country of our children. As far as I am concerned, it is up to us to straighten out what is wrong with her.[2]

The question for the future is this: Can the black church garner enough strength from its rich, fruitful past and its struggles in the present against widespread social turmoil to lead the African American community into a viable future? As the year 2000 approaches, there are strong indications all over the nation that black people will face major challenges. External and internal forces will threaten the viability and well-being of black communities and families in the years ahead.

Each of these challenges embodies the potential of major national crisis. And in each the church can be an agent of social reform. Prominent among these issues is the apparent resurgence of outward manifestations of racism. This can be discerned in the rise of personal attacks on black individuals, the broadside attacks on affirmative action programs, some elements of the welfare reform movement, and most conspicuously in the firebombing of some 200 churches between 1990 and 1995, mostly black churches and primarily in the South.

Not since the 1960s have so many black churches been burned. And as if these events did not fill the plate with challenges, today's black community has another issue to consider, a new schism: the gap between the haves and the have-nots. For the first time in history the bifurcation within the black community between the upper classes and the lower classes has become pervasive and acute.

No problem, real or imagined, though, looms quite as large as the climate and daily reality of within-group violence, particularly among black youth.

Welfare Reform

In the decades ahead, black churches will be called upon to play expanded roles in welfare reform. Churches are close to this issue because many of their members are welfare recipients. There is increasing concern, however, that the much touted welfare reform legislation pushed through Congress by the Republican leadership and signed by the Democratic president just weeks before the 1996 elections may cause as many problems as it solves.

Of course, many large urban black churches with strong leaders are already making a contribution to welfare reform. Even before the passage of the 1996 Welfare Reform Act, the 15,000-member New Birth Baptist Church in Atlanta had developed a plan to adopt three welfare families. The church, said Bishop Eddie Long, the pastor, would provide for all the basic needs of the family—food, closing, shelter, education, counseling, job training, and placement—while nurturing the family toward independence. And while these families are housed in some of the extensive properties owned by the church, Deacon Curtis Crocker Jr. pointed out to the author that the families are required to participate and contribute to their own welfare in appropriate ways.

Another church, the Wheeler Street Baptist Church in Houston, took one of our researchers to visit a house that the church had bought from the city, now home to six female-headed welfare families under the supervision of a married couple as well as staff and volunteer mentors from the church. Again, the church was committed to providing for all the basic needs of these families and guiding them toward independence.

The Union Baptist Church in Washington, D.C., has operated such a home for a number of years. Each time a family is able to go out on its own, another is accepted. In this way the enormous financial, spiritual, and social resources of the church can be enlisted in the welfare reform movement. And in the same city, the giant and rapidly expanding Windsor Village United Methodist Church led by Dr. Kirbyjon Caldwell, continues to break new ground in welfare reform, independent living, and community development.

But there is a limit. Many churches don't believe this is their mission. Many do not have the resources or the leadership to engage in such programs. And even if all churches did so, there would not be enough to meet the needs. The church, then, must serve as example and catalyst for the work which must be done by government and private agencies in collaboration with churches.

Black churches will find their strength as they (1) provide a more equitable place for women in all levels of leadership of the churches; (2) provide strong incentives for men to participate in organized church-sponsored programs; (3) use their enormous financial and economic power in the interest of social reform; (4) honor, learn, and teach the African American heritage as a major component of their mission; and (5) hone and harness their recognized political power to deliver sounder public policies and private programs to their communities—before, during, and after elections, and in non-electoral politics as well.

This is a tall order for individual black churches and organizations of black churches and their leaders. Yet anyone reading this book will see that somewhere, at some time, some black church or group of black churches have done or are doing all five initiatives. And some are doing them extremely well.

Smaller Places

Most of the profiles above are of large churches in major metropolitan areas in the four regions of the nation. Indeed, when thinking of black church activism during the civil rights era, it is common to think of such cities as Montgomery, Birmingham, Selma, and Memphis. Often overlooked is the activity in smaller places before, during, and after the explosions in the larger cities. So it was that in Clarendon County, South Carolina, J. A. De Lane, an A.M.E. minister, initiated action as early as 1949 that led to the *Brigs* v. *Elliott* case challenging inequality in black schools in the county. (This was the first of the regional cases that were absorbed by the U.S. Supreme Court in its landmark ruling in the *Brown* decision outlawing segregation in public schools in 1954.) The Rev. De Lane's church was burned, and his life was threatened. He was finally forced to leave the state after he fired back at vigilantes who shot at his house. Other ministers and other churches were also involved. In Florence, South Carolina, Trinity Baptist Church under the Rev. William P. Diggs, the college teacher turned pastor, led and helped sustain the movement. All of this has led Rev. De Lane's son to write years later that the church was the "crucial instrument" in the struggle. He continued: "The Church, in addition to its primary function of religious teaching, was the only place where we could congregate and address issues ranging from civil rights to social problems."

So it is today that in many smaller cities, towns, and communities around the nation some black churches and church leaders are active in community development beyond their primary religious mission. Indeed a number of these leaders, such as the Rev. Dr. Charles Jackson of Brookland Baptist Church in Columbia, South Carolina, believe that the social reform activities of the church are an integral part of their religious work.

In 1997, Bishop John Hurst Adams, senior bishop of the A.M.E.

churches in South Carolina, was asked if there were any black churches in Columbia that he would consider activist in the arena of social reform. He quickly mentioned three: Bethel A.M.E. Church, newly under the leadership of the Rev. Ronald Brailsford; the Bible Way Church, under the leadership of the Rev. Darrell Jackson, whose father was founder of the church; and the Brookland Baptist Church, under the longtime leadership of Dr. Charles B. Jackson Sr.

Brookland

The Rev. Dr. Charles Jackson Sr. grew up in Brookland Baptist Church. He was ordained to the ministry while still in his teens and succeeded to the pastorate in his early 20s. He has been a leader of this congregation for more than 25 years and is still a young man. Aside from his years at the Morehouse School of Religion at the Interdenominational Theological Center in Atlanta, he has seldom spent time away from the city and his congregation. Still he exhibits an extraordinary cosmopolitan presence, knowledge, and bearing. Over the years he has had a number of offers to lead churches all over the nation, but he has always in the end felt that his calling was at Brookland. The church has grown enormously in membership, programs, finances, and all other ways under his leadership. By 1997 the 3,000-member congregation had to have more space. The church purchased an abandoned shopping center covering at least two square blocks of space and proceeded to built a magnificent sanctuary. Even so it has had to continue two services on Sundays.

Brookland is the mother of all churches in the area of community-outreach programs. The centerpiece of its community work is the Brookland Foundation. This is a separate corporation, owned by the church, with Jackson as chair of the board. The church made a gift of $1,000 to launch the foundation. Other money comes from individuals, organizations, and fund-raising campaigns. The church provides hordes of volunteers that keep the various programs of the foundation operating.

The mission of the foundation is to improve the lives of individuals, families, and communities by developing and promoting their physical, social, and spiritual well-being. Currently the foundation sponsors eight major projects, each of which has a director and cadre of volunteers. They are as follows:

- The HIV/AIDS Project consists of volunteers trained to provide education, prevention, and care for those individuals and families affected.

- The Homeless Project provides volunteers who minister to the physical, social, psychological, and educational needs of the homeless.
- The Tutorial Project brings volunteers together with students to assist the students with homework and to provide other instructional aids.
- The Recreation Project hosts a variety of team sports for youth and adults, male and female, members and nonmembers of the church.
- The Black Male Youth Conference has for 10 years brought together youth and youth leaders from all over the state for several days of intensive learning experiences. The conference recently developed a permanent Male Youth Institute, which will provide year-round mentoring, counseling, education, and guidance for youth and their parents and teachers and other leaders.
- The Brookland Federal Credit Union has become the centerpiece of the foundation's program. The nonprofit savings and banking institution serves the financial needs of residents and businesses in the two surrounding counties. Jackson and his congregation have developed considerable support for the credit union, which serves as a training ground for individuals, families, and the church to learn how to maximize their own and their community's investment potential.

These are just a few of the more than 50 ministries of the church, several of which are outreach ministries focused on social reform. These resources make Jackson's church a powerful resource for good in this community.

Bethel

Bethel is an old, established church, and the Rev. Brailsford is fairly new to it. In less than six years, he has led Bethel to abandon its site downtown, where developments surrounding the church have impeded its growth, and to purchase a church and school buildings encompassing an entire square block previously owned by a large white church. With equal swiftness, despite some initial reluctance, the congregation has rallied behind Brailsford and his wife as they have expanded the church programs enormously, both within the church and in the community. One of the most prominent in the community is the music school and choral group called CaBrailSong, established, taught, and conducted by Mrs. Brailsford. But the heart of the movement of this church into the community is its academic school, which is already established through third grade and is on track to expand to high school. More than 100 students are already enrolled, and there is a waiting list.

According to the Rev. Brailsford, education and spiritual development are keys to the success of African Americans as individuals, families, and communities.

This church is also a partner with two other churches in the operation of housing programs for low-income families. The church has been in the housing business for a very long time, and the housing stock is now aging, prompting Bishop Adams to remark that he hopes the A.M.E. church will not become a slum landlord in the years ahead.

Bible Way

Bible Way Church has also become a fixture in this community. Founded by Bishop A. C. Jackson, it has been led for a decade by Elder Darrell Jackson, who is also a member of the state senate. The church is widely known and admired in the community because of its sponsorship of a home-ownership program. Using its own funds, the church has built nearly 100 homes. These homes are sold to low- and moderate-income families under favorable mortgage arrangements, putting home ownership within reach of people who otherwise might never have dared dream of their own home.

All three of these churches are growing rapidly in membership, programs, and financial resources. Each has a highly educated, seminary-trained minister who is active in community affairs and who sees the church as having a dual mission as spiritual and social resource for the community. Each is a dynamic speaker, able organizer, and rising community leader. Each of these churches also has a very active, growing, and diverse series of youth programs, both in the church and in the community.

An example of the impact a church can have on young people and through them on the larger society can be illustrated by seventeen-year-old honor student, Kara King, who came to public attention in the spring of 1998.[3] Indeed, just as young Lott Carey, Margaret Walker, and L. Douglass Wilder would use the resources of the First Baptist Church in Richmond to catapult them into major contributions to society, King has demonstrated that she can take Bible Way church into the larger society as well.[4] Active in the various youth programs of this church, King is also president of the senior class at Dreher High School. She is among the organizers of the Carolina Youth Network, a statewide group of youth who campaign against guns, substance abuse, and violence in public schools. Rev. Dr. Andrew Chisholm, a local minister, and Professor at the University of South Carolina, who helped King found this Network, considers her among "the brightest young people in the state." Because of this work, King has been appointed to a national advisory committee by U.S. Attorney Janet Reno.

It was King's essay, prepared for a contest by a national magazine, however, that brought her into public acclaim. Her essay on youth contributions to public affairs was judged "one of the best" among the 700 entrants and she was awarded a runner-up prize of $25,000 in merchandise. Characteristically, she donated this prize to the Social Action Foundation of her church. Her pastor, Rev. Senator Darrell Jackson, is extremely proud of her. "Kara is a fantastic young lady," he told a reporter. "She is a shining example of the good that young people do. For every youngster who messes up, we have ten like Kara who don't." He did not need to point out to the reporter that those ten youth who don't "mess up" generally don't get public recognition. King's mother, a retired teacher with the South Carolina Department of Juvenile Justice, where she works to help rescue youth who have gotten into serious trouble, describes her daughter as a "blessed child." "She is simply a great kid, with so much initiative. She has a way of going about things and making them happen." King hopes to take all these blessed gifts into her chosen career as an obstetrician specializing in work with high-risk babies. She will no doubt take with her the nurturing, the values, and the support she continues to receive from her family, her church, her school, and her community. The black church of the future could hardly find a more noble challenge to its historic mission.

These three churches and hundreds of others in our study act consistently on the view that only by paying careful and creative attention to the youth of the church and community can they ensure the viability of both the church and the community in the years ahead. It is the most important contribution they can make to changing the society for the better.

Mt. Nebo

We have pointed to several church initiatives that suggest that economic development, the better utilization of the nearly 400 billion dollars African Americans earn each year which they spend largely on consumer goods offers new challenges for Black Church Activism in the years ahead.

A most instructive example is what happened in 1996 at the

Greater Mt. Nebo A.M.E. Church in suburban Maryland.[3] Like so many other black churches, Mt. Nebo A.M.E. was refused a loan by the bank in which it has long deposited substantial sums. Considering this act a "slap in the face," the Rev. Jonathan L. Weaver, who holds a master's of business administration degree, decided to put it to use. First he threatened to take the church's business to another bank. That got quick results. Then he had an even better idea. And within a few months he had organized 115 black churches of 19 denominations in the Baltimore-Washington area and formed an agreement with four area banks—three black-owned banks and one white-owned bank with a record of investment in the black community. The churches made a covenant to deposit all their funds in these banks. They estimated that they deposited $10 million annually as institutions. They also agreed to urge their 200,000 members to do likewise. In return, the churches, their members, and other sectors of the black community now receive mortgage loans, other kinds of loans, and financial services from these banks. Once a year they consider other banks and churches that wish to join the compact. And they have formed an ongoing association and are teaching other churches and communities how to organize similar compacts.

In closing our reflections on the future social role of the Black Church, we let Bernice King have the last word. The 33-year-old attorney, minister, associate pastor of the Greater Rising Star Baptist Church in Atlanta, leader of a national youth movement, dynamic speaker, lecturer, and preacher, whom many are describing as the semblance of her father, gave the oration of the 1993 celebration of Dr. Martin Luther King Jr.'s birthday at the family's historic Ebenezer Baptist Church.[4] Those who saw and heard her might well have closed their eyes and visualized her famous father as she urged the nation and the black church:

"My brothers and sisters, it is not enough to say that we marched with Dr. King 25 years ago. We need to ask ourselves, 'What are we doing now?' "

In speaking of "the urgency of now" as her martyred father often did, she also challenged black people and the black church to a new era of activism. The response of the black church to her challenge and to the issues described here will, in our view, determine the viability of the African American community and the level of its well-being in the years ahead.

Appendix A:
Project Advisory Committee Members

Bishop John Hurst Adams
African Methodist Episcopal Churches
Charleston, South Carolina

Dr. Diane Brown
Department of Sociology
Howard University, Wayne State University
Detroit, Michigan

Rev. Dr. Alicia Byrd
The Congress of National Black Churches
Washington, D.C.

Vanella Crawford
Washington, D.C.

Sherry Deane
Children's Defense Fund
Washington, D.C.

Dr. Jualynne Dodson
University of Colorado
Boulder, Colorado

The late Rev. Dr. Henry C. Gregory III
Shiloh Baptist Church
Washington, D.C.

Dr. Shirley Hatchett
University of Michigan
Institute for Social Research
Ann Arbor, Michigan

Dr. Lawrence Jones, Dean Emeritus
Howard University
School of Divinity
Washington, D.C.

Dr. Joyce Ladner
Howard University
Washington, D.C.

Rev. H. Michael Lemmons
Congress of National Black Churches
Washington, D.C.

Dr. Harriette McAdoo
School of Human Ecology
Michigan State University

Dr. Wade Nobles, Director
Institute for the Advanced Study of
Black Family Life and Culture, Inc.
Oakland, California

Dr. Suzanne Randolph
Department of Family Studies
University of Maryland
College Park, Maryland

Dr. Shelby Rooks
United Church Board for Home Ministries
New York, New York

Dr. Ida Rousseau-Mukenge
Morehouse College
Department of Sociology
Atlanta, Georgia

Dr. Roger Rubin
Department of Family Studies
University of Maryland
College Park, Maryland

Dr. Stephen Thomas, Director
Minority Health Research Laboratory
School of Public Health
Emory University
Atlanta, Georgia

Dr. Tony Whitehead
Department of Anthropology
University of Maryland
College Park, Maryland

Appendix B:
Studying Contemporary Black Churches

In order to examine empirically the extent and manner in which contemporary black churches are executing the "communal orientation" as set forth by Lincoln and Mamiya, we established the category of "Community Outreach Programs" and studied the sponsorship of these programs by successive samples of black churches. Eventually, more than a thousand black churches were selected and studied through the following surveys:

1. A pilot study was done of 71 black churches on the Eastern Seaboard.
2. Based on results from the pilot study a stratified random sample of 315 black churches in five states in the Northeast were surveyed.
3. A similar study of 320 black churches in five states of the North Central region was conducted.
4. A convenience sample of 80 black churches in Denver were surveyed.
5. A similar study of 150 black churches in Atlanta was conducted.
6. A similar survey of 100 churches in three rural counties in South Carolina was conducted.
7. In all regions follow-up case studies were conducted on a selective basis.

Chapter 7 draws primarily and heavily from the stratified random samples in the two Northern regions of the country.

Table 6 shows the ten communities in five states of the Northeast region from which 315 black churches were drawn and surveyed by telephone. Table 7.3 shows a similar profile of the 320 churches surveyed in the North Central (or Midwestern) region. And Table 7.4 shows the wide range of denominations or faith traditions with which these 635 churches are affiliated.*

The extent, types, and patterning of community outreach programs operated by churches in these surveys can be seen in the series of accompanying figures:

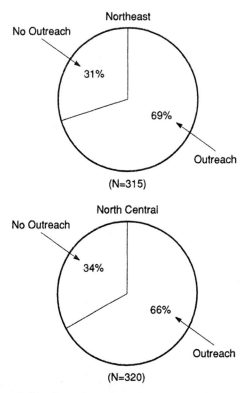

Figure 1 Percent of churches with outreach programs. Upwards of two-thirds of all churches in both regions operate one or more community outreach programs of nonreligious character and extended to members of the community including those not members of the particular church or any church.

*We were assisted with the design of this study by Dr. Shirley Hatchett of the Program for Research on Black Americans, headed by Dr. James Jackson at the Institute for Social Research, University of Michigan, Ann Arbor. Dr. Robert Hill was principal research consultant. Dr. Cleopatra Howard Caldwell was study director, while I served as overall principal investigator. We are grateful for the financial support rendered by The Ford Foundation, The Lilly Endowment, and the University of Maryland, College Park.

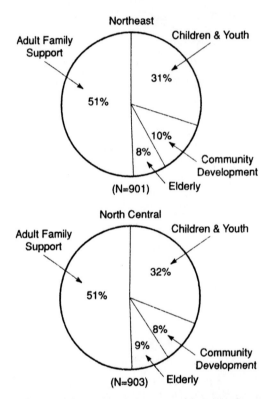

Figure 2 Types of outreach programs sponsored by churches. A majority of programs are family support programs, followed by programs oriented toward children and youth. Programs operated for the elderly and for the total community attract fewer churches.

200

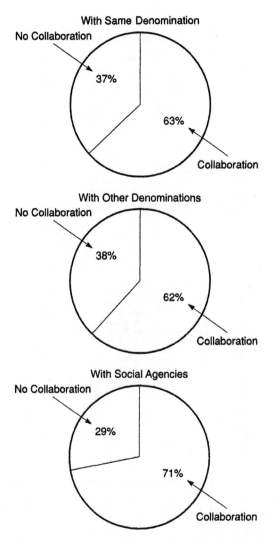

Figure 3 The extensive pattern of collaboration with other community churches and secular social agencies is shown here.

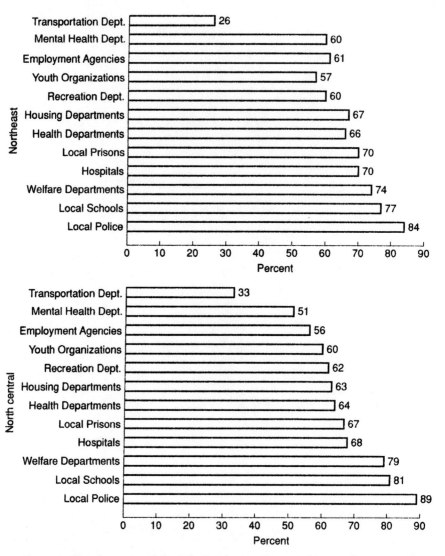

Figure 4 Church cooperation with social agencies most frequently contacted is shown here. These are the local police, local schools, welfare departments, and hospitals, in that order.

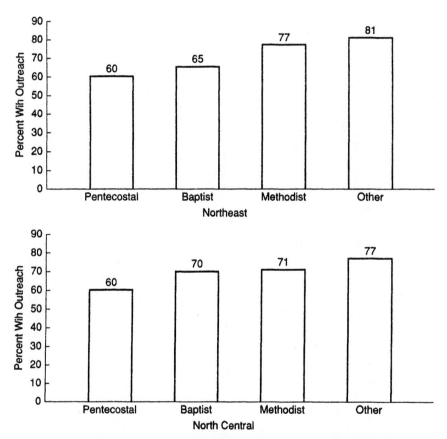

Figure 5 Community outreach by faith traditions. As a group, Methodist churches are more likely to be actively involved in community outreach programs than Baptists or Pentecostal churches. When the Baptist denominations were separated out, it was found that those churches affiliated with the Progressive National Baptist Convention ranked with the Methodist churches in frequency of community outreach programs.

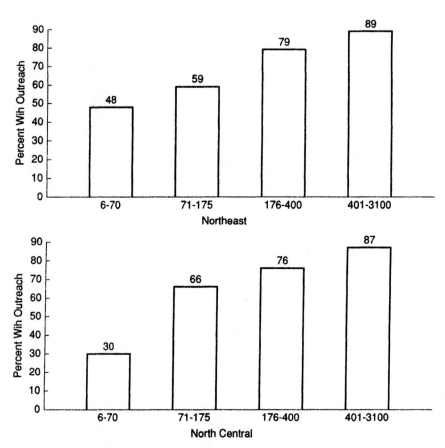

Figure 6 Outreach by church membership size. The larger churches are much more likely to sponsor community outreach programs than smaller ones. This is especially true of the megachurches.

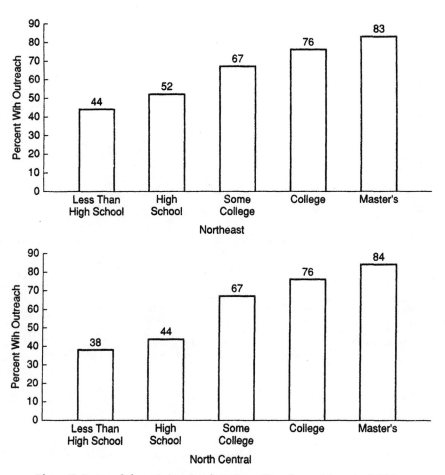

Figure 7 Outreach by minister's education. Churches with more highly educated ministers are much more likely to sponsor community outreach programs.

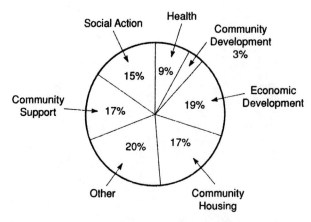

Figure 8 Specific types of community programs offered by various churches. Economic development, housing, and community support are the most frequent.

Appendix C: Tables

List of Tables

Table 1 Pastors of First African Baptist Church in Savannah, 1775–1998

Table 2 Membership and Number Baptized in Three Savannah Baptist Churches, 1818–1857

Table 3 Twenty Black Religious Leaders Who Met With Secretary of War Stanton and General Sherman, January 13, 1865

Table 4 Georgia's Black State Representatives and the Counties They Represented, 1868

Table 5 *Ebony Magazine*'s 15 Greatest Black Preachers, 1993

Table 6 Primary Areas in Northeastern Sample, 1992

Table 7 Primary Areas in North-Central Sample, 1992

Table 8 Denominations Included in the Black Church Sample

Table 9 Types of Family-Support Programs Offered by Northern Churches

Table 10 Types of Support Programs for Elderly Offered by Northern Churches

Table 11 Rank Order Listing of Youth-Support Programs Offered by Northern Churches

Table 12 Student Members of the Jenkins Ten Plus Five, 1993

Table 13 Sources of Death for Blacks and Other Minorities, 1985

Table 14 Characteristics of Black Churches in Denver and Atlanta Samples, 1993

Table 15 Number and Percent of Churches in Denver by Type of Outreach Program, 1993

Table 16 Number and Percent of Churches in Atlanta by Type of Outreach Program

Table 17 Churches and Their Pastors in the Vine City Housing Ministry, 1993

Table 18 *Ebony*'s Runner-Up List of Great Black Women Preachers, 1993

Table 19 *Ebony*'s Runner-Up List of Greatest Black Women Preachers, 1997

Table 20 Megachurches and Their Pastors, 1995

Table 21 Twelve Black Churches Serving as Gateways to the City, and Their Pastors, 1995

Table 1 Pastors of First African Baptist Church in Savannah, 1775–1998

Rev. George Leile	1775–1782
Rev. Andrew Bryan	1783–1812
Rev. Andrew Marshall	1812–1856
Rev. William J. Campbell	1857–1877
Rev. Geroge Gibbons	1878–1884
Rev. Emanuel King Love, D.D.	1885–1900
Rev. James W. Carr, D.D.	1901–1907
Rev. Willis L. Jones, D.D.	1909–1913
Rev. T. J. Goodall, D.D.	1915–1922
Rev. E. G. Thomas, A.B., B.D.	1924–1928
Rev. Mack T. Williams	1929–1931
Rev. J. Alfred Wilson	1931–1939
Rev. Ralph Mark Gilbert, D.D.	1939–1956
Rev. Curtis J. Jackson	1957–1961
Rev. William Franklin Stokes II, D.D.	1963–1973
Rev. Lawrence McKinney	1973–1980
Rev. Thurmond Neill Tillman, M. Div.	1982–

Source: Harry James (ed), The First African Baptist Church celebrating over two hundred years, Savannah First African Baptist Church, 1988.

Table 2 Membership and Number Baptized in Three Savannah Baptist Churches, 1818–1857

Year	First African		Second African		Third African	
	Members	Baptized	Members	Baptized	Members	Baptized
1818	1,712	44	538	11		
1822	854	82	589	41		
1826	2,141	271	1,070	143		
1830	2,417	76	1,047	18		
1832			1,310	122		
1833			1,272	13	155	5
1834			1,264		196	19
1835			1,242	11	224	10
1836			1,233	11	183	10
1837	1,810	110	1,268	31	189	6
1839	1,963	44	1,277	12	250	7
1841	2,296	293	1,454	135	271	46
1843	2,052	69	1,510	39	252	7
1845	1,200	69	578	32	282	2
1847	1,221	55	585	25	298	6
1849	1,233	48	699	78	301	6
1851	1,369	102	841	91	205	15
1853	1,504	68	890	55	205	7
1855	1,051	82	920	54	218	12
1857	1,137	58	1,012	26	241	34

Source: Georgia Baptist Archives: Sunbury Association Files, Mercer University, Macon, Georgia.

Table 3 Twenty Black Religious Leaders Who Met With Secretary of War Stanton and General Sherman, January 13, 1865

Name, Age	Year Freed	Means Freed	Church	Years in Ministry	Number Members	Property Value
Rev. William J. Campbell, 51	1849	will	First African Baptist	10	1,800	$18,000
Rev. John Cox, 58	1849	purchase	Second African Baptist	15	1,222	$10,000
Rev. Ulysses L. Houston, 41	1864	Sherman	Third African Baptist	8	400	$5,000
Rev. William Bentley, 72	1817	will	Andrew's Chapel Method. Epic.	20	36	$20,000
Rev. Charles Bradwell, 40	1851	will	Andrews Meth. Episc.	10	—	—
Rev. James Porter, 39	born free[1]	—	St. Stephen	9	200	$10,000
Rev. James Mills, 56	born free	—	First African Baptist	8	—	—
Rev. Adolphus Delmotte, 28	born free	—	Missionary Baptist Milledgeville	2	350	—
Rev. Garrison Frazier, 67	1856	purchase[2] for $1,000	Baptist	35	—	—
Rev. Charles Bradwell, 40	1851	will	Andrew's Chapel	10	—	—
Rev. William Gaines, 41	1864	Sherman	Andrew's Chapel	16	—	—
Rev. Jame Hill, 52	1864	Sherman	—	16	—	—
Rev. Glasgon Taylor, 72	1864	Sherman	Andrew's Chapel	35	—	—
Rev. Abraham Burke, 48	1844	purchse for $800	—	10	—	—
Rev. Arthur Wardell, 44	1864	Sherman	Baptist	6	—	—
Rev. Alexander Harris, 47	born free	—	Third African Baptist	1	—	—
Rev. Jacob Godfrey,[3] 57	1864	Sherman	Andrew's Chapel	28	—	—
Mr. John Johnson, 51	1864	Sherman	Andrew's Chapel	16[4]	—	—
Mr. Robert N. Taylor, 51	1864	Sherman	Andrew's Chapel	9[5]	—	—
Rev. James Lynch, 26	born free	—	Methodist Episcopal	7[6]	—	—

Source: Berlin, 1992

[1] His mother having purchased her freedom
[2] Himself and wife
[3] His enslaver was a Methodist preacher then serving in the Rebel Army.
[4] Layman, treasurer of the church for 16 years.
[5] Layman, class leader in the church for nine years.
[6] Presiding elder in Methodist Episcopal Church from Baltimore, two years in South.

Table 4 Georgia's Black State
Representatives and the Counties They
Represented, 1868

Name	County
Thomas M. Allen	Jasper
Eli Barnes	Hancock
Thomas Beard	Richmond
Edwin Belcher	Wilkes
Tunis G. Campbell Jr.	McIntosh
Malcolm Clairborne	Burke
George Clower	Monroe
Abram Colby	Greene
John T. Costin	Talbot
Madison Davis	Clarke
Monday Floyd	Warren
F. H. Fyall	Macon
Samuel Gardner	Warren
William A. Golden	Liberty
William H. Harrison	Hancock
Ulysses L. Houston	Bryan
Phillip Joiner	Dougherty
George Linder	Lowndes
Robert Lumpkin	Columbia
Romulus Moore	Columbia
Peter O'Neal	Baldwin
James Porter	Chatham
Alfred A. Richardson	Clarke
James M. Simms	Chatham
Abram Smith	Muscogee
Alexander Stone	Jefferson
Henry McNeal Turner	Bibb
John Warren	Burke
Samuel Williams	Harris

Source: Drago, 1992

Table 5 *Ebony Magazine's* 15 Greatest Black Preachers, 1993
(in order of rank)

Name	Church	City
1. Rev. Gardner C. Taylor	Concord Baptist	Brooklyn
2. Rev. Jeremiah A. Wright	Trinity United Church of Christ	Chicago
3. Rev. Samuel D. Proctor	Abyssinian Baptist	Harlem
4. Rev. Charles G. Adams	Hartford Memorial Baptist	Detroit
5. Rev. Otis Moss Jr.	Olivet Institutional Baptist	Cleveland, OH
6. Rev. H. Beecher Hicks	Metropolitan Baptist	Washington, D.C.
7. Rev. Jesse L. Jackson	National Ministry (Bapt.)	Washington, D.C.
8. Rev. James A. Forbes Jr.	Riverside Church	New York
9. Rev. Caeser A. W. Clark	Good Street Baptist	Dallas
10. Rev. Wyatt Tee Walker	Canaan Missionary Baptist	Harlem
11. Rev. Joseph E. Lowery	United Methodist Churches	Atlanta
12. Bishop John Hurst Adams	African Methodist Episcopal	Columbia, SC
13. Rev. Manuel L. Scott Sr.	St. John Baptist	Dallas
14. Rev. Frederick G. Sampson	Tabernacle Baptist	Detroit
15. Rev. J. Alfred Smith Sr.	Allen Temple Baptist	Oakland, CA

Source: Ebony, November 1993, p. 156.

Table 6 Primary Areas in Northeastern Sample, 1992

State	Primary Area	# of Churches
New York	New York–North East, New Jersey SMSA*	151
	Syracuse SMSA	16
	Buffalo SMSA	9
New Jersey	Trenton	9
	Salem	1
Pennsylvania	Philadelphia	81
	Pittsburgh	13
Massachusetts	Boston	9
Connecticut	Bridgeport	18
	New Haven	8
	Total	315

*SMSA = Standard Metropolitan Statistical Area

Table 7 Primary Areas in North-Central Sample, 1992

State	Primary Area	# of Churches
Michigan	Detroit SMSA	54
	Flint	21
Illinois	Chicago SMSA	81
	Champaign/Urbana SMSA	8
Missouri	St. Louis SMSA	28
	Kansas City (KS & MO)	12
Kansas	Atchinson	1
Ohio	Cleveland SMSA	28
	Cincinnati SMSA	12
	Dayton SMSA	20
	Toledo SMSA	16
	Hamilton SMSA	7
Indiana	Indianapolis	31
	Grant-Blackford	1
	Total	320

*SMSA = Standard Metropolitan Statistical Area

Table 8 Denominations Included in the Black Church Sample

Major Black Denominations Sampled
Major National Black Denominations
National Baptist Convention, U.S.A., Inc.
National Baptist Convention of America
National Primitive Baptist Convention, U.S.A.
Progressive National Baptist Convention, Inc.
National Missionary Baptist Convention of America
Church of God in Christ, Inc. (COGIC)
African Methodist Episcopal Church (A.M.E.)
African Methodist Episcopal Zion Church (A.M.E.Z.)
Christian Methodist Episcopal Church (C.M.E.)
Other Black Faith Traditions
Apostolic
Holiness
Pentecostal

Black Churches Within Major White Faith Traditions Sampled
Church of God
Anderson, Indiana
Cleveland, Tennessee
Episcopal
Lutheran
Presbyterian
Presbyterian Church in America
Presbyterian Church (U.S.A.)
United Methodist
Seventh-Day Adventist
United Church of Christ (Congregational)
Christian Church (Disciples of Christ)

Table 9 Types of Family-Support Programs Offered by Northern Churches

	Northeast	*Central*	*North*
Expressive			
Counseling & Intervention	18%	19%	18%
Family Counseling			
Aid to Incarcerated			
Prisoners & Their Families			
Women's Services			
Child Welfare			
Parenting Workshops			
Sexuality Workshops			
Youth at Risk			
Other			
Social Recreation	10%	9%	10%
General Recreation			
Scouting			
Fellowship/Social			
Other			
Instrumental			
Basic Needs Assistance	41%	39%	40%
Food Distribution			
Clothing Distribution			
Emergency Financial Aid			
Referral Center			
Shelter for the Homeless			
Non-Shelter Services			
Home Care			
Meals-on-Wheels			
Other			
Income Maintenance	5%	6%	6%
Low-Income Housing			
Financial Services			
Youth Employment			
Other			
Instrumental-Expressive			
Education & Awareness	18%	20%	19%
Academic Tutoring			
Child Care			
Bible Classes			
African American Culture			
Head Start			
Mentoring			
Denomination-Sponsored Colleges			
Basic Education			
Life Skills			
Other			

(continued)

Table 9 (*Continued*)

	Northeast	Central	North
Health	8%	7%	7%
Substance Abuse			
General Health			
AIDS			
Other			
Total Number of Programs	836	849	1,685

Table 10 Types of Support Programs for Elderly Offered by Northern Churches

Program	Number of Programs	Percent
Home Care	60	39
Fellowship/Social	27	18
Meals-on-Wheels	16	10
Housing	14	09
Multiservices	07	05
Financial	03	02
Medical	03	02
Other	23	15
Totals	153	100%

Table 11 Rank Order Listing of Youth-Support Programs Offered by Northern Churches (*N* = 176 Churches)

Youth-Support Programs	Number of Programs	Percentage*
Teen Support	69	39%
Sports Activities	55	31
College Student Financial Support	29	16
Parenting/Sexuality	27	15
Youth Substance-Abuse Programs	27	15
Youth-at-Risk	25	14
Role Modeling	14	8
Employment/Job Readiness	13	7
Youth AIDS Support Programs	6	2
Youth Health-Related Services	4	2
Other Youth-Support Programs	24	14

*Percentages do not add up to 100 because respondents were asked to check all that apply. Churches may be conducting a program in more than one category.

Table 12 Student Members of Jenkins Ten Plus Five, 1993

Youth	Juveniles
1. Kevin Mack	1. Anthony McClendon
2. Bernard Wilson	2. Ernest Hunt
3. Brian Green	3. Tony Gary
4. Avery Williams	4. Jamaal Newton
5. Nijumo Smith	5. Ramone Bell
6. Curtis Lovett	
7. John Jones	
8. Samuel Eaddy	
9. Roderick Gardner	
10. Quade Stanley	

Table 13 Sources of Death for Blacks and Other Minorities, 1985

Disease Category	Risk Factors
Cancer	Alcohol, Tobacco, Diet, and Environment
Cardiovascular Disease and Stroke	Tobacco, Diet, Obesity, Sedentary Lifestyle, and Hypertension
Chemical Dependency	Direct Behavioral Outcome of Substance Abuse
Diabetes	Obesity
Infant Mortality	Alcohol, Tobacco, Nutrition, Teen Pregnancy, and Late or No Prenatal Care
Homicide	Alcohol, Drug Abuse, and Poor Conflict-Resolution Skills
Unintentional Injuries	Alcohol
AIDS*	Sharing IV Drug Equipment, Unsafe Sexual Practices

*Not included in the Heckler Task Force Report, 1985.

Table 14 Characteristics of Black Churches in Denver and Atlanta Samples, 1993

	Denver		Atlanta	
	No.	*Percent*	*No.*	*Percent*
Denominations				
Baptist	32	40	66	44
Methodist	8	10	32	21
Church of God in Christ (COGIC)	8	10	4	3
Pentacostal	8	10	3	2
Other	24	30	45	30
Totals	80	100	150	100
Size of Membership				
Fewer Than 100	27	33	14	9.3
100 to 499	39	49	78	52.0
500 to 999	8	10	27	18.0
1,000 or more	6	8	23	15.4
Unknown	—	—	8	5.3
Totals	80	100	150	100.0
Proportion of Female Members				
Half or less	8	10	10	6.6
51% to 74%	46	57	90	60.0
More than 75%	26	33	28	18.7
Unknown	—	—	22	14.7
Totals	80	100	150	100.0
Socioeconomic Status				
Mostly Low Income	28	34	17	11
Mostly Middle Imcome	14	18	69	47
Mixture Low/Middle	25	31	50	33
Mostly High Income	2	3	3	2
All High Income	11	14	11	7
Totals	80	100	150	100
Ownership Status				
Own Church Building Mortgage Paid Off	46	58	77	51
Buying Church Building Mortgage Outstanding	20	25	65	44
Renting Church Building	14	17	8	5
Totals	80	100	150	100
Sponsorship of Outreach Programs				
Yes	60	75	131	87
No	20	25	19	13
Totals	80	100	150	100

Table 15 Number and Percent of Churches in Dever by Type of Outreach Program, 1993

	% of Churches With Outreach	Number With Regular Programs
Children and Youth		
Youth Activities	45%	27
Education	28%	17
Scholarship	DK	DK
Drug/Alcohol Education	13%	8
Head Start	10%	6
Day Care or Before/After		
School Care	8%	5
Total Children and Youth	51%	63
Adults and Families		
Food Bank	33%	20
Clothing Bank	18%	11
Prison Services	37%	22
Physical/Mental Health	3%	2
Total Adults and Families	45%	55
Senior Citizens		
Senior Services	28%	17
Total Senior Citizens	28%	17
Total Number of Churches with		
Outreach Programs		135

DK = Unknown

Source: Jessica Pearson, Ph.D., "Community Outreach in Denver's Black Churches: A Report on the Metro Denver Black Church Initiative." Denver, Center for Policy Research, 1993, unpublished.

Table 16 Number and Percent of Churches in Atlanta by Type of Outreach
Program (*N* = 150 churches)

	% of Churches With Outreach	Number With Regular Programs
1. African American Heritage	70.0	105
2. Character Building/Leadership	74.0	111
3. Christian Education	94.0	141
4. Clothing Banks/Distribution	57.0	86
5. Day Care	11.0	17
6. Drug/Alcohol Education	40.0	60
7. Basic Education/Academic Support	34.0	51
8. Family Enhancement	67.0	101
9. Food Banks/Distribution	7.50	113
10. Head Start	5.0	7
11. Physical/Mental Health Programs	19.0	28
12. Personal Counseling	91.0	137
13. Prison Ministry/Ex-Offender Programs	43.0	64
14. Before/After School Care	20.0	30
15. Programs for Senior Citizens	57.0	85
16. Youth Activities	85.0	128
17. Student Scholarships	64.0	96
18. Credit Unions	4.7	7
19. Housing Developments	23.0	34
20. Health-Care Facilities/Nursing Homes	9.3	14
21. Political Involvement	63.0	95

Table 17 Churches and Their Pastors in the Vine City Housing
Ministry, 1993

Church	Pastor
Beulah Baptist Church	Reverend W. L. Cotrell
Friendship Baptist Church	Reverend William Guy
Grace Covenant	Reverend Charles Strokes
Greater Bethany Baptist	Reverend Curtis Lester
Lindsay Street Baptist	Reverend Anthony A. W. Motely
Mount Vernon Baptist	Reverend Baker (now deceased)
Mount Gilead	Reverend Hall
St. Luke	Reverend Helen Johnson
Central United Methodist	Reverend Rodney Smothers
Cosmopolitan A.M.E.	Reverend Earl Ifill
West Mitchell C.M.E.	Reverend Alex King

Source: VCHM unpublished documents

Table 18 Ebony's Runner-Up List of Great Black Women Preachers, 1993
(in Alphabetical Order)

Name	Church	City
Rev. Katie Geneva Cannon	Temple University	Philadelphia
Rev. Delores H. Carpenter	Michigan Park Christian Church	Washington, D.C.
Rev. Johnnie Coleman	Christ Universal Temple	Chicago
Rev. Susan J. Cook	Mariner's Temple Baptist	New York
Rev. Carolyn A. Knight	Philadelphia Baptist	Harlem
Rev. Vashti M. McKenzie	Payne Memorial A.M.E.	Baltimore
Rev. Prathia Hall Wynn	Mt. Sharon Baptist	Philadelphia

Table 19 *Ebony's* 15 Greatest Black Women Preachers, 1997 (Rank Order)

Name	Affiliation	City
1. Rev. Prathia Hall Wynn	Mt. Sharon Bapt.	Philadelphia
2. Rev. Vashti M. McKenzie	Payne Mem. A.M.E.	Baltimore
3. Rev. Carolyn A. Knight	ITC	Atlanta
4. Rev. Renita J. Weems	Vanderbilt U.	Nashville
5. Rev. Susan J. Cook	Bronx Christian Fellowship	Bronx
6. Rev. Ann Farrar Lightner	Mt. Calvary A.M.E.	Towson, MD
7. Rev. Delores H. Carpenter	Mich. Park Christian	Washington
8. Rev. Claudette A. Copeland	New Creation Fellowship	San Antonio
9. Rev. Jacqueline E. McCullough	Elim Int'l Fellowship Ch.	Brooklyn
10. Rev. Ernestine C. Reems	Center of Hope Comm. Ch.	Oakland, CA
11. Rev. Yvonne Delk	Comm. Renewal Soc. UCC	Chicago
12. Rev. Johnnie Coleman	Christ Universal Temple	Chicago
13. Rev. Ella Pearson Mitchell	ITC	Atlanta
14. Rev. Barbara L. King	Hillside Chapel Truth Center	Atlanta
15. Rev. Jessica K. Ingram	Oak Grove A.M.E.	Detroit
16. Rev. Cynthia Hale	Ray of Hope Christian Ch.	Atlanta
17. Rev. Susan Newman	Georgians for Children	Atlanta
18. Rev. Margaret E. Flake	Allen A.M.E.	Jamaica, NY
19. Bishop Barbara Amos	Faith Deliverance Christ Center	Norfolk
20. Rev. Jacqueline Grant-Collier	ITC	Atlanta
21. Rev. Willie T. Barrow	Rainbow/PUSH	Chicago
22. Rev. Bernice King	Greater Rising Star Bapt.	Atlanta
23. Rev. Brenda J. Little	Bethany Bapt.	Evanston
24. Rev. Cecelia W. Bryant	10th District A.M.E.	Dallas
25. Bishop Leontine Kelly	UMC	San Francisco
26. Rev. Joanne Browning	Ebenexer A.M.E.	Ft. Washington, MD
27. Rev. Clarice J. Martin	Colgate Rochester Div.	Rochester
28. Rev. Leah G. Fitchue	Eastern Bapt. Sem.	Wynewood, PA
29. Rev. Susan K. Smith	Advent UCC	Columbus
30. Rev. Martha Simmons	Pilgrim Community UCC	Grand Rapids
31. Rev. Linda Hollies	UMC	Grand Rapids
32. Rev. Iona Locke	Abyssinia Interdenom. Ch.	Southfield, MI
33. Rev. Addie Wyatt	Vernon Pk. COGIC	Chicago
34. Bishop Barbara Harris	Episc. Diocese of MA	Boston
35. Rev. Cheryl Sanders	Third St. Church of God	Washington

Source: Ebony, November 1997

Table 20 Megachurches and Their Pastors, 1995

Church	Pastor	Size
Full Gospel A.M.E. Zion Temple Hills, MD	John Cherry	18,000
West Angeles COGIC Los Angeles	Bishop Charles E. Blake	15,000
Greater St. Stephens Full Gospel Baptist Church New Orleans	Bishop Paul Morton	14,000
Christian Life Center	Pastor A. R. Bernard	
Windsor Village United Methodist Church, Houston	Dr. Kirbyjon Caldwell	8,000
New Birth Missionary Baptist Church, Atlanta (Full Gospel)	Bishop Eddie Long	14,000
Word of Faith Christian Center Detroit	Pastor Keith Butler	10,000
New Birth Baptist Church Miami (Full Gospel)	Bishop Victor T. Curry	8,000
Trinity United Church of Christ Chicago	Pastor Jeremiah Wright Jr.	4,500
Mississippi Valley Christian Church Memphis	Dr. Alvin O'Neil Jackson	5,000
Brentwood Baptist Church Houston	Pastor Joe Radcliffe	7,500
Center of Hope Christian Church, Oakland	Pastor Ernestine Reems	1,500

Source: Phyl. W. Petrie (1995), "Mega-Churches: Black Americans' New Source of Power," *Gospel Today,* Sept./Oct. 1995, p. 29.

Table 21 Twelve Black Churches Serving as Gateways to the City, and Their Pastors, 1995

Church	Pastor
Three Gates in the East	
Concord Baptist Church, Brooklyn	Rev. Gary Simpson
Abyssinian Baptist Church, Harlem	Rev. Calvin Butts III
Allen A.M.E. Church, Queens	Rev. Floyd Flake
Three Gates in the West	
First A.M.E. Church, Los Angeles	Rev. Cecil L. "Chip" Murray
Second Baptist Church, Los Angeles	Rev. William C. Epps
Allen Temple Baptist Church, Oakland	Rev. J. Alfred Smith Sr.
Three Gates in the North	
Zion Baptist Church, Philadelphia	Rev. Leon Sullivan (Retired)
Hartford Memorial Baptist Church, Detroit	Rev. Charles Adams
Olivet Institutional Baptist Church, Cleveland	Rev. J. Otis Moss
Three Gates in the South	
Third Shiloh Missionary Baptist Church, New Orleans	Rev. Herman C. Forte
Wheat Street Baptist Church, Atlanta	Rev. Michael Harris
Caanan Missionary Baptist Church, Louisville	Rev. Walter Malone Jr.

Notes

Introduction

1. Marty, Martin E., and Blumhofer, Edith I. *Public Religion in America Today*. Chicago: The Public Religion Project, 911 N. Michigan Ave. 60611.

2. Lincoln, C. Eric, and Mamiya, Lawrence H. *The Black Church in the African American Experience*. Durham, NC: Duke University Press, 1990. Ch. 1, *passim*.

3. This has long been the interpretation of the "established" church and it functions as a beachhead for much academic investigation and publication within and outside the Black Sacred Cosmos itself. Cf. Joseph Washington, *Black Religion*, and E. Franklin Frazier, *The Negro Church*.

4. The missionary agency of the Church of England.

1. The Storm Is Passing Over

1. "The Birmingham Civil Rights Institute," undated pamphlet. See also Andrew Young, *An Easy Burden: The Civil Rights Movement and the Transformation of America* (New York: HarperCollins, 1996). For details of the most devastating experience of this church and the movement, see Frank Sikora, *Until Justice Rolls Down: The Birmingham Church Bombing Case* (Tuscaloosa: University of Alabama Press, 1991).

2. Most of the extensive literature on the civil rights movement documents the role of the black church. See especially Aldon D. Morris, *The Origins of the Civil Rights Movement: Black Communities Organizing for Change* (New York:

The Free Press, 1984). Morris has argued that the modern civil rights move-ment—which he says began in June 1953 with the successful bus boycott in Baton Rouge, Louisiana, led by the Rev. T. J. Jemison, and ended in 1963 with the successful Birmingham campaign led by Dr. Martin Luther King Jr.—like the Garvey movement before it, could not have possibly succeeded without the moral, financial, practical, and personnel support of the indigenous black church. See also Vincent Harding, *Hope and History: Why We Must Share the Story of the Movement* (Maryknoll, NY: Orbis Books, 1990).

3. W.E.B Du Bois (ed), *The Negro Church* (Atlanta: Atlanta University Press, 1903). Indeed, as we shall see, Du Bois found the church to be the center of African American community life, and he made the church a central feature of his sociology. See his *The Philadelphia Negro: A Social Study* (New York: Schocken Books, 1970) and *The Souls of Black Folk* (New York: American Library, 1969).

4. Dan S. Green and Edwin D. Driver (eds), *W.E.B. Du Bois on Sociology and the Black Community* (New York: Basic Books, 1978).

5. Ibid., 214.

6. Ibid., 215.

7. Ibid.

8. E. Franklin Frazier, *The Negro Church in America* (New York: Schocken Books, 1964).

9. Ibid., p. 40.

10. Ibid., p. 47.

11. Ibid., p. 49.

12. Ibid., p. 50.

13. C. Eric Lincoln and E. Franklin Frazier, *The Negro Church in America: The Black Church Since Frazier* (New York: Schocken Books, 1974).

14. C. Eric Lincoln and Lawrence Mamiya, *The Black Church in the African American Experience* (Durham, NC: Duke University Press, 1990). Lincoln and Mamiya build on the previous extensive scholarship of Lincoln on the black church and black religion to produce the first comprehensive, theoretically grounded, national survey of churches in the seven historically black-controlled denominations that they estimate have some 85 percent of all black church members.

15. Ibid., p. 2.

16. Ibid., p. 10.

17. Ibid., p. 13.

18. Peter Paris, *The Social Role of the Black Church* (Valley Forge, PA: Judson Press, 1985).

19. Hans A. Baer and Merrill Singer, *African American Religion* (Nashville: University of Tennessee Press, 1992), p. xviii. Baer has given particular em-phasis to the great diversity of both structures and missions among black churches. Hans A. Baer, *The Black Spiritual Movement: A Religious Response to Racism* (Knoxville: University of Tennessee Press, 1984).

20. Ibid.

2. *If Tombstones Could Talk*

1. Letters from George Leile in Jamaica to W. H. Leicestershire of England in 1786 and 1791. Copies in the archives, First African Baptist Church, Savannah.

2. Emanuel King Love, *A History of the First African Baptist Church From Its Organization, January 20, 1788 to July 1, 1888* (Savannah: The Morning News Print, 1888). See also James M. Simms, *The First Colored Church in North America* (Philadelphia: J. B. Lippincott, 1888); Edgar D. Thomas, *The First African Baptist Church of North America* (Savannah: Self-published, 1925); and Albert J. Raboteau, *Slave Religion: The Invisible Institution in the Antebellum South* (New York: Oxford University Press, 1978).

See also Harry James (ed), *The First African Baptist Church Celebrates Over Two Centuries 1773–1988: Souvenir Journal* (Savannah: First African Baptist Church, 1988); and Margaret Delores Williams (ed), *First Bryan Baptist Church Bicentennial Anniversary 1788–1988* (Savannah: First Bryan Baptist Church, 1988).

In addition to our research in the archives of First African Baptist Church in Savannah and the Georgia State Baptist Archives at Mercer University in Macon, we are indebted to the following for extensive and often repeat interviews over a three-year period. They include current pastors of the three historic churches that grew out of George Leile's vision and work in Savannah: the Rev. Thurmond Tillman of First African Baptist Church on Franklin Square, the Rev. James H. Cantrell of Second African Baptist Church on Greene Square, and the Rev. Edward L. Ellis Sr. of First Bryan Baptist Church in Yamacraw. We are also indebted to the Rev. Leonard Smalls of Littway Baptist Church, the Rev. Henry Delaney of St. Paul C.M.E. Church, and numerous other ministers whom we saw for briefer periods. In addition, Dr. Otis Johnson, executive director of the Savannah Chatham County Youth Futures Authority; Dr. Lillian Reddick of Savannah State University; and preeminently, W. W. Law, longtime community leader and historian of Savannah, were, among others, extraordinarily generous and helpful with their time and information.

3. Benjamin Quarles, *The Negro in the American Revolution* (New York: W. W. Norton, 1961).

4. Jesse Galphin, a.k.a. Jesse Peter, was held in slavery by one George Galphin, who allowed him considerable freedom of movement and encouraged him in his religious work. Jesse Galphin had been an original member of the Silver Bluff Church, where George Leile preached between 1773 and 1775. During the British occupation Galphin went to Savannah and served with Leile in the church there. After the British evacuation he returned to Augusta and established the Springfield Baptist Church there in 1789. See Raboteau, *Slave Religion*; see also Edward J.Cashin, *Old Springfield: Race And Religion in Augusta, Georgia* (Augusta: Springfield Village Park Foundation, 1995), pp. 139–40. Meanwhile David George, another associate of Leile's at Silver Bluff and at Savannah, departed Savannah with the British and went with other black emi-

gres to Nova Scotia, where he established another Baptist church. Ten years later, he led 1,200 of these emigres to Sierra Leone, where he established yet another Baptist Church. A group of his followers later went to Nigeria to do missionary work, and a group of their descendants returned to the United States and established another Baptist church in South Carolina.

5. Thomas, *The First African Baptist Church of North America.*

6. Ibid., p. 33.

7. Ibid., p. 34.

8. Ibid.

9. From "Lift Every Voice and Sing," by James Weldon Johnson and his brother, J. Rosamond Johnson, still often referred to as the African American national anthem. See James Weldon Johnson and J. Rosamond Johnson (eds), *The Book of American Negro Spirituals* (New York: Viking, 1925).

10. Thomas, *The First African Baptist Church of North America,* p. 37.

11. Ibid.

12. Sunbury Association minutes, 1833. Courtesy Georgia Baptist Association Papers, Mercer University, Macon, GA.

13. Ibid.

14. Marshall would continue as pastor for 24 years, for a total of 44 years, passing away in his 100th year while on a trip up North to raise funds for the construction of the new building in 1856.

3. General Sherman and the Black Church

1. See William S. McFeely (ed), *Memoirs of General William T. Sherman* (New York: Da Capo, 1984), on the Kennesaw Mountain campaign. A couple of expertly guided tours through the Kennesaw Mountain monument grounds brought home the solemnity and savagery of that campaign. Casualties on both sides were extraordinarily heavy. A dispatch to Sherman from one of his field commanders on July 24, 1864, would recount the cost of a successful engagement two days before.

Our total loss	3,521
Enemy's dead delivered to them	3,220
Total prisoners sent North	1,017
Total prisoners wounded in our hands	1,000
Estimated loss of the enemy, at least	10,000.

Major General John A. Logan summarized his report: "Total loss, killed, wounded, and missing, thirty-five hundred and twenty-one and ten pieces of artillery." McFeely, *Memoirs,* vol. 2, pp. 83–84.

It was during this campaign that Sherman used the (white) First Baptist Church of Marietta as a Union hospital, and set free the (black) Zion Baptist Church, which was growing restless in its midst. I am indebted to Judith Crocker for this extensive history lesson. See Crocker-Burris, "Zion Baptist Celebrates 120th Anniversary Sunday," *The Marietta Daily Journal,* May 17, 1986, p. 6-A, and Judith Crocker, "Upon this Rock: The History of Zion Baptist

Church," *Georgia Baptist* (Winter 1984), pp. 4–5. The play *Zion* based in part on Crocker's research has been referenced in a number of publications. See E. Cleland-Pero, "Church's History Again Being Relived on Stage: Zion Reprised at Theater on the Square," *Atlanta Journal/Constitution*, July 18, 1996, p. JF-6.

2. The story of Zion Baptist was documented in a report by Judith Crocker that inspired a play produced by the resident Marietta "Theatre on the Square" in 1990. The play, titled "Zion," got an enthusiastic response and ran for a record 12 weeks. Written by Beverly Trader and commissioned by Michael Horne and Palmer Wells, "Zion" also was produced off Broadway in 1991. A revival of "Zion" at Theatre on the Square was produced in 1996.

3. McFeely, *Memoirs*, vol. 2, p. 109.

4. Gregory D. Coleman, *We're Heaven Bound* (Athens: C. of Georgia Press, 1992). A dramatization of this church's historical evolution, titled "We're Heaven Bound," has become a major annual event at the church on Auburn Avenue and elsewhere in the nation.

5. In 1992, as a result of some additional pioneering research by Judith Crocker, Bethseder's story would be placed in the National Archives in Washington.

6. A History of Bethlehem Baptist Church, Covington, pamphlet, undated. Sherman's march out of Atlanta also liberated another underground black church. After he passed through Stone Mountain, the jubilant blacks set free by him named their section of town "Sherman town" in his honor. Their church became the historic Bethseder Baptist Church, and its history was put in the National Archives, based on the research conducted by Judith Crocker. See Cathy Tyler, "Church History Recorded," *The Daily News*, Stone Mountain, Georgia, January 31, 1992, p. 1; Carlous Daniel, "Preserving Their History," *Atlanta Journal/Constitution*, January 31, 1992, p. B-1; and Duane D. Sanford, "Stone Mountain Parish a Link in History of the Black Church," *Atlanta Journal/Constitution*, Dekalb Extra, July 23, 1993.

7. Benjamin Quarles, *The Negro in the Civil War*, p. 314.

8. Ibid., p. 318.

9. Ibid., p. 317.

10. Ibid., p. 319.

11. Ira Berlin et al., *Free At Last: A Documentary History of Slavery, Freedom, and the Civil War* (New York: The New Press, 1992), p. 310.

12. An undated brochure describes it as "of the country's finest examples of residential Gothic Revival architecture, the detail of the interiors being as sumptuous as any to be found in America." The stately mansion still stands today. It was built for Green by the distinguished architect John S. Norris, of New York, in 1861. See also Donald L. Grant, *The Way It Was In The South* (New York: Carol Publishing Group, 1993).

13. McFeely, *Memoirs*.

14. Sherman's ornate bedroom as late as 1995 held the original marble fireplace, chandeliers, and two Victorian love seats. All else had been restored. Personal tour for the author.

15. In April 1993, as the local historian and tour guide, longtime com-

munity leader W. W. Law approached the Green House with two researchers in tow and assumed the posture of extreme reverence, the same reverence he had shown when touring the historic black churches of Savannah and Laurel Grove Cemetery. "Here," he said to us, "is where history was made. And not many Americans and not many black Americans seem to know or care about what happened in this house in January 1865. It is not too much to suggest," he continued, "that the foundation for the implementation of the Emancipation Proclamation was laid right here in this house by 20 black leaders in their historic meeting with General Sherman and Secretary of War Stanton."

16. McFeely, *Memoirs*.

17. Berlin, *Free at Last*.

18. Episcopal Church, pamphlet undated.

19. Quarles, *The Negro in The Civil War*, p. 320.

20. Ibid., p. 321.

21. Ibid., p. 322. It must be remembered that at this time President Lincoln's cabinet held some of the ablest men in the nation, including Stanton's fellow abolitionists, Treasury Secretary Salmon P. Chase, and John Jay, who would go on to become chief justice of the U.S. Supreme Court.

22. McFeely, *Memoirs*, vol. 2, p. 295.

23. Quarles, *The Negro in the Civil War*, p. 326.

24. McFeely, *Memoirs*, p. 250.

25. Berlin, *Free at Last*.

26. McFeely, *Memoirs*, p. 251.

27. Ibid., p. 252.

28. Ibid.

29. Ibid. The date on which this meeting took place is in some dispute. It most certainly occurred, however, between the meeting with the 20 religious leaders on January 12 and Sherman's departure from Savannah on January 22, 1865. It probably did not occur before Secretary Stanton's departure on January 15. The two generals who addressed the meeting were in all likelihood Sherman and Saxton, who was already known and admired by the black community in Savannah because of his leadership in the liberation of blacks across the river in Beaufort, South Carolina.

30. John Conyers, HR 40. Congressman Conyers has introduced this legislation, written in 1990, repeatedly over the past few years without any substantial support.

31. Chester Hartman (ed), *Poverty and Race: Journal of the Poverty and Race Research Action Council*, vols. 3, 4, 5, and 6 (Washington, D.C., 1994). The publication of this discussion by such a reputable nonblack journal suggests that the issue has a certain saliency and might come alive under a more timely venue.

32. The Rev. Mac Charles Jones devoted the last few years of his remarkably productive life to the issue of reconciliation growing out of the church burnings. He spoke eloquently about the need for the communities to come together as they did during the latter days of the modern civil rights movement.

33. McFeely, *Memoirs*.

34. James M. McPherson, *Marching Toward Freedom: Blacks in the Civil War, 1861–1865* (New York: Facts on File, 1994), p. 85.

35. Ibid., p. 90.

4. Crisis of Emancipation and Reconstruction

1. Robert Perdue, *The Negro in Savannah, 1865–1900* (New York: Exposition Press, 1973).

2. Quarles, *The Negro in the Civil War.*

3. Edmund L. Drago, *Black Politicians and Reconstruction in Georgia: A Splendid Failure* (Baton Rouge: Louisiana State University Press, 1992), p. 27. Jones, who has chronicled the role of the white missionaries from the North who came later, has recognized the early role of the Africans in this regard.

4. Donald L. Grant, *The Way It Was in The South: The Black Experience in Georgia* (New York: Carol, 1993).

5. Ibid., p. 223.

6. Ibid.

7. Ibid.

8. After the war Jane was instrumental in assisting her husband, John Deveaux, the political leader and businessman who founded Savannah's first black newspaper, *The Savannah Tribune*, in 1875. See Grant, *The Way It Was*, p. 129.

9. Grant, *The Way It Was*. See also Susie King Taylor, *Reminiscences of My Life in Camp with the 33rd United States Colored Troops, Late 1st S.C. Volunteers* (Boston: Self-Published, 1904).

10. Grant, *The Way It Was*, p. 220.

11. William Craft and Ellen Craft, *Running a Thousand Miles for Freedom* (London, 1860; reprint, Boston: Beacon Press, 1969).

12. Grant, *The Way It Was*, p. 225.

13. Ibid., p. 226.

14. Ibid.

15. Drago, *Black Politicians*, p. 27.

16. Grant, *The Way It Was*, p. 228.

17. James, *The First African Baptist Church Celebrates*, p. 42.

18. Thomas, *The First African Baptist Church of North America*, p. 87.

19. Ibid., p. 88.

20. Charles Elmore, personal conversation with the author. See also Elmore, *Richard R. Wright, Sr. at Georgia State Industrial College, 1891–1921* (Savannah: Atlantic Printing Co. and the King-Tisdell Foundation, 1996). See also Elizabeth Toss Haynes, *R. R. Wright: Black Man of Atlanta* (Edenborough: Edenborough Press, 1952).See further, Preston Russell and Barbara Hines, *Savannah: A History of Her People Since 1733* (Savannah: Frederick C. Bell Publishers, 1992); Kevin, Meredith, (1990) *Savannah State College Centennial Celebration: 1890–1990.*

21. Grant, *The Way It Was*, p. 246.

22. Ibid, p. 247.

23. Ibid.
24. Elmore, *Richard R. Wright Sr.*
25. Ibid.
26. Ibid.
27. Grant, *The Way It Was*, p. 258.
28. Ibid, p. 259.
29. Ibid.
30. John Blassingame, *The Slave Community: Plantation Life in the Antebellum South* (New York: Oxford University Press, 1972).
31. Grant, *The Way It Was*, p. 259.
32. Ibid.
33. Ibid.
34. Ibid.
35. Quarles, *The Negro in the Civil War*, p. 327.
36. Perdue, *The Negro in Savannah.*
37. Drago, *Black Politicians*, p. 73.
38. Ibid.
39. Ibid.
40. Ibid.
41. Thomas, *The First African Baptist Church of North America.*
42. Ibid., p. 106.
43. Drago, *Black Politicians*, pp. 26–27.
44. Ibid, pp. 27–31.
45. Ibid, p. 27.
46. Ibid, p. 52.
47. James A. Jahannes, Lecture on Bishop Henry McNeil Turner, July 4, 1997, at Savannah.

5. Rev. Ralph Mark Gilbert and the Civil Rights Movement in Savannah

1. The museum to commemorate the civil rights movement, opened in 1996, is named the Ralph Mark Gilbert Civil Rights Museum. Though Gilbert has been referred to in recent years as the Dr. Martin Luther King Jr. of Savannah, it is worth noting that Gilbert began his crusades in Savannah when King was only 10 years old.
2. James, *The First African Baptist Church Celebrates*, p. 45.
3. Otis Johnson, "The Social Welfare Role of the Black Church" (Ph.D. diss., Brandeis University, 1980).
4. James, *The First African Baptist Church Celebrates,*p. 45.
5. Johnson, "The Social Welfare Role," pp. 109–119.
6. When Dr. James A. Jahannes gave a lecture on Bishop Henry McNeil Turner at the 1997 annual celebration at a site near Turner Boulevard, he remarked that Turner would be disappointed about the schism which developed in the church over the years but proud as punch of the activism which led to it.

7. Marty, Shuter, "Savannah's Civil Rights Story: Ralph Gilbert Museum to Tell of 'Finest Hour,' " *Savannah News Press*, September 1, 1996, p. 12-A. See also W. W. Law, "The Ralph Mark Gilbert Civil Rights Museum" (Savannah: Savannah Area Convention and Visitors Bureau, 1995). Dr. Johnson should know: He was part and parcel of the whole transition. He emerged as scholar, educator, political leader, social worker, and now is leader of a wide movement, the Chatham County Savannah Youth Futures Authority, to help all the children of the area live up to the premise in accordance with the content of this chapter. And just as the black church was a central engine for the civil rights movement, so it is an agent of social reform for today.

8. Johnson, "The Social Welfare Role."

6. First African Baptist Church, Richmond

1. Quarles, *The Negro in the Civil War*. R.J.M. Blackett (ed), *Thomas Morris Chester: Black Civil War Correspondent: His Dispatches from the Virginia Front* (New York: Da Capo, 1989), p. 1. McPherson, *Marching Toward Freedom*, p. 90.

2. Quarles, *The Negro in the Civil War*, p. 330.

3. Among the ironies of Lumpkin's existence is that at the same time he was trading in slave markets, he was "married" to a black women with whom he lived. She too was left behind as he fled for his life. Still another irony is that this black woman inherited his property, including his infamous Lumpkin Jail. When black educators and their supporters went looking for a place to start a college for blacks after emancipation, she sold the Lumpkin Jail to them for the purpose of beginning Virginia Union College, which continues to the present day as a college primarily for black students. The late Dr. Samuel DeWitt Proctor, former president of Virginia Union University, cited this story in numerous personal appearances, including his address at the 1975 inauguration of the author as president of Morgan State University in Baltimore.

4. Blackett, *Thomas Morris Chester*, p. 314.

5. Quarles, *The Negro in the Civil War*, p. 331.

6. Blackett, *Thomas Morris Chester*, p. ix. Nor was it the first black troops that had captured a Confederate stronghold. McPherson reports that they had done so earlier in February 1865 in Charleston. Moreover, black troops had also led the capture and occupation of nearby Petersburg. See McPherson, *Marching Toward Freedom*, p. 90.

7. Quarles, *The Negro in the Civil War*, p. 331.

8. Ibid., p. 333.

9. Ibid., p. 334.

10. Ibid., p. 335.

11. Ibid.

12. Blackett, *Thomas Morris Chester*, p. 302.

13. "History of the First Baptist Church, Richmond, on the Occasion of its 100th Anniversary, 1880." See also "The First Baptist Church, Richmond, 1780–1955: One Hundred Seventy-Five Years of Service to God and Man."

Both documents were made available to the researchers by Trustee Daniel R. Perkins Jr. from the archives of the First African Baptist Church, Richmond, together with extensive discussions and interpretations.

14. John O'Brien, "Slave Labor and the Black Church in Richmond," *Journal of Southern History*, vol. 44, no. 4 (November 1978): pp. 509–36. See also Luther P. Jackson, *Free Negro Labor and Property Holding in Virginia, 1830–1860* (New York and London: 1942), pp. 158–59.

15. Ibid., p. 509.

16. Ibid., p. 534. The event was also carried in the *New York Times* of June 17, 1865.

17. Daniel Perkins Jr. (ed), "The 115th Anniversary of the First African Baptist Church and the 8th Anniversary of our Pastor, Rev. Y. B. Williams, and the Dedication of the Present Building of First African Baptist Church, Sunday November 4th through Friday, November 30, 1956." Richmond, 1956.

18. "History of the First Baptist Church, Richmond," p. 61.

19. Perkins, "The 115th Anniversary."

20. Ibid.

21. "History of First Baptist Church, Richmond."

22. Ibid.

23. Robert Ryland, "Origins and History of the First African Baptist Church, Richmond," in Henry A. Tupper, *The First Century of the First Baptist Church, Richmond* (1880), pp. 271–72.

24. "History of First Baptist Church, Richmond."

25. Ibid.

26. Perkins, "The 115th Anniversary."

27. Ibid.

28. Proceedings of the Church Conference, 1928.

29. Gertrude W. Marlow, "Maggie Lena Walker, 1867–1934," in Darlene Clark Hines, *Black Women Pioneers*, p. 1219. See also Gertrude W. Marlowe, *Ransom For Many: A Life of Maggie Lena Walker* (New York: Carlson Publisher, 1996), and Wendell P. Dabney, *Maggie L. Walker: Her Life and Deeds* (Washington: Eastern National Park and Monument Association, 1994).

30. Daniel R. Perkins Jr., personal interview with the author, 1994–95.

31. Ibid. Perkins is a senior member of this church, chairman of the board of trustees, church archivist, and historian. He spent numerous hours with the two researchers on at least four different occasions and was as informative as he was generous with his time.

32. Interview with former Gov. Wilder at his Richmond law office, September 2, 1995. Wilder was gracious and informative, and he provided a copy of his résumé. Additional information was derived from newspaper articles and from *Who's Who in America*.

33. The Rev. Dennis E. Thomas, personal interview with the author in 1994. Thomas gave the researchers copies of his résumé and other church documents. He has also visited with the researchers on several subsequent occasions, including Sunday, Sept. 14, 1997, together with Trustee Daniel R. Perkins Jr.

7. New-Time Religion

1. Editorial, *New York Times*, May 23, 1988.

2. "The 15 Greatest Black Preachers: Expert and Leading Blacks Name Select Group of Ministers," *Ebony*, November 1993, pp. 156–68.

3. Lloyd Gite, "The New Agenda of the Black Church: Economic Development for Black Enterprise," *Black Enterprise*, December 1993, pp. 54–59.

4. Ingrid Sturgis, "Urban Seminary: New York Theological's Mission Down Town," *Emerge*, February 1995, pp. 56–59.

5. Billingsley et al., "Tradition and Change: The Black Church and Family Oriented Community Outreach Programs," a report to the Ford Foundation and the Lilly Endowment, 1992.

6. The methods by which we arrived at this conclusion are detailed in Appendix B. In general, we undertook the following activities beginning in fall 1987: First, we read widely in the literature of church-sponsored outreach programs. These references are listed in the Appendix. Second, we conducted unstructured face-to-face interviews with some two dozen "informants." These were usually religious leaders with broad experience and knowledge of community outreach activities of black churches.

On the basis of our findings, we developed a questionnaire and conducted a pilot study of 72 black churches along the East Coast in New York, Pennsylvania, Maryland, Washington, D.C., Atlanta, and New Orleans. Dr. Robert B. Hill was research consultant on this survey.

Then, on the basis of findings from the pilot study, we developed a questionnaire and pretested it in a focus group of black ministers in Washington, D.C., in a meeting at Shiloh Baptist Church.

Once the questionnaire was revised after the focus group, we then conducted a stratified random sample of 312 black churches in six Northeast regions: Massachusetts, Connecticut, New York, New Jersey, Pennsylvania, and Delaware. The churches represented 20 different denominations.

Next, we conducted a similar stratified random sample of 315 black churches in six Midwestern states: Ohio, Illinois, Minnesota, Indiana, Michigan, and Kansas. Dr. Cleopatra Howard Caldwell was study director for both the above surveys.

Survey of a nonrandom sample of 80 black churches in metropolitan Denver was conducted using a modified version of the same questionnaire. Grant Jones, Dr. Jessica Pearson, and others conducted this survey.

Additionally, a similar survey of 150 black churches was conducted in the Southern gateway city of Atlanta. We are indebted to Professor Naomi Ward, Judith Crocker, and my students at Spelman College for assistance.

Finally, in the fall of 1997, a similar study of nearly 100 churches was conducted in three largely rural counties of South Carolina. These surveys were supplemented by extensive ethnographic case studies of selected churches in all regions of the nation.

7. C. Eric Lincoln and Lawrence Mamiya, *The Black Church in the African American Experience* (Durham, NC: Duke University Press, 1990).

8. Otis Johnson, The Social Welfare Role of the Black Church. Ph.D. Dissertation, Brandeis University, 1980.

9. Andrew Billingsley, *Black Families in White America* (New York: Simon & Schuster, [1968] 1988).

10. Roger Rubin, Andrew Billingsley, and Cleopatra Howard Caldwell, "The Role of the Black Church in Working with Black Adolescents." *Adolescence* 29, no. 114 (1994): 251-66. See also Rubin, Billingsley, and Caldwell, "The Black Church and Youth at Risk of Incarceration," in *Monograph on Youth in the 1990s* (Dalhousie University, 1995). Still another version of this paper appeared as Rubin, Caldwell, and Billingsley, "The Black Church and Adolescent Sexuality," *National Journal of Sociology*, vol. 8, nos. 1 and 2 (Summer and Winter 1994): 131-48. Still another analysis of the data was reported in Billingsley and Crocker, "The Role of Black Churches in the U.S. in the Prevention of Deviant Behavior Among Youth," delivered at the International Symposium on Youth, England, July 1995.

11. T. A. Turner and K. McFate, "Community Programs that Serve Young Black Males" (Washington, D.C.: The Joint Center for Political and Economic Studies, 1994).

12. Harriette P. McAdoo and Vanella Crawford conducted this assessment on behalf of the Council of National Black Churches, Washington, D.C.

13. Brewer Wilson et al., "Violence Prevention Strategies Targeted at Populations of Minority Youth" (Atlanta: Centers for Disease Control and Prevention, 1990).

14. Cleopatra Howard Caldwell, Linda M. Chatters, Andrew Billingsley, and Robert Joseph Taylor, "Church-Based Support Programs for Elderly Black Adults: Congregational and Clergy Characteristics," in Melvin A. Kimble et al. (eds), *Aging, Spirituality and Religion: A Handbook* (Minneapolis: Fortress Press, 1995).

15. Ibid.

16. Ibid.

17. Joseph M. Shopshire, "The Methodist Church and Community Outreach," in Billingsley et al., *Tradition and Change* (unpublished, 1992).

18. Wardell J. Payne (ed), *Directory of African American Religious Bodies* (Washington, D.C.: Howard University Press, 1991), pp. 48–55.

19. Willie F. Tolliver, "A Model For Church Based Social Services" (New York School of Social Work, Hunter College, 1994).

8. The Black Church and the Male Youth Crisis

1. Jewell Gibbs (ed), *Young, Black and Male in America: An Endangered Species* (Dover, MA: Auburn House, 1988).

2. This report and much of the field work for this study in Savannah were conducted by Judith Denise Crocker, LMSW, who was principal research assistant for the Southern states.

3. For a detailed study on this topic see Judith Denise Crocker, "The Role of the Black Church in the Prevention of Violence Among Black Youth," Master's Thesis, Clark Atlanta University School of Social Work, 1997.

9. The Black Church Confronts the HIV/AIDS Crisis

1. "HIV/AIDS Surveillance: U.S. AIDS Cases Through September 1994." Atlanta: Centers for Disease Control and Prevention, 1994.

2. Maureen Downey, "AIDS and the Black Community," *Atlanta Journal/Constitution*, Nov. 30, 1995, p. 1.

3. Debra Frazier-Howze (ed), Black Leadership Commission on AIDS Progress Report, 1994. I am indebted to Frazier-Howze, Dr. James Dumpson, and other staff and board members of BLCA for the opportunity of working briefly with a major initiative of the organization during 1995 and 96.

4. BLCA, "Choose Life," an agency brochure, 1994.

5. Sandra Crouse Quinn and Stephen B. Thomas, "Results of a Baseline Assessment of AIDS knowledge Among Black Church Members," *National Journal of Sociology*, vol. 8, nos. 1 and 2 (Summer/Winter 1994): 89–108.

6. Suzanne Randolph, "Studying Black Churches and Family Support in the Context of HIV/AIDS," *National Journal of Sociology*, vol. 8, nos. 1 and 2 (Summer/Winter 1994): 109–30.

7. Ibid.

8. Stephen B. Thomas, Sandra Crouse Quinn, Andrew Billingsley, and Cleopatra Howard Caldwell, "The Characteristics of Northern Black Churches with Community Health Outreach Programs," *American Journal of Public Health 84*, no. 4 (1994): 575–79.

9. Louis Sullivan (ed), "Healthy People 2000" (Washington, D.C.: Department of Health and Human Services, 1991).

10. Stephen B. Thomas and Sandra Crouse Quinn, "The Tuskegee Syphilis Study, 1932–1972: Implications for HIV Education and AIDS Risk Reduction Programs in the Black Community," *American Journal of Public Health 81*, no. 11 (1991): 1498–1505.

10. A Tale of Two Cities

1. I am indebted to Grant Jones and the Piton Foundation in Denver for organizing and supporting the Metro Denver Black Church Initiative, which gave rise to this study. For results of the Denver survey see Jessica Pearson and Jane Anhalt, "Community Outreach in Denver's Black Churches" (Denver: Center for Policy Analysis, 1993). I am indebted to Judith Crocker and seven other Spelman women for assistance with the Atlanta survey. For a report of the Atlanta survey, see Naomi Ward et al., "Black Churches in Atlanta Reach Out to the Community," *National Journal of Sociology*, vol. 8, nos. 1 and 2, (Summer/Winter, 1994). Other students who assisted were Lila Anderson, Gail Armstrong, Pauline Greeter, Glenda Hodges, Tamara Mann, Jo Ellen Page, Wanda Perry Hardeman, and Helen Richmond. Dr. Pauline Drake, dean of

continuing education at Spelman, helped students with this study. Ward was research consultant. The study was funded by the Ford Foundation and by Spelman College. Professors Coye Williams, LeConya Butler, Norman Rates, Daryl White, Harry Leffever, and Evelyn Chisholm in the departments of sociology, psychology, and religion were also helpful to the students and to me. For all this support and assistance, I express my deep gratitude.

2. Pearson and Anhalt, *Community Outreach in Denver's Black Churches.* See also Grant Jones, "Metro Denver Black Church Initiative: Churches Working Together to Build Strong Communities" (Denver: The Piton Foundation, 1995).

3. Grant Jones, "Grant Awards, Denver Black Church Initiative" (Denver: The Piton Foundation, 1996).

4. Ibid.

5. Walter V. Collier, "The Piton Foundation's Metro Denver Black Church Initiative: An Interim Evaluation Report: 1995–1996," final version, October 25, 1996.

6. Ward et al., "Black Churches in Atlanta."

7. Ibid.

8. Alma E. Hill, "Hotel Could Revitalize Vine City," *Atlanta Journal/Constitution*, February 8, 1995, p. 1.

11. *Often Seen, Seldom Called: The Legacy of Jerena Lee*

1. Material in this section is taken from Jerena Lee, "The Life and Religious Experience of Mrs. Jerena Lee as Written by Herself," 1836, self-published, reprinted in Milton Sernett, *Afro-American Religious History: A Documentary Witness* (Durham, NC: Duke University Press, 1985).

2. Jualynne Dodson, *19th Century A.M.E. Preaching Women*, Ph.D. diss., University of California, Berkeley, 1990.

3. Lincoln and Mamiya, *The Black Church*, p. 280.

4. Ibid., p. 281.

5. Ibid., p. 279.

6. Ibid.

7. Church Bulletin, First A.M.E. Church, Los Angeles, undated. Church founder Biddy Mason is memorialized along with other notable persons and events in African American history in the impressive mural, which spans the entire length of the wall behind the pulpit.

8. Though the original congregation was nondenominational, it joined forces with the A.M.E. mission as it moved to the West Coast.

9. Lincoln and Mamiya, *The Black Church*, p. 275.

10. Ibid.

11. Such a list can only be suggestive of the rich potential for blossoming forth of this remnant element in the black church.

12. Jacquelyn Grant, "Womanist Theology: Black Women's Experience as a Source of Doing Theology with Special Reference to Christology," *Journal of the Interdenominational Center 13* (Spring 1986). See also Jacquelyn Grant, "Black Women and the Church," in Gloria T. Hull et al. (eds), *All the Women*

Are White and All the Blacks Are Men, But Some of Us Are Brave: Black Women's Studies (Old Westbury, NY: Feminist Press, 1982), pp. 141–52.

13. Lincoln and Mamiya, *The Black Church*, p. 292–93.

14. Ibid.

15. Delores Carpenter, "The Effect of Sect Typeness Upon the Professionalization of Black Female Master's of Divinity Graduates 1972–1984," Ph.D. diss., 1986. Dr. Carpenter has also graciously shared with the author others of her unpublished materials.

16. James Cone, *Martin and Malcolm and America: A Dream or a Nightmare?* (Maryknoll, NY: Orbis Books, 1991).

17. Vincent Harding, *Hope and History: Why We Must Share the Story of the Movement* (Maryknoll, NY: Orbis Books, 1990).

18. James Cone, *A Black Theology of Liberation* (New York: Orbis, 1990). When *Ebony Magazine* conducted a poll among certain of its readers in 1993 and selected the 15 Greatest Black Preachers, women did not make the list. In a measure of compensation, however, respondents to *Ebony*'s poll did place women preachers in the second-tier honor roll of recognized black preachers. Among 46 preachers on this second-tier honor roll, seven were women. By 1997 Ebony would conduct a special survey of the 15 Greatest Black Women Preachers and 20 follow ups. (See Tables 18 and 19.)

Ebony has pioneered in profiling individual black women preachers. See, for example, Marilyn Marshall, "Leentyne, Kelly: First Black Woman Bishop," *Ebony*, November 1984.

12. Twelve Gates to the City

1. For some 25 years *Black Enterprise* has been the authoritative source of information of business enterprises in the African American community. For much of that time, the Rev. Wyatt Tee Walker has tried, without success, to persuade or cajole the magazine to write about the black church as the premier economic enterprise in the community. He once told a meeting of the Association of Black Sociologists in New York that the black church collectively owned more property, employed more people, provided more housing, fed more people, collected more money, banked more money, spent, saved, and invested more money, and turned around more money within the community than any other category of black institution they might know. "And that's not our main business," he taunted them. "Our main business is saving souls. But on top of that we do more economic business than any other institution." He challenged them to conceptualize and study the black church as an economic and social institution as well as a religious one, instead of ignoring the church as many sociologists do. See also Wyatt Tee Walker, "The Black Church and the Revolution of the '60s: The Essay that the NAACP Refused to Publish" (self-published, 1982), p. 6.

2. Gregory J. Reed, *Economic Empowerment Through the Church* (Detroit: Zondervan Publishing House, 1993), p. 17.

3. Ibid.

4. Walter Malone Jr., *From Holy Power to Holy Profits: The Black Church and Community Economic Empowerment* (Chicago: African American Images, 1993).

5. See Billingsley et al., *Tradition And Change*, pp. 561–64.

6. See Gary Simpson, "The Concord Baptist Church Christ Fund" (1993), unpublished paper made available to the author. Simpson, who was at the time associate pastor and is now pastor, was most gracious in providing information and materials during this site visit. See also Gardner C. Taylor, *The Scarlet Thread* (Chicago: The Progressive National Baptist Publishing House, 1981).

7. Simpson, "Concord Baptist."

8. Rev. Gardner C. Taylor to the *Baltimore Afro-American Newspaper*, 1988.

9. Calvin Butts, "The Abyssinian Development Corporation," unpublished. See Billingsley et al., *Tradition and Change*, p. 361.

10. Ishmael Lateef Ahmad, "An Evening of Elegance," *The St. Louis American*, Sept. 17–23, 1998, pp. A1, A6.

11. Cecil L. Murray (ed), *History of the First African Baptist Church*, Los Angeles, unpublished. The Rev. Murray and his staff were most cordial and helpful during the two site visits. I am indebted to Dr. Jeanne Giovannoni of UCLA for introducing me to this church.

12. Cecil L. Murray (ed), annual reports of First A.M.E. Church, Los Angeles, 1993 and 1994, made available to the author during site visits.

13. Ibid.

14. Murray, *A History of First A.M.E. Church*, Los Angeles, undated.

15. *Black Enterprise* (Sept. 1993), p. 57.

16. William S. Epps (ed), annual reports of Second Baptist Church, Los Angeles, for 1991, 1992, made available to the author during site visit. Rev. Epps and his staff were most gracious in providing information during this site visit and subsequently. The average size of the activist churches in this study was around 500 members.

17. J. Alfred Smith Sr. and J. Alfred Smith Jr., annual reports and extensive interviews and documents made available to the author during site visits. Both the father and son have been very generous in providing information for this study. See also Alfred J. Smith Sr., *Preach On* (Chicago: The Progressive Baptist Publishing House, 1981).

18. Annual reports made available to the author during two site visits in 1994–95. See also Leon Sullivan, *Build Brother Build* (Philadelphia: Mcrae Smith, 1989).

19. Charles Adams (ed), annual reports and other items made available to the author during site visit.

20. Ibid.

21. In addition to my visits to this church and my discussions with Rev. Moss I am indebted to Rev. Mark C. Olds and Ms. Beverly Gaffney for special assistance in data collection.

22. In addition to our three site visits to this church and community, written reports on the progress of the outreach ministries were made available. See Billingsley (1992), p. 357. See also Frank Marcus Frances, "New Orleans Jour-

nal: Project on Piety Street Reclaims Crack House," *New York Times*, May 12, 1989, p. 8.

23. Letter to the author, dated May 15, 1993.

24. Annual reports and interview with the Rev. Michael Harris. See also Lincoln and Mamiya, *The Black Church*, p. 176; *Black Enterprise* (Sept. 1993), p. 58; and *Ebony* (November 1993), p. 156.

25. Lincoln and Mamiya, *The Black Church*, p. 176.

26. Michael Harris recounts this story.

27. Annual reports and interviews made available during site visit. See also Walter J. Malone, *From Holy Power to Holy Profits: The Black Church and Community Economic Empowerment* (Chicago: African American Images, 1994).

28. *Black Enterprise* (Sept. 1993), p. 59.

29. Ibid.

13. Unashamedly Black and Unapologetically Christian

1. Jeremiah Wright (ed), Trinity United Church of Christ Annual Report, 1991.

2. Ibid., 1987.

3. Jeremiah Wright (ed), "Unashamedly Black and Unapologetically Christian," a booklet (1986).

4. See Roy C. Nichols, "Components of a Vital Congregation," in Report of the Consultation on Vital Congregations, Council of Bishops, United Methodist Church, November 15, 1987, p. 109.

5. *Ebony* (November 1993), p. 157.

6. Personal communication to the author from Pastor Wright.

14. One More River to Cross

1. Vincent Harding, *There Is a River: The Black Struggle for Freedom in America* (New York: Harcourt Brace Jovanovich, 1981).

2. Sullivan, *Build Brother Build*.

3. Bill McDonald, "A Fantastic Young Lady," *The State Newspaper*, Columbia, SC. May 24, 1998, p. E-1.

4. The Rev. Bernice King, address to the annual Dr. Martin Luther King Day Celebration, Ebenezer Baptist Church, Atlanta, January 15, 1993.

References

Abernathy, Ralph David. *And the Walls Came Tumbling Down*. New York: Harper & Row, 1989.

African-American Religion: Research Problems and Resources for the 1990s. New York: The Schomburg Center for Research in Black Culture, 1990.

African American Religious Studies. Durham, NC: Duke University Press, 1989.

Askew, Glorya, and Gayraud Wilmore, eds. *Reclamation of Black Prisoners: A Challenge to the African American Church*. Atlanta: ITC Press, 1992.

———. *From Prison Cell To Church Pew*. Atlanta: ITC Press, 1993.

Baer, Hans A., and Merrill Singer. *African-American Religion in the Twentieth Century*. Nashville: University of Tennessee Press, 1992.

Baldwin, Lewis V. *There Is a Balm in Gilead*. Minneapolis: Fortress Press, 1991.

———. *To Make the Wounded Whole*. Minneapolis: Fortress Press, 1992.

Battle, Michael A., Sr., ed. *The African-American Church at Work*. St.: Hodale Press, 1994.

Berendt, John. *Midnight in the Garden of Good and Evil*. New York: Random House, 1994.

Billingsley, Andrew. *Climbing Jacob's Ladder*. New York: Simon & Schuster, 1992.

Boritt, Gabor S., ed. *Why the Confederacy Lost*. New York: Oxford University Press, 1991.

Branch, Taylor. *Parting the Waters*. New York: Simon & Schuster, 1988.

Butler, John Sibley, ed. *National Journal of Sociology*, vol. 8, nos. 1 and 2 (Summer/Winter 1994).

Carson, Clayborne, David J. Garrow, Gerald Hill, Vincent Harding, and Darlene Clark Hine, eds. *Keep Your Eyes on the Prize*. New York: Penguin, 1991.

Carter, Harold A. *Prayer in the Life of Black People*. Baltimore: Gateway Press, 1994.

Carter, Weptanomah W. *The Black Minister's Wife, as a Participant in the Redemptive Ministry of Her Husband*. (Detroit: Progressive Baptist Publishing House, 1976.

Cashin, Edward J. *Old Springfield: Race and Religion in Augusta, Georgia*. Augusta: The Springfield Village Park Foundation, 1995.

Chester, Thomas Morris. *Black Civil War Correspondent*. New York: Da Capo Press, 1989.

Cleage, Albert B., Jr. *Black Christian Nationalism*. Detroit MI: Luxor Publishers of the Pan-African Orthodox Christian Church, 1987.

———. *The Black Messiah*. Trenton, NJ: Africa World Press, 1989.

Coan, Josephus R. "The Expansion of Missions of the African Methodist Episcopal Church in South Africa, 1896–1908." Hartford Seminary, 1961.

Coleman, Gregory D. *We're Heaven Bound*. Athens: U. of Georgia Press, 1992.

Cone, James H. *The Spirituals and the Blues*. New York: Orbis Books, 1972.

———. *A Black Theology of Liberation*. New York: Orbis Books, 1990.

———. *Martin and Malcolm and America, A Dream or a Nightmare*. Maryknoll, NY: Orbis Books, 1991.

Dabney, Wendell P. *Maggie L. Walker—Her Life and Deeds*. Cincinnati, OH: The Dabney Publishing Co, 1927.

Davis, Burke. *Sherman's March*. New York: Vintage, 1988.

Davis, Cyprian. *The History of Black Catholics in the United States*. New York: Crossroad Publishing, 1990.

Drago, Edmund L. *Black Politicians and Reconstruction in Georgia—A Splendid Failure*. Baton Rouge: Louisiana State University Press, 1992.

Du Bois, W.E.B. *On Sociology and the Black Community*. Chicago: University of Chicago Press, 1978.

Evans, Zelia S. and J. T. Alexander, eds. "Dexter Avenue Baptist Church 1877–1977," Dexter Avenue Baptist Church, 1978.

Fitts, Leroy. *A History of Black Baptists*. Nashville: Broadman Press, 1985.

Frazier, E. Franklin. *The Negro Church in America*. New York: Schocken, 1964

———. *E. Franklin Frazier on Race Relations, Selected Writings*. Chicago: University of Chicago Press, 1968.

Frazier, E. Franklin, and C. Eric Lincoln. *The Black Church Since Frazier*. New York: Schocken Books, 1974.

Freedman, Samuel G. *Upon This Rock*. New York: HarperCollins, 1984.

Futch, Abie. *Business and Life History From 1800 Thru 1995*. Savannah: Self-Published, 1995.

Garrow, David J. *Protest at Selma*. New York: Yale University Press, 1978.

George, Yolanda S., Vincent Richardson, Marsha Lakes-Matyas, and Frederick Blake. *Saving Minds: Black Churches and Education*. Washington, DC: American Association for the Advancement of Science.

Glide Foundation, a national conference, "To Heal a Wounded Soul," 1992.

Grant, Donald L. *The Way It Was in the South*. New York: Carol Publishing, 1993.

Harding, Vincent. *Hope and History: Why We Must Share the Story of the Movement*. Maryknoll, NY: Orbis Books, 1990.

Hicks, H. Beecher, Jr. *Preaching Through a Storm*. Detroit: Zondervan Publishing House, 1987.

Higginbotham, Evelyn Brooks. *Righteous Discontent*. Boston: Harvard University Press, 1993.

Hilliard, Asa G. *The Maroon Within Us*. Baltimore: Black Classic Press, 1995.

Hopkins, Dwight N., and George Cummings. *Cut Loose Your Stammering Tongue*. New York: Orbis Books, 1992.

Howze, Joseph L., et al. "What We Have Seen and Heard, A Pastoral Letter on Evangelization From the Black Bishops of the United States." New York: St. Anthony Messenger Press, 1993.

King, Coretta Scott. *My Life With Martin Luther King, Jr*. New York: Holt, Rinehart and Winston, 1969.

Kunjufu, Jawanza. *Countering the Conspiracy to Destroy Black Boys*. Chicago: African American Images Press, 1985.

————. *Adam! Where are you? Why Most Black Boys Do Not Go to Church*. Chicago: African American Images Press, 1994.

Lincoln, C. Eric, and Lawrence H. Mamiya. *The Black Church in the African American Experience*. Durham, NC: Duke University Press, 1990.

Logan, Rayford W., and Michael R. Winston. *Dictionary of American Negro Biography*. New York: W. W. Norton, 1982.

Long, Richard A., ed. *Black Writers and the American Civil War*. Secaucus, NJ: The Blue & Grey Press, 1988.

Lucas, Lawrence E. *Black Priest/White Church*. Trenton NJ: Africa World Press, 1989.

Malone, Walter, Jr. *From Holy Power to Holy Profits: The Black Church and Community Economic Empowerment*. Chicago: African American Images, 1994.

McAdam, Doug. *Freedom Summer*. New York: Oxford University Press, 1988.

McFreely, William S., ed. *Memories of General William T. Sherman*. New York: Da Capo, 1984.

McPherson, James J. *Marching Toward Freedom*. New York: Facts on File, [1965] 1994.

Mitchell, Henry H. *Black Preaching*. New York: J. B. Lippincott, 1970.

Morris, Aldon D. *The Origins of the Civil Rights Movement: Black Communities Organizing for Change*. New York: The Free Press, 1984.

"115th Anniversary of the First African Baptist Church and the 8th Anniversary of our Pastor, Rev. Y. B. Williams, and the Dedication of the present building of First African Baptist Church, Richmond, Virginia, Sunday, November 4th through Friday, November 30, 1956." Richmond: First African Baptist Church, 1956.

Paige, Carol. "Bishop Henry McNeal Turner and the 'Ethiopian Movement' in South Africa 1896–1904," MA thesis. Roosevelt U., Chicago, 1973.

Paris, Peter J. *The Social Teaching of the Black Churches*. Minneapolis: Fortress Press, 1985.

————. *Black Religious Leaders; Conflict in Unity*. Louisville, KY: Westminster/ John Knox Press, 1991.

Payne, Wardell J., ed. *Directory of African American Religious Bodies*. Washington, D.C.: Howard University Press, 1991.

Philanthropy and the Black Church. Washington, D.C.: Council on Foundations, 1990.

Platt, Anthony M. *E. Franklin Frazier Reconsidered*. New Brunswick, NJ: Rutgers University Press, 1991.

Porter, Horace. *Campaigning With Grant*. New York: Konecky & Konecky, 1992.

Proctor, Samuel D., and William D. Watley. *Sermons From the Black Pulpit*. Valley Forge, PA: Judson Press, 1984.

Quarles, Benjamin. *The Negro in the Civil War*. New York & Boston: Da Capo, 1953; Boston: Little, Brown, 1969.

————. *The Negro in the American Revolution*. New York: W. W. Norton, 1961.

Raboteau, Albert J. *Slave Religion*. New York: Oxford University Press, 1978.

Reed, Gregory J. *Economic Empowerment Through the Church*. Grand Rapids, MI: Zondervan, 1993.

Reid, Frank M., III. *The Nehemiah Plan*. Shippingburg Treasure House, 1993.

Sanneh, Lamin. *West African Christianity—The Religious Impact*. New York: Orbis Books, 1983.

Sikora, Frank. *Until Justice Rolls Down: The Birmingham Church Bombing Case*. Tuscaloosa: University of Alabama Press, 1991.

Smith, Edward D. *Climbing Jacob's Ladder*. Washington, D.C.: Smithsonian Institution Press, 1988.

Smith, J. Alfred. *Preach On!* Nashville, TN: Broadman Press, 1984.

Smith, Wallace Charles. *The Church in the Life of the Black Family*. Valley Forge, PA: Judson Press, 1985.

Stampp, Kenneth M. *The Causes of the Civil War*. Englewood Cliffs, NJ: Prentice Hall, 1965.

The Study Guide to Dr. Cain Hope Felder's Troubling Biblical Waters, Race, Class, and Family. Morristown, NJ: Aaron Press, 1990.

Sullivan, Leon H. *Build Brother Build*. PA: Macrae Smith, 1989.

Taylor, Gardner C. *How Shall They Preach*. Elgin, IL: Progressive Baptist Publishing House, 1977.

————. *The Scarlet Thread*. Elgin, IL: Progressive Baptist Publishing House, 1981.

Wade-Gayles, Gloria, ed. *My Soul Is a Witness*. Boston: Beacon, 1995.

Walker, Wyatt Tee. *The Soul of Black Worship*. New York: Martin Luther King Fellows Press, 1984.

————. *Spirits That Dwell in Deep Woods*. New York: Ray Leonardo & Sons, 1987.

Ward, Naomi. "Employment Needs Assessment in the Vine City Community, A Community Job Skills and Employment Opportunity Survey." Atlanta: Vine City Housing Ministry, 1991.

Washington, Preston Robert. *From the Pew to the Pavement*. Morristown, NJ: Aaron Press, 1986.

————. *God's Transforming Spirit: Black Church Renewal*. Valley Forge, PA: Judson Press, 1988.

West, Cornel. *Race Matters*. Boston: Beacon, 1993.

Wilmore, Gayraud, ed. *Women in Ministry—Four Views*. Downes Grove, IL: InterVarsity Press.

Williams, Cecil. *No Hiding Place*. San Francisco: Harper, 1992.

Williams, Juan. *Eyes on the Prize*. New York: Penguin Books, 1987.

Young, Henry J. *The Black Church and the Harold Washington Story*. Bristol, IN: Wyndham Hall, 1988.

Index

A.L.I.V.E., 167
Abernathy, Ralph David, 12, 60
Abyssinian Baptist Church (NYC),
    88, 113, 146, 148–49
Academic School, 192–93
Activist churches, 95–98, 186
Adams, Charles, 88
Adams, Charles Francis, 63
Adams, John Hurst, *xvii*, 190
Adams, John Quincy, 63
Adero, Malaika, *xviii*
African American Family, national
    conference on, 158
African Americans: cultural values
    of, 112; heritage of, 157, 170, 183
African American Studies Program,
    USC, *xvii*
African Baptist Church, 109
African colonization, 52, 69
African Methodist Episcopal Zion
    Church, 137, 141
Afrocentric/Christocentric creed,
    180, 183
Afrocentricity, 181
Agape Christian Church, 121, 123

Agape House, 156
AIDS, 70, 92, 110–18
Alabama Civil Rights Institute, 5
Alabama Voting Rights League, 4
Alford-Smith, Daisy, 158
Allen, Barbara, 175, 180
Allen, Richard, *xxi*, 133–34, 135,
    136, 173
Allen A.M.E. Church, 146, 150
Allen Temple Baptist Church, 150,
    153–54, 176
All Nations Pentecostal Church (Chi-
    cago), 138
All Nations Pentecostal Church
    (Denver), 124
Alston, Walter, *xvi*
Alvin Ailey Dance Workshop, 165
A-MEN Enterprise, 105
American Ballet Theater, 165
American Baptist College, 163
American Baptist Home Mission So-
    ciety, 49
American Colonization Society, 52
American Friends Service Commit-
    tee, 125

American Missionary Association, 38, 39, 40

Anchor of Hope Christian Church, 123

Anderson, Andrea, *xvii*

Anderson, Margaret, 79

Anderson, Marian, 176

Anderson, Thomas, 21

Aniton, Emmett, 93

Antioch Baptist Church-North, 127

Apartheid, 155–56

Armstrong State College, 56, 59

Arrington, Richard, 5–6

Ashley, Sandra Kay, *xviii*

Atlanta, GA, 23, 119–31

Atlanta Economic Development Corporation, 130

Atlanta Journal Constitution, 110, 131

Atlanta University, 42, 44, 128, 138

Augusta Baptist College, 42

Augusta Institute, 41

Augusta Weekly Sentinel, 41, 43

Auto repair school, 156

Auxiliaries, 179

Baer, Hans A., 10

Baker, T., 23

Baltimore United in Leadership Development (BUILD), 146

Banks, black-owned, 45

Bankston, Gene, 165

Baptist denominations, 137, 141

Baptist Truth, The, 41

Barr, Sylvia, *xviii*

Beach Institute, 40

Beasley, Matilda, 37

Bell, Derrick, 143, 187

Beloved (Morrison), 71

Benedict College, 102

Bentley, William, 26

Berlin, Ira, 24, 31–32

Bethany Baptist Church (Detroit), 90–91

Bethel A.M.E. Church (Columbia, SC), 96, 190, 192–93

Bethel A.M.E. Church (Philadelphia), 133

Bethel Baptist Church, 56

Bethlehem Baptist Church, 109

Bethseder Baptist Church, 23

Beulah Baptist Church, 129

Bible Way Church, 190, 193

Big Bethel A.M.E. Church, 23, 96, 120, 128

Billingsley, Angela, *xviii*

Birchett, Colleen, 180

Black Christian Nationalist Church, 127

Black church(es): as agent of social control, 8; challenge to, 171; collaboration of, 130–31; community outreach programs, of, 88–89; and Confederacy, 35; contemporary mission of, 103, 189; culture of, *xxi*; as economic enterprises, 8, 144–69; educational mission of, 8; and elderly, 93–94; emphasis of, *xxiii*; females in, 120; and HIV/AIDS, 110–18; and male youth crisis, 102–9; membership of, 119–20; missions of, *xxii-xxiv*, 8, 171; orientations of, 10; origins of, *xx*; as political institution, 8; as power base, 168–69; protest tradition among, 10; as refuge, 9; renewal of community action in, 87–89; role of, for African Americans, 185–88; rural economic development of, 167–68; in secular crises, 186–87; and social/community programs, 131; socioeconomic mix in, 120; as support for black-owned enterprises, 80; types of, 186

Black Church Activism, 193–94

Black Enterprise Magazine, 88, 144, 152

Blackett, R.J.M., 63–64

Black History Museum, 78

Black Madonna shrines, 183

Black Male Youth Conference, 192

Black Minister Summit on AIDS, 113

Black Muslims, *xiii*

Black Prayer, A, 178–79

Black Religion and Black Radicalism (Wilmore), 180

Black religious leaders: Sherman/ Stanton meeting with, 24–34; as spokespersons, 31

Blacks: Northern, as educators, 38–40; Sherman's use of, 23–24

"Black Sacred Cosmos," *xix*, 10

Blacksheer, Jesse, 58–59

Black Summit, 59

Black Theology of Liberation, A (Cone), 140

Black Value System, 172–74, 181

Black women, 132–33, 136–43, 171

Black worship program, 174–84

Blake, Charles E., 97, 150

Blassingame, John, 45

Bolton Street Church, 109

Borders, William Holmes, 162

"Boxcar schools," 42

Boyd, Ramsford, 120

Bracken, Linda, *xvii*

Bradley, Tom, 151

Brailsford, Ronald, 96, 190, 192–93

Braxton, Tony, 176

Brewer, T.H., 54

Bridge Street A.M.E. Church, 146

Brigs vs. Elliott case, 190

Brock, Annette K., 40

Bronner Brothers Cosmetic enterprises, 163

Brookland Baptist Church, 102, 190, 191–92

Brown, Kelly, 140

Brown, Morris, 34

Brownlee, Henry, 55

Brown vs. Board of Education of Topeka, Kansas, 4, 190

Bryan, Andrew, 14, 16–19, 20, 21, 53, 60, 61, 86

Bryan, James, 60

Bryan, Joan Tyson, 55

Bryan, Jonathan, 17, 18

Bryan, William, 18

Bryant, J.E., 46

Burt, John, *xvi*

Burton, Jacqui, *xviii*

Bus boycott, 4, 11, 145

Bush, George, 151

Butler, La Conya, *xvii*

Butts, Calvin III, 113, 149

C.M.E Church, 137, 141

Caldwell, Cleopatra Howard, *vi, xvi, xviii*

Calvin, Sandra, 164

Campbell, Alexander, 20

Campbell, Tunis G., Sr., 39

Campbell, W.L., 49

Campbell, William J., 24, 25–26, 53

Campbell Chapel A.M.E. Church, 124

Canaan Baptist Church , 7, 169

Canaan Missionary Baptist Church, 145, 159, 163–67

Cannon, Katie Geneva, 139, 140

Cantrell, James H., 50

Carey, Lott, 68–70, 83, 84

Carpenter, Delores, 139, 140, 141–42

Carson, Emmett, *xvii*

Carter, Pamela, *xvi*

Carver, George Washington, 43

Central Baptist Church (Denver), 123

Central Baptist Church (Savannah), 109

Chester, Thomas Morris, 63, 65

Chicago Theological Seminary, 171

Children's Defense Fund (CDF), 92, 187

Chisholm, Andrew, 193

Chisholm, Evelyn, *xvii*

Christian Commission, 65

Christocentricity, 181

Christ Our Redeemer A.M.E. Church, 124

Christ Universal Temple, 138

Church of God in Christ (Brooklyn), 97, 146

Church of God in Christ denominations, 137

Church of the Holy Redeemer, 123

Civil rights movement, 53–61

Claremont College, 151

Clark, Ben, 57

Clark College, 44

Cleage, Albert, 183
Clergy Commission on AIDS, 116
Clinton, William Jefferson, 81
Coleman, Johnnie, 138
Collier, Walter V., 126
Collins, Addie Mae, 5
Colored American, 37–38
Colored Tribune, 45
Community development corporation, 164–67
Community outreach programs, black churches, 121–31
Community Renewal Society, 171
Community Revitalization Housing Project, 160–62
Computer Literacy and Education Program, 164, 165
Concerned Black Clergy, 110
Concord Avenue Baptist Church, 88, 146–48
Condoms, 92, 111, 114
Cone, James, 140, 142, 143
Congregation size, 97–98, 100
Congress of Black Churches, 92, 115–16
Connor, Bull, 4
Conservative churches, 95, 186
Conyers, John, 33
Cooper, Curtis V., 55
Cottrell, W.L., 129, 130
"Council of Elders," 112
Couples Ministry, 90–91
Cox, John, 26, 47
Craft, William & Ellen, 37
Cram, James C., 69
Crane, William, 68–69
Crawford, Vanella, 91
Credit union, first black, 55
Crocker, Curtis, Jr., 189
Crocker, Judith Denise, *vi, xvi, xvii, xviii*
Crogman, William Henry, 44
Cunningham, Henry, 14, 19, 44, 61
Cure D'Ars Catholic Church, 124

Dance Ministry, 177–78
Daniel A. Payne Memorial A.M.E. Church, 132

Daugherty, Herbert, 146
Davis, Darwin N., Sr., 113
Davis, Jefferson, 62–63
Davis, Oliver, *xvii*
Davis, Terrikay, 158
Davis, Ulysses, 40
Dawson, Mabelle, 57
DeLane, J.A., 190
Delaney, Henry, 107, 109
Delaney, Martin, 173
Delk, Yvonne, 180
Delmotte, Adolphus, 26
Denny, Reginald, 151
Deveaux, Jane, 36–37
Deveaux, John H., 45
Dexter Avenue Baptist Church, 11–12
Diggs, William P., 190
Dodson, Jualynne, 137, 140
Dougherty, William, 97
Downey, Maureen, 110–11
Drago, Edmund L., 35–36, 51–52
Draper, Elizabeth, 76
DuBois, W.E.B., 6–7, 35, 43, 178, 180, 186, 187
Durley, Gerald, 50, 102, 110–11, 120

Eaddy, Samuel, 106
East Denver Church of God, 123
Eastern Baptist Theological Seminary, 83
Eastern College, 83
East Savannah Church, 109
Ebenezer Baptist Church, 91, 113, 120, 128, 131, 194
Ebony Magazine, 88, 139, 157, 174–75
Edelman, Marion Wright, 92, 187
Education, 35–44, 115
Edwards, Benjamin, Jr., 160
Edwards, Benjamin, Sr., 160–61
Edwards, Luke, 167–68
87 Years Behind the Black Curtain (Wright, Jr.), 44
Elderly, black church and, 93–94
Ellis, Edward L., Jr., 50
Elmore, Charles, 41
Emancipation, 35–52

Emancipation Proclamation, 19, 25, 31
Emani Temple African American Catholic Congregation, 183
Emanuel A.M.E. Church, 34
Emerge Magazine, 88
Emory University, 110
Epps, William S., 152–53
Epworth Methodist Church, 122–24
Evans, Joseph W., 173–74

Family(ies): functions of, 89–90; support programs for, 89–91
Farajeje-Jones, Elias, 116
Farrell, Walter, 109
Fege, Hartmut, *xviii*
Felder, Cain Hope, 175, 180
Female ministry, 135–36
Ferguson, Elaine, 179
First A.M.E. Church (Hampton, GA), 105
First A.M.E. Church (Los Angeles), 87, 92, 111, 138, 150, 151–52
First African Baptist Church (Richmond), 62–84
First African Baptist Church (Savannah), 13, 20, 21, 26, 27, 36, 40–44, 49, 50, 57, 59; and male youth crisis, 102–6, 109
First African Baptist Church (Thomasville, GA), 43
First African Baptist Church of North America, The (Simms), 49
First Baptist Church (AL), 12
First Baptist Church (Kingston, Jamaica), 15
First Baptist Church (Marietta, GA), 22
First Baptist Church (Monrovia, Liberia), 70
First Baptist Church (Richmond), 81
First Baptist Church of Liberia, 69
First Bryan Baptist Church, 49–50, 109
First Christian Assembly of God Montbello, 125
First Foreign Missionary Society, 69
First Tabernacle Church, 109

Fisher, Sam, 23
Flack, Roberta, 176
Flake, Floyd H., 150
Foote, Julia A., 137
Ford Foundation, *xv*, 93, 122, 125, 148
Forte, Herman C., 159–62
Francis, Henry, 19
Franklin, Aretha, 176
Franklin, Robert, *xvii*
Frazier, E. Franklin, 6, 7–9, 186
Frazier, Garrison, 25–29, 35
Frazier-Howze, Debra, 111–13
Freedman's Bureau, 30, 38–39, 51; "boxcar schools" of, 42
"Frenzy," *xxiii*, 7, 178
Friendship Baptist Church, 93
From Holy Power to Holy Profits: The Black Church and Community Economic Empow- erment (Malone), 145, 163
Frotaine, Julian, 36
Frye, Teresa, *xvii*

Gallmon, Albert, 116
Galphin, Peter, 16
Gardner, Roderick, 106
George, David, 15
Georgia Constitutional Convention, 46, 51, 52
Georgia Dome, 128, 129, 130
Georgia Education Association (GEA), 39
Georgia legislature, 39
Georgia Negro State Fairs, 43
Georgia World Congress Center, 129
Geter, Pauline, *xviii*
Gibbons, Thomas, 18
Gilbert, Ralph Mark, 53–61
Gilkes, Cheryl, 140
Giovannonni, Jeanne, *xvi*
Glide Memorial U.M.C. Church, 153
Grace, C.M. ("Daddy"), 145
Grace and Truth Full Gospel Pentecostal Church, 124
Graham-Hill, Peggy, 152
Grant, Donald, 37
Grant, Jacquelyn, 140

Grant, Ulysses S., 34, 64
Greater Christ Temple Church, 167–68
Greater East Denver Ministerial Alliance, 124
Greater Mt. Nebo A.M.E. Church, 194
Greater Rising Star Baptist Church, 194
Green, Charles, 24
Greenbriar Orphanage, 54
Greene, Angela Dungee, *vi, xvi*
Greene, Carol, 40
Gregory, Henry C. III, *viii, xv*

Hacker, Andrew, 143
Haley, Alex, 167
Hall, Arsenio, 151
Hardemann, Wanda Perry, *xviii*
Harding, Rachael, *xvii*
Harding, Vincent, 142–43, 185
Harris, Alexander, 48
Harris, Michael, 128, 159, 162
Hartford Memorial Baptist Church, 88, 156–57
Head Start, 92
Healthy People 2000: National Health Promotion and Disease Prevention Objectives, 117–18
Heckler report, 117
Henry, Patrick, 81
Hill, Robert B., *vi, xvi, xviii*
Hillside International Truth Center and Chapel, 138–39
HIV/AIDS project, 110–18, 191
Hodges, Glenda, *xviii*
Holcombe, Henry, 18
Holiness of Pentecostal tradition, 138
Holmes, Clairborne, 74
Holmes, Delphia, 74
Holmes, James R., 66, 73–77, 84
Holy Spirit Lutheran Church, 109
Homans United Methodist Church, 150–51
Hood, James Walker, 137
Hopson, Helen, *xvi*
House of Joy Miracle Deliverance Church, 123

House of Prayer Deliverance, 123
Houston, Ulysses L., 26, 36, 47, 48
Houston, Whitney, 176
Hovey, Alvah, 65–66
Howard, Otis, 30, 38–39, 42, 51
Howard University, 30, 116, 132
Hugely, Bobby, 164, 166–67
Hughes, Langston, 185
Huntley, Lynn Walker, *xv, xviii*

Imani Fellowship program, 166
"Imani Ya Watume," 176
Inner City AIDS Network, 116
Interdenominational Theological Center, 191
International Theological Seminary, 102
Israel A.M.E. Church, 51

Jackson, Brian, *xvi*
Jackson, Charles, 190–92, 193
Jackson, Curtis L., 55, 56
Jackson, Darrell, 190, 192
Jackson, Fleda Mask, *vi*, 91
Jackson, Maynard, 130
Jackson, Duane, 91
Jacobs, Harriet Brent, 38
James, Harry, 40, 54
Jefferson, Thomas, *xxii*, 81
Jeffries, James M., 74
Jenkins, Rebecca, 57
Jenkins High School, 104–6
Jewish culture, 166–67, 182
Johns, Vernon, 11–12
Johnson, Adam Arguile, 21
Johnson, Andrew, 32, 67
Johnson, Gail Armstrong, *xviii*
Johnson, H.V., 76, 78, 84
Johnson, James Weldon, 17
Johnson, Otis S., *vi, xviii*, 54, 56–57, 59
Johnson, Sol C., 45
Johnson, Susan, 139
Johnson, Whittington B., 47
Joiner, Philip, 39, 46
Jones, Grant, *xvii*, 121, 123
Jones, John, 106
Jones, Juliette, *xvi*

Jones, Lawrence N., *xiii-xiv*, 99
Jones, Mac Charles, 33
Jones, Michelle, 165
Jordan, Vallmer E., 172, 178
Jordan, Vernon, 148
Jordan A.M.E. Church, 124

Karinga, Maulama, 180
Kelly Ingram Park, 4, 5
Kente, 112
Kilgore, Thomas, Jr., 153
King, Barbara, 138–39
King, Bernice, 194
King, Joel, 23
King, Kara, 193
King, Martin Luther, Jr., *xvi*, 4, 12,
  19, 52, 57, 97, 105, 173, 194; and
  Abernathy, 60; ancestors of, 23;
  assassination of, 172; and capacity
  to grow, 142–43; on redemptive
  death, 103
King, Primus, 54
King, Rodney, 151
Kiwanuka, N. Jorinda, 122
Knight, Carolyn Ann, 139
Knight, Gladys, 176
Koblinsky, Sally, *xvi*
Kwanzaa, 180

Labor unions, 46–47
Ladd, Mary, *xviii*
Lafayette, Sandra, 165
Land, as secret, 28, 32–34
Laney, Lucy, 52
Langford, Joseph, 69
Laurel Grove South Cemetery, 13–
  14, 21, 36, 44, 109
Law, W.W., 14, 38, 40, 60, 61; and
  NAACP, 55, 56, 58
Lawson, James, 151
Lee, Jerena, 133–36, 173
Lee, Joseph, 135
Lee, Robert E., 63, 64
Lefevre, Harry, *xvii*
Leile, George, 14–16, 18, 21, 53,
  109, 173, 186
"Letter from a Birmingham Jail"
  (King), 5

Liberia, 69–70
Lighthouse Community Church, 124
Lilly Endowment, *xviii*
Lilly Foundation, 116, 122, 125
Lincoln, Abraham, 32, 38–39, 64
Lincoln, C. Eric, *xix–xxiv*, 6, 9–12, 35,
  186; on black church, 89, 139–40,
  141, 144, 184, 187
Littway Baptist Church, 19, 106
Long, Eddie, 111, 189
Long, Jefferson, 46
Lott Carey Society, 70
Love, Emanuel King, 40–45, 50, 53
Lovett, Curtis, 106
Lucas, Barbara, 146
Lucas, Lawrence, 146
Lucas, Lila Anderson, *xviii*
Lumpkin (slave broker), 63
Lynch, James, 28, 31

McAdoo, Harriette P., 91
McCain, Dorothy, 104–5
McCormick, Robert Eugene, 164
McFate, K., 91
McGill, Lillie, *xviii*
McKenzie, Vashti Murphy, 132–33,
  139, 183
McKinley, William, 43
McNair, Denise, 5
Malone, Walter, Jr., 144–45, 159,
  163–64
Mamiya, Lawrence, *xv*, 10, 35, 89,
  139–40, 141, 184
Manesa, Brooks, *xvi*
Manly, Albert E., 139
Mann, Tamera, *xviii*
Marsalis, Wynton, 177
Marshall, Abraham, 18
Marshall, Andrew, 14, 19–21, 44,
  49, 53, 61, 186
Martin and Malcolm and America
  (Cone), 142
Martin Street Church of God, 127
Marty, Martin, *xix*
Maryland, University of, *xvii*
Mason, Biddy, 138, 151
Mason Temple Church of God in
  Christ, 97

Maxwell, May, 26
Mendenhall Bible Church, 167
Men of Shiloh, *xv*, 93
Methodist churches, 96, 99; and role of women in, 137, 141
Methodist Episcopal Church, Andrew's Chapel of, 26
Methodist Ministers Fellowship, 124
Metro Denver Black Church Initiative, 121–27
Michigan Park Christian Church, 139
Ministerial Alliance, 58, 59
Missionary Baptist Church, 26
Mitchell, Margaret, 158
Mitchell, William, 76
Mobley, Hardy, 38
Mochtari, Mitch, *xvi*
Monrow, Dale, 60–61
Monrow, George, 61
Montgomery, Andrew, 23
Montgomery Pinpoint Group, 109
Morehouse College, 41, 106, 120, 149, 156, 157, 191
Morris, Aldon, 10–11
Morris Brown College, 52, 137
Morrison, Toni, 71, 143
Morrison-Rodriguez, Barbara, *xviii*
Moss, J. Otis, 88, 157–59, 163
Motley, Anthony, 116
Mt. Ephraim Baptist Church, 128
Mt. Gilead Baptist Church, 125
Mt. Sharon Baptist Church, 139
Mount Sinai Holy Church, 138
Murphy, Melus, 23
Murray, Cecil "Chip," *ix*, 4, 87, 100, 151–52, 183, 187
Myers, Samuel S., 74
Myricks, Noel, *xvi*

NAACP, 54–60, 78, 99, 112
National Association for the Advancement of Colored People. *See* NAACP
National Baptist Convention of America, 96
National Baptist Convention USA, Inc., 96
National Baptist Ministers Conference, 112
National Black Leadership Commission on AIDS, 111–13
National Cancer Institute, 110
National Football League, 112
National Rainbow Coalition, 112
National Urban League, 99
National Watchman, 41
Nation of Islam, 128
Negro Church in America, The (Frazier), 8
Negro Labor Union, 46
Nehemiah Houses, 145–46
New Bethel A.M.E. Church, 183
New Birth Missionary Baptist Church, 111, 128, 189
New Hope Baptist Church, 124
New York City Mission Society, 113
New York Newsday, 118
New York Times, 87
Nguzo, Saba, 180
Nichols, Roy, 180
Night marches, 57
Nixon, A.D., 12
Nuttall, Annie and George, 60

O'Brien, John, 67
Olds, Mark C., 158
Olivet Institutional Baptist Church, 88, 157–59
"One More River to Cross," 185
"One More Sunday in Savannah," 13
Open Door Church of God in Christ, 124–25
Opportunities Industrialization Centers (OIC), 155
Order of St. Luke, 77
Origins of the Civil Rights Movement (Morris), 10–11
Osbourne, Chief Justice, 17
Outreach to the Diaspora, 182

Paige, Jo Ellen, *xviii*
Paris, Peter, 10
Park Hill Christian Church, 125

Park Hill Congregational Church, 125

Park Hill United Methodist Church, 125

Parks, Rosa, 11, 12

Payne, Polly, 79

Payne, A.M.E. Church, 139, 183 *See also* Daniel A. Payne Memorial A.M.E. Church

Pearson, Jessica, *xvii*

Pentecostal church, 97, 137, 141

Peoples Presbyterian Church, 123

Perdue, Robert, 35

Perkins, Daniel R., Jr., 76, 79, 81–82

Peters, Jesse, 18

Philadelphia Church of Christ, 139

Phillips, Joe Lee, 165

Phillips, Karen, 149

Phillips, Mona, *vi, xvii*

Piton Foundation, 121, 123–25

Poinsett, Alex, *ix*

Political action, black, 47–52

Porter, James, 26, 37–39, 47, 48

Powell, Adam Clayton, 148

Pressley, Calvin O., 113

Princeton Theological Seminary, 10

Proctor, Samuel D., 88, 148–49, 163

Progressive National Baptist Convention, 96–97, 141, 154

Protestant Episcopal Church, 38

Providence Baptist Church (Atlanta), 50

Providence Baptist Church (Liberia), 69

Providence Missionary Baptist Church, 102, 110–11, 120

Quarles, Benjamin, 29, 64

Quillion, Carolyn, 55

Quinn, Sandra Crouse, *vi*, 114

Racism, 9, 143, 188

Ralph Mark Gilbert Civil Rights Museum, 59–61

Randolph, Suzanne, *vi, xvi*

Rates, Norman, *xvii*

REACH, Inc., 168

Reagon, Bernice, 187

Redeeming Love Fellowship Church, 124

Reducing AIDS Through Community Education, 113–15

Reed, Frank Madison, 183

Reed, Gregory, 144

Rehobath International Baptist Church, 124

Resettlement, for blacks, 32–33

Rice, Gwendolyn, 92

Richards, Jane, 70–72, 83, 84

Richmond, Helen, *xviii*

Richmond, VA, 34, 62–64

Richmond Council of Colored Women, 78

Rites of Passage program, 164, 166–67, 182

Rivers, Al, 57

Robb, Chuck, 8

Roberts, Joseph, 91, 113, 128

Robertson, Carole, 5

Robinson, Ernest, 55

Robinson, Ida, 138

Robinson, Jo Ann, 12

Rockefeller Foundation, *xvii*

Roots (Haley), 167

Rouse, Victor, *xvi*

Royal Church of Christ, 109

Rubin, Roger, *vi, xvi, xviii*

Rucker, Ephraim, 22–23

Rutgers University, 149

Ryland, Robert, 65, 66, 71–73, 83, 84

St. Agnes Catholic Church, 127–28

St. Andrews Episcopal Church, 123

St. Ignatius Loyola Catholic Church, 123

St. James A.M.E. Church, 109

St. James Baptist Church, 3, 11

St. John Baptist Church, 145

St. Mark United Methodist Church, 92

St. Mattthew's Episcopal Church, 27

St. Paul A.M.E. Church, 128

St. Paul Academy, 106–8

St. Paul C.M.E. Church, 106, 107–8, 109

St. Paul Community Baptist Church, 145, 146

St. Paul's Church, 63

St. Philip's A.M.E. Church (Atlanta), 127

St. Philip's A.M.E. Church (Savannah), 47, 52

St. Stephen's Protestant Episcopal Colored Church, 26, 27

Sanders, Cheryl, 140

Savannah, GA, 15, 21, 24, 186,187; civil rights in, 53–61

Savannah Baptist Association, 18, 19, 20

Savannah Education Association, 36, 39, 40

Savannah Negro Laborer Union, 46–47

Savannah News, 56

Savannah State College, 39, 43, 45, 57, 59

Savannah Tribune, 44, 45

Saxon, Rufus, 33

Scarlet, Frank M., 56

Scott United Methodist Church, 124

Second African Baptist Church, 19, 21, 26, 27, 31, 33, 47, 50, 57

Second Baptist Church, 150, 152–53

Second Bethlehem Baptist Church, 109

Senior ministers, 98–100

Sexism, 141–43

Sherman, William Tecumseh, 22–34, 47

Shiloh Baptist Church, 92–93, 166

Shiloh Temple, 124

Shopshire, James, *vi, xviii*

Shorter A.M.E. Church, 120, 124, 176

Shrine of the Black Madonna, 127

Shropshire, Joseph, 96

Shuttlesworth, Fred, *xvi*, 4, 5

Simms, James M., 36, 44, 47, 48, 49

Simon, Alicia, *vi, xvii*

Simone, Nina, 13

Simpson, Gary V., 148

Singer, Merrill, 10

16th Street Baptist Church, *xvi*, 4, 176

Slaves and slavery, 16, 27

Small, Mary J., 137

Smalls, Robert, 32

Smith, Gregory, 123

Smith, J. Alfred, Jr., 154

Smith, J. Alfred, Sr., 154

Smith, Charles, *xviii*

Smith, Kenneth B., *ix*, 171–72

Smith, Lucy, 138

Smith, Nijiumo, 106

Smith, Ozzie, 176

Smith, Wallace Charles, *vi*

Snead, Henry S., 147

Snell, L. Scott, 56

Society for the Propagation of the Gospel in Foreign Parts (Anglican), *xx–xxi*

South Carolina, University of, *xviii*

Southern Baptist Theological Seminary, 163

Southern Christian Leadership Conference, 57, 113–15

Speller, Julia, 180

Spelman College, 106, 139

Spottswood A.M.E. Zion Church, 124

Springfield Baptist Church, 16, 38, 41

Stallings, Bishop, 183

Stanley, Quade, 106

Stanton, Edwin, 25–32, 47

Stephens, Terry, *vi, xvi, xviii*

Stokes, Louis, 157, 159

Stokes, William Franklin, 55

Streisand, Barbra, 151

Strickland, Henry, 23

Sullivan, Leon, 154–56, 187–88

Sullivan, Linda and John, *xviii*

Sullivan, Louis, 117

Sullivan Principle, 155–56

Sunbury Baptist Association, 20, 50

Tabernacle Baptist Church, 43

Taft, William Howard, 43

Taylor, Gardner, 88, 146–48, 164

Taylor, James, *xvi*
Taylor, Susie King, 36, 37
Teague, Collin, 68–70
Temple Baptist Church, 139
Temple University, 139
"10/36 Plan," 154–55
Texas Southern University, 138
There Is a River (Harding), 185
Third African Baptist Church, 21, 26, 27, 36, 47, 48, 49–50
Third Shiloh Missionary Baptist Church, 159–62
Thomas, Dennis E., 80, 83–84
Thomas, E.G., 16, 18
Thomas, E.K., 50
Thomas, Franklin, 148
Thomas, Stephen, *vi*, 110, 113–15
"Tiger Woods syndrome," *xxiv*
Tillman, Thurmond, 41, 50, 102–6, 109
Tolliver, Willie F., *vi*, *xviii*, 100–101
Townsend, Adjutant-General, 25
Travis, Harris, 171
Trinity Baptist Church, 190
Trinity United Church of Christ (Chicago), 7, 166, 170–74, 177–78, 180–81
Trinity United Church of Christ (Detroit), 88
Troubling Biblical Waters (Felder), 175
Truth, Sojourner, 140, 173
Tubman, Harriet, 173
Tucker, Frank, 116
Turner, Alice, *xvii*
Turner, Henry McNeal, 8, 39, 46, 48, 50–52, 58, 136–37, 173
Turner, Nat, 67
Turner, T.A., 91
Turrentine, Stanley, 177
Tuskegee Study of Untreated Syphilis in the Negro Male, 117–18

U.S. Army, blacks in, 32–33
U.S. Congress, 33
U.S. Peace Corps, 149
U.S. Public Health Service, 117
Underground railroad, *xxiii*

UNESCO, 7
Union Baptist Church, 183, 189
Union Church, 23
United Church of Christ denomination, 181
United House of Prayer for All People, 145
United Theological Seminary, 163
Unity School of Christianity, 138
Usher boards, 179

Van Lew, Elizabeth, 76
Vesey, Denmark, 34
Villagio Center for Scholars, *xvii*
Vine City Housing Ministry, 128–31
Virginia Union College, 66
Virginia Union University, 78, 82, 149
Vivian, C.T., 57

Wage Earners Bank, 45, 60
Walker, C.T., 42, 43
Walker, Maggie Lena, 75–80, 83, 84
Walker, Wyatt Tee, 7, 169
Wallen, Jacqui, *xvi*
Ward, Catherine, *xviii*
Ward, Naomi, *xvii*
Ware, Vine, 23
Washington, Booker T., 43
Washington, James M., 187
Weary, Dorcus, 167
Weaver, Jonathan L., 194
Welfare reform, 188–90
Wells, Ida B., 173
Wesley, Cynthia, 5
Wesleyan Theological Seminary, 96
West Angeles Church of God in Christ, 97, 150
Western Reserve University, 158
Whalun, Kirk, 177
Wheat Street Baptist Church, 120, 128, 159, 162–63
Wheeler Street Baptist Church, 189
White, Michael R., 157
White, William Jefferson, 39
Whitlock, Mark, 152

Whittier, John Greenleaf, 42
Wilberforce University, 44
Wilder, Eunice, 82
Wilder, Lawrence Douglass, 80–84
Williams, A.D., 23
Williams, C., 153–54
Williams, Delores, 140
Williams, Hosea, 57
Williams, L.A., 45
Wilmore, Gayraud, 180
Wilson, Willie, 183
Winans, Vickie, 177
Wolfolk, Robert, *xvii*, 121
World Trade Center, 129
Worship programs, 146
Wragg, Cecilia, *xvi*
Wright, Emanuel Crogman, 44

Wright, Jeremiah A., Jr., 7, 88, 171,
    172, 174–75
Wright, Mercedes, 55
Wright, Richard R., Jr., 44
Wright, Richard R., Sr., 41–44, 45
Wright, Whittier, 44
Wynn, Prathia Hall, 139

Young, Andrew, 157
Youngblood, Johnny Ray, 145, 146
Youth, programs for, 91–93, 105,
    109, 179

Zion Baptist Church (Marietta, GA),
    22, 171
Zion Baptist Church (Philadelphia),
    154–56